MW00995629

Harley-Davidson

100 YEARS

Celebration of a Legend

Harley-Davidson

100 YEARS

Celebration of a Legend

Tod Rafferty

MBI Publishing Company

Dedication: *Once again, for Bronwyn, without whom the author would be just a dust-bunny in the corner of a storage shed behind a Harley shop in Pittsburgh.*

Tod Rafferty *has been riding and racing motorcycles for 40 years and writing about them for 30. His work has appeared in Cycle News, Roadracing World, American Roadracing, Cycle World, Hot Bike, Rider and The Robb Report magazines. His earlier books include "Harley: The Ultimate Machine" (1994, 1999, 1902), "The Complete Harley-Davidson" (1996), "Harley Memorabilia" (1997), "The Indian" (1998, 1901), "The Encyclopedia of American Motorcycles" (1999) and "Ducati" (2000). Rafferty is the proprietor of MotorSports Media Productions and lead rider for Team Geezer Vintage Racing. He and his wife live on the central coast of California.*

COMMISSIONING EDITOR: Will Steeds

PROJECT MANAGER: Jo Richardson

DESIGNER: Philip Clucas MSIAD

COMMISSIONED PHOTOGRAPHY: Neil Sutherland

COLOR ARTWORK: Hector Cademartori (page 214, BL); Glynn Kerr (page 214, TL, page 215, T); Steve Posson (page 215, B)

INDEX: Chris Bernstein

COLOR REPRODUCTION: Media Print (UK) Ltd.

PRINTED AND BOUND IN CHINA

This edition first published in 2002 by MBI Publishing Company, Galtier Plaza, Suite 200, 380 Jackson Street, St. Paul, MN 55101-3885 USA

Produced by Salamander Books Ltd., 8 Blenheim Court, Brewery Road, London N7 9NT, U.K.

A member of Chrysalis Books plc
© 2002 Salamander Books Ltd.

The name Harley-Davidson, and certain model designations, are properties of the trademark holder. They are used herein only for purposes of identification. This is not an official Harley-Davidson publication.

Photographs identified as such in the text and picture credits are copyright Harley-Davidson Motor Company and are provided courtesy of Dr. Martin Jack Rosenblum, Historian, Harley-Davidson Juneau Avenue Archives.

All rights reserved. With the exception of quoting brief passages for the purpose of review, no part of this publication may be reproduced without prior written permission from the publishers.

The information in this book is true and complete to the best of our knowledge. All recommendations are made without any guarantee on behalf of the author or publisher, who also disclaim any liability incurred in connection with the use of this data or specific details.

MBI Publishing Company books are available at discount bulk quantity for industrial or sales-promotional use. For details write to Special Sales Manager at Motorbooks International Wholesalers & Distributers, Galtier Plaza, Suite 200, 380 Jackson Street, St. Paul, MN 55101-3885 USA.

Library of Congress Cataloging-in-Publication Data Availiable.

ISBN 0-7603-1308-3

HARLEY-DAVIDSON®
1930

contents

introduction

The Harley-Davidson Motor Company is 100 years old in 2003. As the sole-surviving manufacturer of more than 300 motorcycle builders before World War I, the Milwaukee firm is certifiably unique in the industry.

Longevity is not the company's only distinction, although more than a half-century as the only American motorcycle company is achievement in itself. But Harley-Davidson became more than a producer of motorized vehicles. Until the 1950s and the demise of Indian motorcycles, Milwaukee was one half of a national rivalry between the two companies. The contest had all the adversarial trappings of hometown baseball-cheering sections—the New York Yankees vs. the Brooklyn Dodgers—but extended across the country and beyond.

This rivalry was not always friendly. The tension between Harley guys and Indian guys (the gals were seldom so belligerent) could escalate beyond shouting matches. The companies themselves eventually declared a truce on economic grounds, and indulged in some price-fixing for their common benefit. Nonetheless, the spirit of warring tribes (pun intended) served to promote both brands in the showrooms, on the race tracks and in the hearts of supporters on both sides.

Ultimately the advantage turned to Harley-Davidson, whose solid family foundation prevailed when Indian passed through various corporate hands. Milwaukee would face stronger rivals in the second half-century, but the standards set by William Harley and the Davidson brothers had moved the company beyond business success into the realm of popular legend. And carried it forward when the economics appeared to be entirely hopeless. This is that story.

Tod Rafferty,
San Luis Obispo, California, 2002; traff@thegrid.net

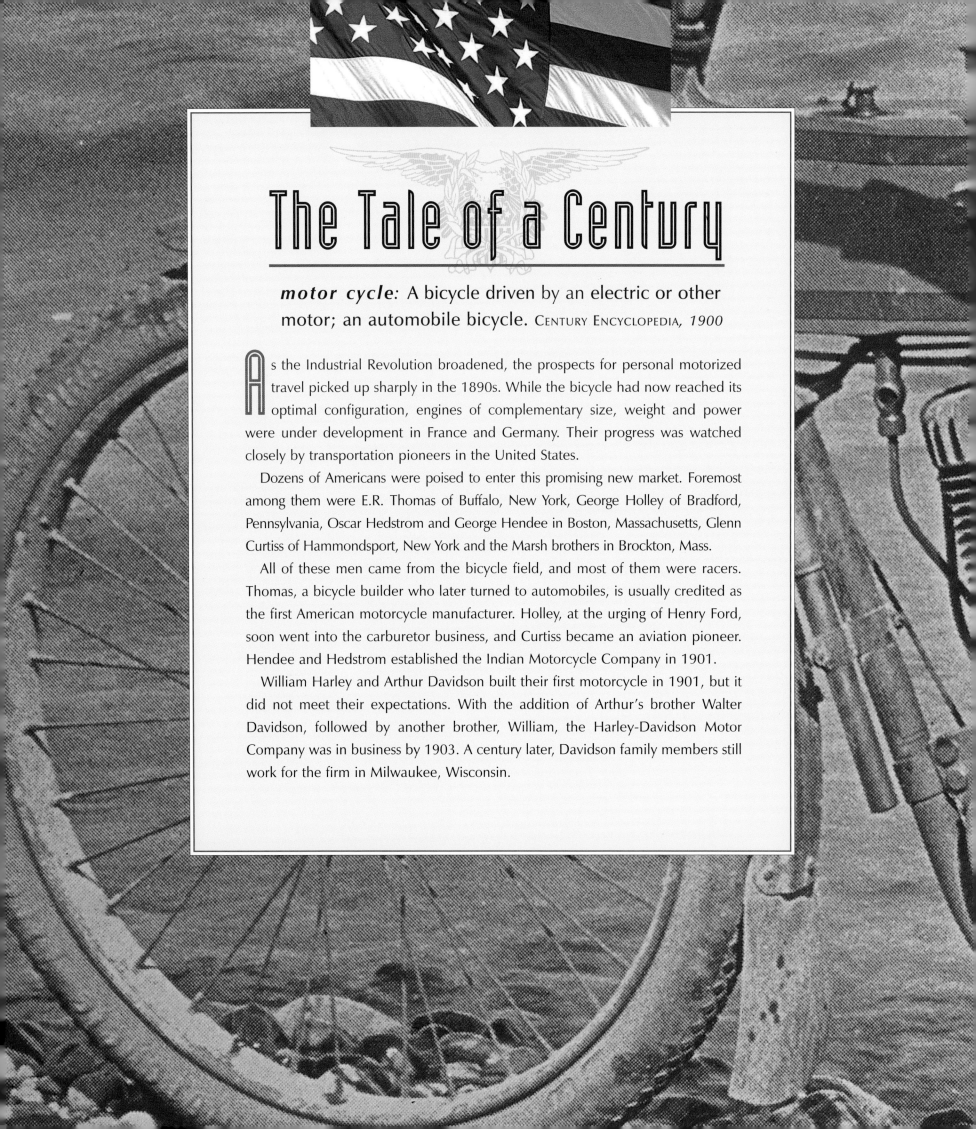

The Tale of a Century

motor cycle: A bicycle driven by an electric or other motor; an automobile bicycle. CENTURY ENCYCLOPEDIA, *1900*

As the Industrial Revolution broadened, the prospects for personal motorized travel picked up sharply in the 1890s. While the bicycle had now reached its optimal configuration, engines of complementary size, weight and power were under development in France and Germany. Their progress was watched closely by transportation pioneers in the United States.

Dozens of Americans were poised to enter this promising new market. Foremost among them were E.R. Thomas of Buffalo, New York, George Holley of Bradford, Pennsylvania, Oscar Hedstrom and George Hendee in Boston, Massachusetts, Glenn Curtiss of Hammondsport, New York and the Marsh brothers in Brockton, Mass.

All of these men came from the bicycle field, and most of them were racers. Thomas, a bicycle builder who later turned to automobiles, is usually credited as the first American motorcycle manufacturer. Holley, at the urging of Henry Ford, soon went into the carburetor business, and Curtiss became an aviation pioneer. Hendee and Hedstrom established the Indian Motorcycle Company in 1901.

William Harley and Arthur Davidson built their first motorcycle in 1901, but it did not meet their expectations. With the addition of Arthur's brother Walter Davidson, followed by another brother, William, the Harley-Davidson Motor Company was in business by 1903. A century later, Davidson family members still work for the firm in Milwaukee, Wisconsin.

the birth of a legend

"It has always been Walter's way that whatever he goes into, he goes into it right." ARTHUR DAVIDSON, 1916

BELOW: *Walter Davidson's skills as a machinist, rider and forceful organizer moved the fledgling company quickly into contention with the market leaders.*

RIGHT: *The original home of The Harley-Davidson Motor Company was moved to the factory and long preserved until mistaken instructions led to its unintentional demolition.*

Bill Harley and Art Davidson are often cited as the original founders of the Harley-Davidson Motor Company. They did start building a prototype in 1901, but it wasn't until brother Walter Davidson came aboard in 1903 that theirs could be properly called a motorcycle company. A third brother, William, worked for the Chicago, Milwaukee & St. Paul Railway at the time.

On the occasion of Bill Davidson's impending marriage, Arthur wrote to Walter who was then working for the Missouri, Kansas & Texas Railway in Parsons, Kansas. "When you come home for Bill's wedding, we will have a motorcycle for you to ride." The news so encouraged Walter that rather than take time off for the wedding, he resigned his job as a machinist and headed for Milwaukee.

The first of the Scottish family to be born in the USA, Walter Davidson had an inquiring mind and a meticulous nature. By age 14 he had converted the family basement into a shop and built an electro-plating device. Fascinated by electricity and intrigued by Milwaukee's first electric street cars, Walter proceeded to build his own storage battery when he was 15 years old. He bought his first bicycle at 17, a used Remington, and took up the racing sport, at which he proved adept.

"One time I wanted to see how fast I could ride the 90 miles [145km] from the state capital at Madison," Davidson recalled in 1916. "I was so tired after I made the trip that I couldn't stand up or even lie down with comfort. But I satisfied my curiosity as to how long the trip would take with my 35-pound [16kg] Remington. It took ten hours."

That curiosity, and the conviction that things should be done right, formed both the foundation and future of Harley-Davidson. Neither Bill Harley nor Arthur Davidson were too pleased with Walter's critical response to their second-generation motorcycle, which still employed a bicycle frame. If he could build something better, they said, go to it. So Walter took a job with the local railway company and put his spare time into the motorcycle.

By the fall of 1903 the Harley-Davidson engine had improved carburetion and electrics, was making three horsepower and housed in a full-loop frame with forged lugs

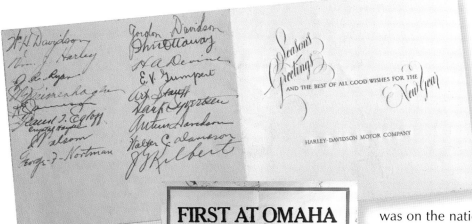

FIRST AT OMAHA

Otto Ramer, riding his stock Harley-Davidson twin, took first place in each of the four events he entered at Omaha, July 4th.

The races were held over a course laid out from Fairacres to Fifty-second and Dodge Streets.

According to Omaha newspapers young Ramer climbed hills like a streak and distanced his competitors by thirty feet at every goal.

In two events Mark Schwerin finished second, also riding a Harley-Davidson.

HARLEY-DAVIDSON MOTOR COMPANY

Producers of High-Grade Motorcycles for More Than Twelve Years

Milwaukee, Wis., U. S. A.

ABOVE: *The tradition of sending Christmas cards to dealers and friends of the company was instituted in the early years. Arthur Davidson insisted on regular contact between Milwaukee and the dealerships.*

ABOVE: *The factory formed its first official professional racing team in 1914, and continued to proclaim the achievements of amateurs around the country.*

"The fast Harley-Davidsons startled the world with their speed and stamina. Time and time again it was a Harley-Davidson procession in long-distance races in America when the famous racing team won victory after victory."

FLOYD CLYMER, RACER/DEALER/ENTREPRENEUR

RIGHT: *Red Parkhurst, one of the best factory team riders before and after the war, set many records and later worked for the Firestone Tire & Rubber Company.*

and a stout fork. In 1904 Walter became a full-time motorcycle builder; the backyard plant was enlarged from 150 to 300 square feet (14–28m²) and production output climbed to eight machines. Arthur came on full time in '06, followed by the eldest brother William. Bill Harley completed his engineering degree in 1908 and became the last of the founding four to join the company.

When Walter Davidson won the Catskill–New York City endurance run in 1908, with a perfect score, Harley-Davidson was on the national map. From production that year of 450 motorcycles, the young Milwaukee firm turned out 1,149 the following year and more than 3,000 for the next three years. In 1913 Harley-Davidson built nearly 13,000 machines. Indian of Springfield, Massachusetts produced almost 32,000 motorcycles that year, the highest number they would attain.

Milwaukee continued to close the gap on Springfield, and when Arnold-Schwinn and Company of Chicago acquired Excelsior in 1910, the three-way battle for motorcycle supremacy was on. Indian and Excelsior had achieved prominence in the racing game, while Harley-Davidson avoided direct factory involvement until 1914. Under the direction of Bill Harley and racing engineer William Ottaway, formerly of Thor Motorcycles, the well-organized Harley Wrecking Crew went on to dominate professional racing in the next two seasons. Racing was suspended with the advent of U.S. participation in World War I and Milwaukee's shift to military production.

post-war promotion

The effects of World War I would ripple for some time through the American economy. The motorcycle industry, which between 1900 and 1917 had numbered some 300 manufacturers, had been cut to fewer than a dozen. Among them only Indian, Harley-Davidson and Excelsior could be considered major contenders.

Milwaukee had supplied U.S. and allied forces with 20,000 motorcycles during the war, but Indian had consigned virtually its total production—some 50,000 machines—to the military. This ruptured relations with customers and dealers, and had a lasting effect on Indian's fortunes. By 1920, Harley-Davidson was the world's largest motorcycle company with 2,000 dealers around the world, nearly 17 percent of its production built for export. The percentage went higher as the domestic market went flat in 1921, Milwaukee production dropping from 27,000 to 11,000 machines.

Professional racing resumed in what had appeared a booming post-war economy, and Harley-Davidson again fielded its powerful factory team. In

ABOVE: *The Harley-Davidson Wrecking Crew: second from left is Ray Weishaar with his pet pig; far right is Red Parkhurst, who rode Harleys throughout his career; and next to him is Maldwyn Jones, who rode for Merkel, Harley and Excelsior.*

"The World's Champion: That is the name and the fame the Harley-Davidson motorcycle has gained. It is preferred for its performances all over the world—and adopted by the United States government after its wonderful war work on the fields of France."

1920 ADVERTISEMENT

FAR RIGHT: *The two Bills, Harley on the bike, Davidson in the sidecar, were both fisherman but didn't likely go fishing in coats and ties. The photo suggests the importance attached to the image of motorcycling.*

1920 Ohioan Jim Davis won the brutal 300-mile (483km) Dodge City classic for Milwaukee, followed by Gene Walker on the Indian eight-valve and Harley's Ray Weishaar in third. Davis and Weishaar swapped positions in the 1921 race, an Indian again coming second.

Indian president Frank Weschler congratulated Bill Harley on the victory. "I picked the winner before the race started," Harley said. "I put up $10 on Weishaar, who didn't have the fastest machine, and Bill Lister picked one of our riders who had the fastest one in the team. I simply figured that the fastest wouldn't win over this kind of going." Ray Weishaar, usually accompanied by his pet pig named Hog (who enjoyed Coca Cola), was popular with the fans. Jim Davis, who rode for both Indian and Harley-Davidson, remained involved in motorcycle racing his whole life. He died a few years ago at the age of 103.

"Speed in every line – strength in every curve – low hung for safety and easy control – better-sprung and bigger-tired for luxurious comfort – that's Harley-Davidson's latest and greatest motor-cycle, the 'Stream-Line'!" 1925 ADVERTISEMENT

BELOW: *Fuel mileage became the major selling point. "…one is inclined to estimate the upkeep cost of a Harley-Davidson as on a par with that of the automobile. Such is, however, far from the case."*

RIGHT: *This ad lists the Harley advantages. Founder photos were taken much earlier.*

BOTTOM: *An ad from 1925 stresses the open-air charms of a ride in the country.*

By then the expense of factory team racing had outstripped its marketing returns, and Harley-Davidson dropped its professional program at the end of the 1921 season. But the lessons learned on engine tuning, lubrication, metallurgy and component durability transfered gradually to production motorcycles. The two-wheelers could no longer compete with the automobile as primary transportation, and the shift began to advertising appeals of sporting recreation.

Arthur Davidson headed the sales department and instituted a national advertising campaign stressing fun, companionship and economy. Ads pictured men riders and women sidecar passengers in the "Chummy Car," with the tag of "40 to 60 Miles per Gallon of Gasoline." The new Seventy-four (1200cc) engine was well suited for sidecar duty, especially the new two-passenger model. Noting that motorcycling had a growing image problem, created by irresponsible "hooligans and boobs" who rode unmuffled machines, Walter Davidson joined his brother in the public relations effort. Harley-Davidson dealers were urged to keep tidy showrooms and promote local motorcycling activities and civic goodwill. Sales slowly began a steady climb to pre-war levels, aided by direct mail advertising, more streamlined styling in 1925 and reduced prices.

By 1928, when Milwaukee adopted its first front brake, production was above 20,000 motorcycles and the prospects for continued growth appeared bright. With the introduction of the new side-valve Forty-five (750cc) twin in 1929, built to contest the Indian Scout and Excelsior's sporty Super X, Harley-Davidson had a solid lineup of models. Plans were underway to build a four-cylinder motorcycle, and Everett DeLong, designer of the Cleveland Four, was hired on in Milwaukee.

But the bright future dimmed sharply with the 1929 crash of the stock market in New York, and the advent of the Great Depression. Excelsior expired in 1931 and the American motorcycle market had come down to Indian and Harley-Davidson, with Milwaukee holding a much stronger position.

out of depression into war

BELOW: *In 1931 the New York Police Department had a contract with Indian Motorcycles of Springfield, Mass. The city used both Chiefs and Indian Fours.*

Hard times had settled on Milwaukee in 1931. But while motorcycle production and sales were down, Harley-Davidson management did their best to keep as many employees as possible on the job, though some had only two days' work a week. By 1933 production had fallen to 3,700 machines, the lowest output since 1910.

The Depression reinforced the need to cultivate and maintain government and commercial service accounts, especially fleet sales to police departments around the country. The competition between Harley and Indian for these sales became bitter contests of political maneuvering, backroom deals and, according to some reports, even offering motorcycles at below cost. The Servi-Car, introduced in 1932, was adopted by many police departments, auto shops and light delivery services for its economical advantages over cars.

Harley-Davidson and Indian did manage to agree on regulations for a new racing class, since professional board track racing had gone to history. In 1934 the motorcycle trade association and the American Motorcycle Association (AMA) established the Class C formula based on production motorcycles. The division stipulated slightly modified 750cc flatheads (Harley Forty-five and Indian Scout), and 500cc overhead-valve engines were included. In the 500cc single-cylinder division, former Excelsior rider Joe Petrali joined Harley-Davidson and won five national championship titles. When his racing career was over, Petrali went to work in the aircraft industry and served as flight engineer on Howard Hughes' famous wooden seaplane "The Spruce Goose."

RIGHT: *The Servi-Car found immediate acceptance in all manner of light-duty commercial enterprises. The tow bar made it especially useful for auto repair shops.*

IT PAYS TO GIVE.... ...**service** with a HARLEY-DAVIDSON **servi-car**

HARLEY-DAVIDSON [¼ Ton Capacity] *Package Truck*

FAR RIGHT: *Harley-Davidson's Package Truck was offered in a number of configurations. Using a modified version of the sidecar chassis, the frame and body were just a few dollars more than the sidecar versions. The trikes were popular during the Depression.*

While Class C offered one economical manner of keeping the Harley-Davidson banner in public view, the revival of cross-country record runs was another. In 1935 Earl Robinson, riding a Harley Forty-five (750cc), set a new record from New York to Los Angeles in three days, six hours. Earl and his wife Dot Robinson also established the cross-country sidecar time of 89 hours, 58 minutes, a record that

would stand for 23 years. In 1936 Pasadena, California policeman Fred Ham averaged nearly 60mph (96.5km/h) on a Harley Seventy-four between Canada and Mexico, covering the distance in just over 28 hours.

Then as the Depression began to lift, and the prospects of war loomed once again, Harley-Davidson turned more attention to the design and production of new military models. During the process, William A. Davidson, eldest of the founding four, died in April, 1937, at age 66. The only founder who didn't become a motorcyclist, as works manager Big Bill was the backbone of actual motorcycle production in Milwaukee. He had established the most comprehensive and efficient factory in the business, and was respected throughout the industry. His son, William H., started in the factory, became an accomplished rider and within five years would succeed his uncle Walter as president of the company.

With the success of the OHV Knucklehead, the addition of a 74-inch (1200cc) version in 1941 and continuing popularity of the big twin flatheads, Harley-Davidson was in command of the heavyweight motorcycle market. Orders for military models from the U.S. and allied forces were rising, and with America's entry into the war the factory service school was converted to the Quartermaster School to train military mechanics.

ABOVE: *The U.S. Army Service School at Fort Knox, Kentucky trained mechanics to maintain and rebuild Harley engines during the war.*

RIGHT: *Actors Tyrone Power (left) and Preston Foster were among Hollywood's active motorcyclists in the 1940s.*

FAR RIGHT: *Joe Petrali set a speed record of 136mph (219km/h) on the new Knucklehead in 1937.*

"Walter Davidson was a man of forceful personality, dynamic enthusiasm and keen judgement. These qualities, combined with his thorough knowledge of motorcycles and interest in motorcycling, made him an outstanding figure in the world of business."

THE ENTHUSIAST, *1942*

Unfortunately, two more of the original founders would not survive to see Harley-Davidson return to peacetime production. Walter Davidson, 66, died in 1942. He had been the keystone of the company's success—a man of exceptional energy with an uncommon combination of athletic skill, mechanical abilities and business acumen. Walter knew every aspect of the motorcycle business, and his forceful personality ensured that his recommendations were usually followed.

William S. Harley, the company's creative force, died in 1943 at age 63. In terms of lasting influence, he was the foremost motorcycle engineer of the 20th century. But Bill Harley was also a complex man with an expansive range of talents and interests. Rather shy socially, he was a dedicated fisherman and hunter as well as an accomplished artist and photographer. A rider who tested his own designs, Harley was also a racing enthusiast who was largely responsible for Milwaukee's competition successes. He was succeeded by his son, William J., as chief engineer.

progress and prosperity

"Harley-Davidson's achievements over the years, including the announcement of our splendid Golden Anniversary models, now in full production, are adequate evidence that we are firmly committed to an aggressive program of steadily moving forward. Harley-Davidson is sharply conscious of our ever-shifting economy, and the need for intelligent and constant change."

WILLIAM J. DAVIDSON, 1953

ABOVE: *Arthur Davidson and his wife, Clara, died in an automobile accident five days after Christmas in 1950. Davidson reportedly turned in front of another car, in which two occupants also died.*

World War II did little damage to Harley-Davidson. Much like Milwaukee's situation in the previous mechanized combat chapter, the conflict proved helpful for Harley and detrimental to Indian. Only the 74ci (1200cc) Chief remained on the Springfield roster for 1947, and while Indian built 7,000 motorcycles that year, Harley production was nearly triple that. New Indian owner Ralph Rogers had invested heavily in new lightweight models that appeared in 1949, but the enormous development costs were never recovered.

So Harley-Davidson stood in firm command of the heavyweight motorcycle division, and with the "spoils of war" award of manufacturing rights to the German DKW two-stroke had a ready-made lightweight

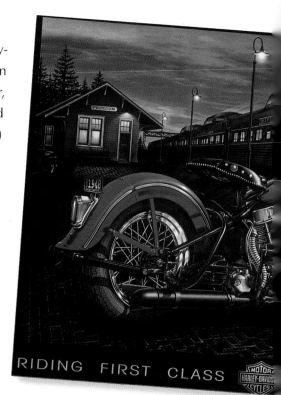

contender. With the Panhead succeeding the venerable Knucklehead in 1948, the Hydra-Glide telescopic fork on the menu the following year, the debut of the new K model Forty-five (750cc) and foot shift for the big twins in 1952, Milwaukee was on a progressive track. And the purchase of a new engine plant on Capitol Drive forecast continued brightness for the future.

The saddest note was struck in 1950, when Arthur Davidson and his wife were killed in an automobile accident. Last survivor of the founding four, Arthur was the youngest, and smallest, of the Davidson brothers. But his physical stature belied the reservoir of organizational and marketing abilities he brought to the family enterprise. He is credited with founding the Harley-Davidson service school for training mechanics, and pioneered installment buying in the motorcycle business. Establishing and maintaining the company's extensive dealer network and spearheading the national advertising campaigns were his paramount contributions.

Within the business, and among sporting riders, rumors of Milwaukee's forthcoming sport model had run throughout the grapevine for more than a year. At the dealer convention in November, 1951, Chief Engineer William J. Harley put the rumors to rest. "Some time ago we began the development of a completely new motorcycle," he said to the assembled hall. "This has now become a production reality." The stage curtains parted to reveal two sparkling white K model Forty-fives; telescopic suspension at both wheels, internal four-speed transmission and clean, classy looks. The dealers, who had campaigned for a middleweight sport bike, were unanimously enthused.

Class C racing had grown in popularity since the war, but despite the flathead's displacement advantage in the rulebook, the 500cc OHV British machines had

LEFT: *This nostalgic illustration of a 1948 Panhead parked at the train station portrays an era of simple pleasures. Critics would later say Harley was lost in the 1940s for a bit too long.*

RIGHT: *Dealers were provided with posters heralding the arrival of the Duo-Glide in 1958. As Harley-Davidson's first big twin with rear suspension, the new model created quite a stir; especially among skeptics who predicted bad wobblies.*

outpaced the aging WR model. Nortons had won the prestigious Daytona Beach race from 1949 through 1952. By 1953 the KR racing version of the new Forty-five was ready to go, and Paul Goldsmith recaptured the Daytona glory for Milwaukee, setting a new speed average in the process.

The K model continued its development for the next few years, gaining power and reliability in the hands of independent tuners like Tom Sifton. But race-wise fans and sportbike enthusiasts knew that eventually Harley-Davidson would come forth with an overhead-valve version. When their hopes were answered by the 54ci (883cc) Sportster in 1957, the response was even more enthusiastic. Likewise, touring riders were all but uniformly pleased by the adoption of rear suspension on the big twins, when the Duo-Glide appeared in 1958.

With the demise of Indian in 1953, Milwaukee's return to racing prominence and a new generation of sport and touring machines, Harley-Davidson had done quite well in the '50s. In 1960 they were emboldened to step outside tradition and introduce a motor scooter called the Topper. Little attention was paid to a little 50cc step-through that had just arrived in America, built by a Japanese company named Honda.

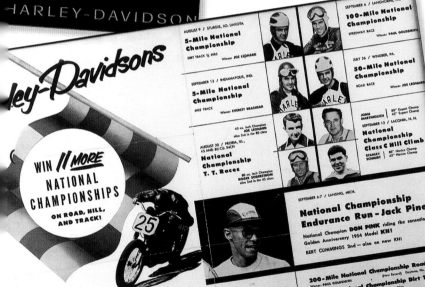

ABOVE: *Milwaukee hadn't had a Daytona victory since 1940, but Paul Goldsmith won the race for Harley in 1953 on the 750 KR. Goldsmith later became a winning stock car driver.*

RIGHT: *Brochures for the Duo-Glide portrayed the adventures awaiting riders of the new, improved (and most powerful) big twin from Harley. Note the casual riding togs.*

markets and mergers

"It was obvious when they went public in '65 that Harley was in trouble. And hooking up with AMF looked like it would be the last chapter for the family business. Luckily that's not how it would turn out, but it looked mighty shaky in the '70s."

FAT BURNS, MOTO PUNDIT

The second-generation members of the Harley and Davidson families were now charged with charting the company's future. The influx of British and European motorcycles was now in full flood. None of them posed any immediate threat to Milwaukee's commanding position in the heavyweight division, but the imported sportbikes and lightweights were another matter. Those who buy small bikes often move up to larger ones.

Harley-Davidson managers had begun scouting sources abroad for lightweight machines in the late '50s, since high U.S. labor costs prohibited building their own. Most European builders had their hands full meeting the requirements of their own markets, especially those who had discovered the growing appetite among Americans for dirt bikes. Thus Harley-Davidson came to acquire a half interest in the Italian firm Aeronautica Macchi, which built two- and four-stroke singles. The first Aermacchi model in the States was the 250cc Sprint.

Milwaukee also established Harley-Davidson International in Switzerland, which would serve the factory's export distribution in Europe's new Common Market, and coordinate purchasing and personnel for Aermacchi. The Italian OHV single was expected to serve the lightweight sport and commuter markets in the U.S., and compete in the smaller displacement AMA racing classes. Assured that they now had a comprehensive product roster, Milwaukee set to work on the next generation of motorcycles.

ABOVE: *In 1965 Roger Reiman piloted this 14-foot (4.3m) streamliner powered by a 250cc Sprint engine to a new record of 177mph (285km/h) on the Bonneville salt flats. While the Sprint engine was outpaced in roadracing by the two-strokes, it was still effective in short dirt track events.*

When company President William H. Davidson asked his son, William G., if he'd like to work for the company as styling director, young Willie replied, "I'll bring my crayons and be right down." With the imminent celebration of Harley-Davidson's 100th anniversary, he will have been on the job for 40 years. A rider, like his father and grandfather, Willie G. also seemed to inherit some of the art and design talent of Bill Harley. His abilities would serve the company well in the tumultuous times ahead.

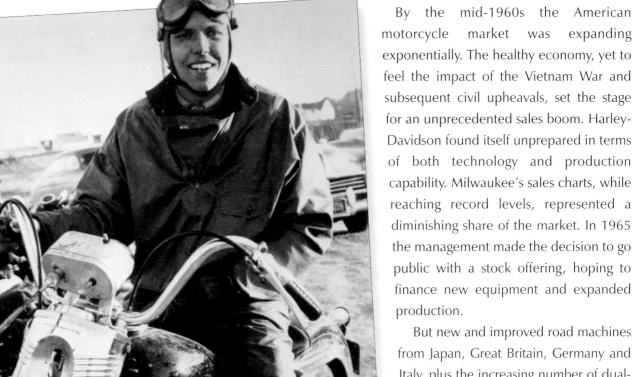

RIGHT AND ABOVE:
Willie G. Davidson was all smiles after winning an endurance run on the new K model in 1952. He appeared just as pleased some 35 years later at Sturgis, South Dakota, overlooking a sea of Harley-Davidsons he had designed.

By the mid-1960s the American motorcycle market was expanding exponentially. The healthy economy, yet to feel the impact of the Vietnam War and subsequent civil upheavals, set the stage for an unprecedented sales boom. Harley-Davidson found itself unprepared in terms of both technology and production capability. Milwaukee's sales charts, while reaching record levels, represented a diminishing share of the market. In 1965 the management made the decision to go public with a stock offering, hoping to finance new equipment and expanded production.

But new and improved road machines from Japan, Great Britain, Germany and Italy, plus the increasing number of dual-purpose and dirt bikes from Spain, Sweden and Czechoslovakia, put Milwaukee further behind. Upgrades to the aging Panhead engine had little effect overall, and sales of the big twins lingered at 7–8,000 a year, with the Sportster at 4–5,000. Harley-Davidson would need help to compete in a changed market.

Confronted with the threat of a hostile takeover by industrial giant Bangor-Punta, in 1969 Harley-Davidson merged with American Machine and Foundry (AMF), a large recreation industry firm. While it would no longer be a family business after 65 years, the partnership did allow the company to maintain its current management and control its own design and development decisions. Milwaukee had effectively bought time, and a source of funding, to bring new models to market. While the arrangement wasn't to flourish in the long term, it ensured Harley-Davidson's survival in the 1970s.

LEFT: *The AMF-Harley-Davidson logo of the '70s was patterned on the AMA's Number One number plate awarded to the Grand National Champion each year. While it did not signify Milwaukee's position in the market then, the design did reflect the sense of purpose and pride in the product they were striving for.*

investing in the future

"Bless their hearts, they pulled out of the death dive and made it. Those people really busted their asses to make it work, starting with Vaughn Beals. They took a hell of a risk and it paid off. Beals has been paid very handsomely, but he risked just about everything he had, and put in Herculean effort and considerable intelligence. I think it's a marvelous business story."

BILL DUTCHER, FORMER PR MANAGER

The merger with American Machine and Foundry (AMF) was to develop in various and not always mutually satisfactory ways. But it did provide working capital and the opportunity to recreate some of Harley's former glory. And it didn't hurt that AMF Chairman Rodney Gott had learned to ride on a Harley-Davidson in the 1930s.

Another fortuitous boost came from Hollywood in the form of films based on varying aspects of the motorcycling lifestyle. Within just a few years, the movies "Easy Rider," "On Any Sunday," "Hell's Angels '69," "Little Fauss and Big Halsey" and "Electra Glide in Blue" gave audiences a graphic taste of life on two wheels. And the already growing market for custom bikes and choppers opened even wider. For Harley, the timing was perfect.

Willie G. Davidson was ready with designs that reflected existing trends among several segments of the motoring public. First among them was the FX 1200 Super Glide, with a "Sparkling America" paint scheme of red, white and blue. Combining the Electra Glide (F) engine and chassis with the Sportster (X) front end accomplished several goals; using mostly existing parts eliminated delays and expensive tooling, and the instant custom would appeal to those without the know-how and/or money to build their own cruiser. And although the styling didn't attract legions of buyers, it did draw attention to Harley-Davidson, and the fact that they were still in the game.

Milwaukee's publicity quotient was also kept current by the exploits of motorcycle jumper Evel Knievel, whose daring leaps and sometimes disastrous landings guaranteed wide coverage in the national media. Riding the Harley XR 750 racing model, Evel's daredevil entertainments played to large audiences at home and abroad. Meanwhile, racer Mark Brelsford used the new alloy-engine XR to recapture the national championship for Harley-Davidson in 1972. Though no longer a force in roadracing, Milwaukee maintained its domination of the more popular American sport of dirt track competition.

But by the mid-1970s, despite the increased production afforded by the corporate merger, AMF Harley-Davidson faced a growing roster of problems. The parent company had divided the plant between Milwaukee's Capitol Drive facility, now responsible for building engines and transmissions, and a final assembly factory in York, Pennsylvania. The federal government issued an edict that motorcycle engines would contribute less pollution to the atmosphere,

LEFT: *Walter C. Davidson, son of founder and former company president Walter, served as secretary and sales manager before retiring in '71. "Junior" was unhappy with the direction AMF was taking the company, and made this known.*

ABOVE AND RIGHT: *Robert Redford and Michael J. Pollard starred in the racing movie "Little Fauss and Big Halsey," a light-hearted treatment of the sport. "Electra Glide in Blue" featured veteran film actor Robert Blake as a patrolman.*

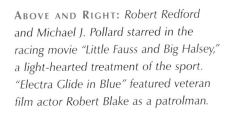

BELOW: *Evel Knievel provided Harley-Davidson with considerable international publicity, not all of it positive. His personal life and dramatic crashes attracted lawyers and physicians.*

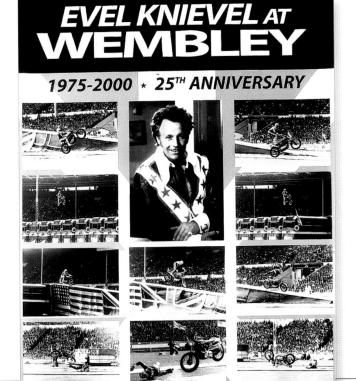

and gave manufacturers a strict deadline to meet stringent emissions standards. Then opposing factions in the Middle East effected what came to be called The Oil Crisis, creating gasoline shortages and higher prices, which some thought would improve motorcycle sales, but didn't. And finally, union workers at the Capitol Drive plant went out on strike for three months over a wage dispute.

Also, in 1975 the Honda Gold Wing arrived. The water-cooled four-cylinder touring bike set a new industry standard, and cost far less than a Harley.

AMF now began to reconsider its commitment to Harley-Davidson, one of its least profitable divisions, and decided to put more emphasis on industrial products and services. Soon the word was out that the only remaining American motorcycle company was for sale. There were few takers.

To its credit, and Harley-Davidson's ultimate good fortune, AMF hadn't meddled with the design and engineering process. Willie G. was left to his own devices, and two of them—the XLCR Cafe Racer and the FXS Low Rider in 1977—served as indicators that there was life in the old hog yet. The task at hand was to find the money, and the management, to rebuild Harley-Davidson and capitalize on its unique position in the world of motorcycling. No one thought it would be easy, and few thought it would even be possible.

The few and the brave turned out to be 13 Harley managers, led by President Vaughn Beals and including William G. Davidson, who mortgaged their futures and bought the company from AMF in 1981. Then the restoration process was begun.

from survival to success

"Harley-Davidson is a great example of a respected American manufacturer bouncing back from adversity. It's great to see another fine Wisconsin company take the offensive in our global economy."

TOMMY THOMPSON, GOVERNOR OF WISCONSIN

Even though 1981 was the first year for the eagle to soar alone, getting off the ground was no simple matter. A nationwide recession put motorcycle sales in the dumpster, and some of the buyback team's financial lenders got nervous. Faced with finding themselves at the mercy of bankers, Harley-Davidson appealed to Washington for relief in the form of tariffs on imported motorcycles. The company had made the same attempt five years earlier and failed, and few observers held much hope for success this time. But the Reagan administration looked more favorably on Milwaukee's plight, and slapped a 45 percent duty on Japanese heavyweight machines.

The decision had little tangible effect on the U.S. sale of Japanese motorcycles, but it did represent a symbolic victory for Harley-Davidson and served to reassure the financiers that recovery was still possible. Given some breathing room, Milwaukee stepped up the program to replace the maligned Shovelhead engine with a thoroughly modern V-twin. Success or failure hinged on the new motor, dubbed the V2 Evolution, which appeared in 1984 after seven years of development and testing.

Its success was not immediate. A residue of suspicion remained in the marketplace, and it would take time to convince buyers that Harley-Davidson had produced a reliable product. Just as the persuasion process had gotten underway, Milwaukee's financial footing found gravel on the road. Citicorp, leader of the four lenders financing the corporate buy-back deal, wanted out. The vote of no confidence created a quick scramble for new money.

Harley's Chief Financial Officer, Richard Teerlink, was able to secure new financing, but additional security would be required. So in 1986 the company went public once again, offering two million shares of common stock and $70 million in high-yield bonds that would come due in 1996. With the bacon pulled from the fire, Milwaukee could focus again on winning the hearts and minds of American riders.

In 1983 Harley's total production was below 30,000 machines; in 1988 it topped 47,000 and by '91 was over 65,000 motorcycles. In the same period, the Harley Owners Group (HOG) had grown to more than 90,000 members. By 1993 the factory was unable to keep up with the demand for motorcycles, and began to expand its production facilities. Those who bought $5,000 worth of Harley-Davidson stock in 1986 now had a $35,000 share in the company.

LEFT: *A signal event in Harley history occurred on July 16, 1986, when the company was listed on the U.S. Stock Exchange. Chairman Vaughn Beals (on bike) celebrates the occasion with Exchange President Arthur Levitt.*

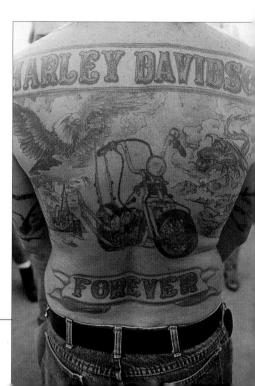

RIGHT: *One measure of devotion to the Harley brand is the permanent recording of it on the epidermis of thousands of fans, male and female, around the world.*

WE'VE SURVIVED FOUR WARS, A DEPRESSION, A FEW RECESSIONS, SIXTEEN U.S. PRESIDENTS, FOREIGN AND DOMESTIC COMPETITION, RACETRACK COMPETITION, AND ONE MARLON BRANDO MOVIE. SOUNDS LIKE PARTY TIME TO US.

Live in the wind for 90 years and a lot of turbulence blows by. But that which is good, endures. Like family. And Harley-Davidson. And we think it's time to celebrate: The Harley-Davidson® 90th Anniversary. The party starts with a cross-country Reunion Ride for MDA that covers the continent. Then we'll thunder into Milwaukee on June 12, 1993 for a huge family reunion built with live music, food, fun, and acres of soul-satisfying machinery. The journey begins at your Harley-Davidson dealer, where the tickets are limited and time is already running short. So sign up now. Because even something as big as our 90th Anniversary will soon fade into the wind. And we'll have the memory of what we've enjoyed together.

ABOVE: *Foreign competition was both threat and salvation, and Brando didn't hurt that much. Ninety years deserved a party.*

BELOW AND RIGHT: *The house that Willie built, the Harley design center. Memorial plaque is in the walkway at the Juneau Avenue plant.*

And the numbers continued to rise for the rest of the decade. The traditional Harley-Davidson 45-degree V-twin, still an air-cooled pushrod motor in a world of high-tech rocket-bikes, was chooglin' along into the 21st century, attracting more enthusiasts along the way. Willie G., joined in the company ranks by his children, has remained the creative keystone and directs an international team of designers and stylists. The design center is now a modern, sprawling complex with tight security and no public access, but the motorcycles retain something of that down-home quality that Bill Harley and the Davidson brothers invested them with 100 years ago.

Surely they could not have predicted that their work would survive more than a century, or that it would create such numbers of dedicated fans, aftermarket businesses, racing heroes, books, movies and more than a few millionaires. One day Milwaukee will get around to building a statue of those guys, as a way of saying thanks. They deserve it.

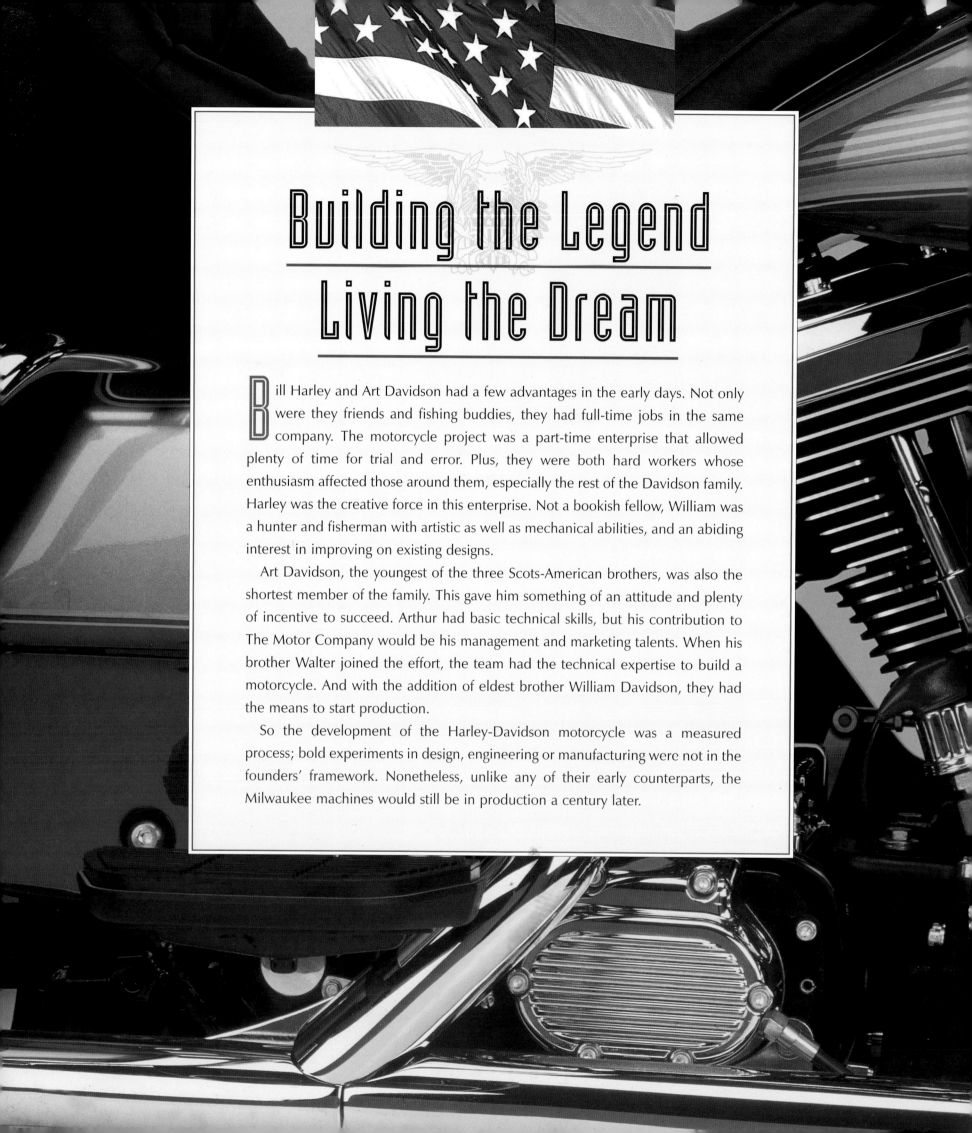

Building the Legend
Living the Dream

Bill Harley and Art Davidson had a few advantages in the early days. Not only were they friends and fishing buddies, they had full-time jobs in the same company. The motorcycle project was a part-time enterprise that allowed plenty of time for trial and error. Plus, they were both hard workers whose enthusiasm affected those around them, especially the rest of the Davidson family. Harley was the creative force in this enterprise. Not a bookish fellow, William was a hunter and fisherman with artistic as well as mechanical abilities, and an abiding interest in improving on existing designs.

Art Davidson, the youngest of the three Scots-American brothers, was also the shortest member of the family. This gave him something of an attitude and plenty of incentive to succeed. Arthur had basic technical skills, but his contribution to The Motor Company would be his management and marketing talents. When his brother Walter joined the effort, the team had the technical expertise to build a motorcycle. And with the addition of eldest brother William Davidson, they had the means to start production.

So the development of the Harley-Davidson motorcycle was a measured process; bold experiments in design, engineering or manufacturing were not in the founders' framework. Nonetheless, unlike any of their early counterparts, the Milwaukee machines would still be in production a century later.

1903—10: The First Years

decade design evolution

"In making our motorcycle we have not endeavored to see how cheap we could make it, but how good, and nothing but the best materials are used throughout its construction."

ARTHUR DAVIDSON

Motorcycle design at the end of the 19th century focused almost exclusively on engine development. The bicycle frame was the obvious choice for chassis, so the object was the construction of an engine that made sufficient power with the least weight, to allow motoring without pedaling.

The first Harley-Davidson engine, begun in 1901 and finished in 1902, wasn't quite sufficient. The 10.2ci (167cc) single generated enough urge to propel bike and rider to about 15mph (24km/h) on level ground, but went wheezing at the slightest incline, forcing the rider to pedal a heavier bicycle. So the first problem Bill and Art had to solve was the power issue. Establishing what would become an abiding American tradition, they made the engine bigger.

The pocket-valve engine, so called for the pouch cast for the exhaust valve, employed an atmospheric intake valve atop the cylinder. Often called the IOE (inlet over exhaust) engine, the cast-iron cylinder was fitted to an aluminum crankcase which included a flywheel to keep the engine turning between power strokes. The intake valve was sucked open by the descending piston, closed by compression on its return and aided by a light spring.

Two other co-workers would figure in the development of the first real production engine. Emil Kroger, a draftsman recently emigrated from Germany, had worked on the first De Dion engines, and Ole Evinrude had some notions for a carburetor. Harley redesigned the engine with increased bore and stroke, bringing displacement to 24.74ci (405cc), and more than doubled the size and weight of the flywheel. The bicycle diamond frame gave way to a loop frame, then in use by several manufacturers.

Model two worked, and with the addition of Arthur's brothers, Walter and William Davidson, the Harley-Davidson Motor Company was up and running in 1903. Bill Harley continued his design work while attending engineering classes at the university in Madison.

In 1906 Harley-Davidson took license on the Keating patent for a "Spark and Valve Controlling Device for Explosion Engines." Proper delivery of ignition was followed in 1907 by license to use the Sager-Cushion spring fork design, modified

ABOVE: *Patent drawing for the Keating spark advance mechanism. Keating built motorcycles under his own name in Connecticut in 1902.*

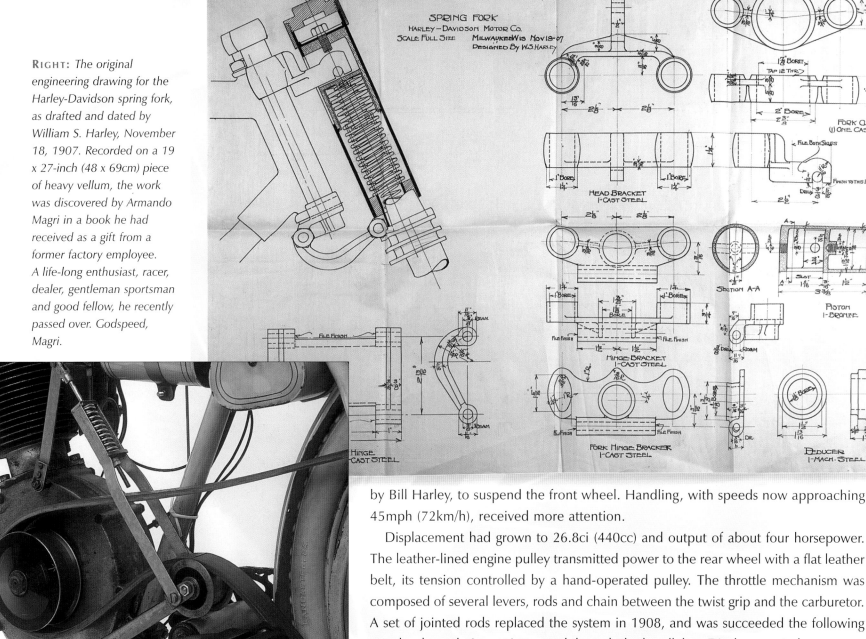

RIGHT: *The original engineering drawing for the Harley-Davidson spring fork, as drafted and dated by William S. Harley, November 18, 1907. Recorded on a 19 x 27-inch (48 x 69cm) piece of heavy vellum, the work was discovered by Armando Magri in a book he had received as a gift from a former factory employee. A life-long enthusiast, racer, dealer, gentleman sportsman and good fellow, he recently passed over. Godspeed, Magri.*

ABOVE: *The spring-loaded belt tensioner was controlled by a lever adjacent to the fuel tank. The early version of a clutch featured a simple pulley on an arm attached to the base of the engine.*

by Bill Harley, to suspend the front wheel. Handling, with speeds now approaching 45mph (72km/h), received more attention.

Displacement had grown to 26.8ci (440cc) and output of about four horsepower. The leather-lined engine pulley transmitted power to the rear wheel with a flat leather belt, its tension controlled by a hand-operated pulley. The throttle mechanism was composed of several levers, rods and chain between the twist grip and the carburetor. A set of jointed rods replaced the system in 1908, and was succeeded the following year by sleeved piano wire routed through the handlebar. Displacement also went up again, now at 30.16ci (494cc), and magneto ignition was offered as an option.

As production tripled in 1907 and again in '08, with factory facilities growing apace, Harley-Davidson's reputation was growing likewise. In the April, 1908 issue of *Bicycling World and Motorcycle Review*, the editor stated, "Of the latter day motorcycles, none so quickly earned a reputation as the Harley-Davidson."

Bill Harley had now taken his bachelor of science degree in engineering at the University of Wisconsin, and returned to work full time with the co-founders in Milwaukee. He had already begun work on his next engine design in response to rider requests for more power; the first Harley V-twin was on the drawing board.

1903—05 Single

After some 18 months of research, trial-and-error engineering and machining, by early 1903 Bill Harley and Art Davidson were in the motorcycle business. Thorough studies of existing models from Indian, Curtiss, Thomas and Marsh convinced the partners on the benefits of the loop frame, single-cylinder engine and belt drive.

The production engine had more than doubled the displacement of the prototype—from 10.2 to 24.74ci (167 to 405cc)—and the flywheels had grown to more than twice the original size. Horsepower for the IOE single hovered somewhere between 2 and 3, and the 178-pound (81kg) machine could, on a good day, achieve a top speed of about 35mph (56km/h). Deceleration was handled by a rear coaster brake.

The Harley-Davidson Motor Company produced three machines in 1903 and the same number the following year. By 1905, production had risen to eight motorcycles, encouragement enough for Walt Davidson to quit his railroad job and become the company's first full-time employee. The factory had grown to 300 square feet (28m²), and aunt Janet Davidson applied her artistic talents to the lettering and pinstriping on the motorcycles, which were painted black with gold trim.

Bill Harley and the Davidson brothers had embarked on a road none of them could have predicted would travel so far.

BELOW: *The first Harley-Davidsons adopted the full-loop frame, while some manufacturers stuck with the less stout bicycle diamond design. The founders established build quality and durability as priorities early on.*

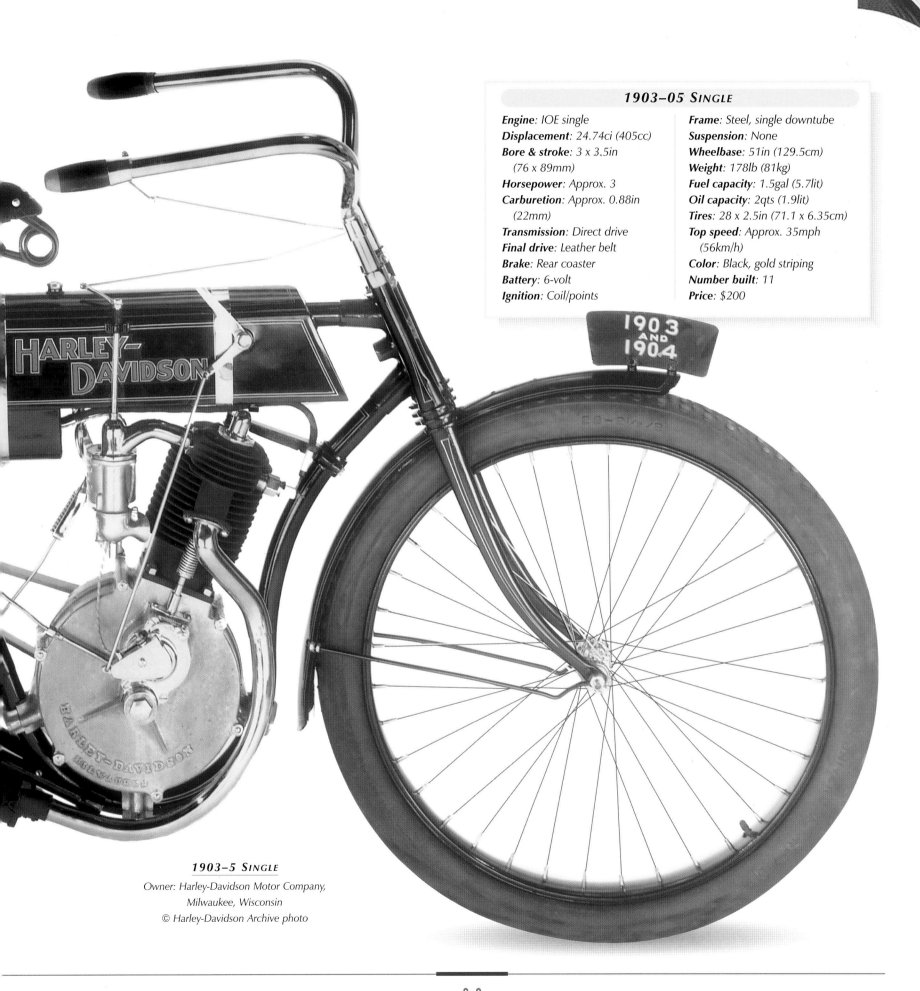

1903–05 SINGLE

Engine: IOE single
Displacement: 24.74ci (405cc)
Bore & stroke: 3 x 3.5in (76 x 89mm)
Horsepower: Approx. 3
Carburetion: Approx. 0.88in (22mm)
Transmission: Direct drive
Final drive: Leather belt
Brake: Rear coaster
Battery: 6-volt
Ignition: Coil/points
Frame: Steel, single downtube
Suspension: None
Wheelbase: 51in (129.5cm)
Weight: 178lb (81kg)
Fuel capacity: 1.5gal (5.7lit)
Oil capacity: 2qts (1.9lit)
Tires: 28 x 2.5in (71.1 x 6.35cm)
Top speed: Approx. 35mph (56km/h)
Color: Black, gold striping
Number built: 11
Price: $200

1903–5 SINGLE
Owner: Harley-Davidson Motor Company,
Milwaukee, Wisconsin
© Harley-Davidson Archive photo

1906—07 Single

The Motor Company, as fans would come to call it, hit its stride in 1906. Word of mouth on the motorcycle's reliability, and Arthur's advertising and promotion efforts, had moved Harley-Davidson into the motorcycling mainstream. The 1906 model had a larger engine, 26.8ci (440cc), better twistgrip controls and a new color—Renault gray, which effected the machine's first promotional subtitle, The Silent Gray Fellow.

Despite his good manners, the Fellow's top speed was up to 45mph (72km/h), which soon illustrated the shortcomings of the front fork. This led to the adoption of the leading-link Sager-Cushion spring fork in 1907 and improved high-speed handling. Braking was still provided by backpedal effort at the rear coaster, and the 1.5-gallon (5.7lit) fuel tank was good for a range of over 100 miles (161km). The price for a 1906 Harley-Davidson was $210, one of the more expensive machines on the market.

Production jumped from 50 in 1906 to 150 the following year, and any doubt that the company was up to speed was dispelled by the appearance of a prototype V-twin engine designed by Bill Harley. But it was the middle Davidson boy—Walter, the first of the Scots immigrant family born in the U.S.—who proved himself as the new driving force in Milwaukee. Walt, in addition to his mechanical skills, turned out to be a damn good motorcycle rider. His perfect score in the New York national endurance run in 1908 caught the attention of growing numbers of sporting riders.

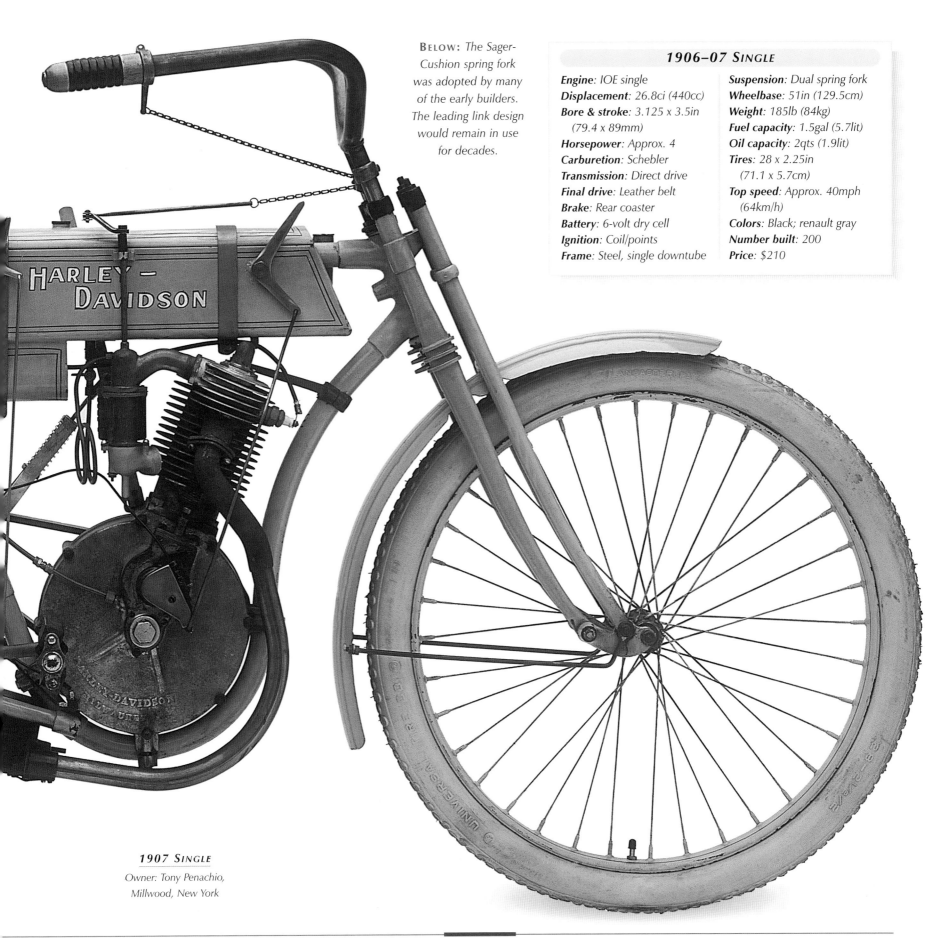

BELOW: *The Sager-Cushion spring fork was adopted by many of the early builders. The leading link design would remain in use for decades.*

1906-07 SINGLE

Engine: *IOE single*
Displacement: *26.8ci (440cc)*
Bore & stroke: *3.125 x 3.5in (79.4 x 89mm)*
Horsepower: *Approx. 4*
Carburetion: *Schebler*
Transmission: *Direct drive*
Final drive: *Leather belt*
Brake: *Rear coaster*
Battery: *6-volt dry cell*
Ignition: *Coil/points*
Frame: *Steel, single downtube*

Suspension: *Dual spring fork*
Wheelbase: *51in (129.5cm)*
Weight: *185lb (84kg)*
Fuel capacity: *1.5gal (5.7lit)*
Oil capacity: *2qts (1.9lit)*
Tires: *28 x 2.25in (71.1 x 5.7cm)*
Top speed: *Approx. 40mph (64km/h)*
Colors: *Black; renault gray*
Number built: *200*
Price: *$210*

1907 SINGLE

Owner: Tony Penachio,
Millwood, New York

1909 Model 5

Production swelled to 1,300 machines in 1909, showing The Motor Company's steady growth. Milwaukee's motorcycle output had yet to provoke much concern in Springfield, Massachusetts, where Indian rolled nearly 5,000 motorcycles off the assembly line. But other midwestern manufacturers were feeling the impact of Harley-Davidson's achievement, and the contest to prevail in the quickly evolving market gathered momentum. Some of the thrust was being provided by the increasingly popular drama of board track motorcycle racing.

The 1909 Harley-Davidson was the fifth generation design from Milwaukee, and the first to be numerically designated. The Model 5 engine displaced 30.16ci (494cc) and was rated at 4.3 horsepower, good for about 45mph (72km/h). The machine sold for $210 with a battery and $250 for the magneto model. Color choices were still black or gray, and riders could choose 26- or 28-inch (66 or 71.1cm) tires. Wire hand controls (throttle and spark) replaced the external linkage of the first models.

Harley-Davidson's first V-twin appeared in 1909, but only 27 examples were built. The pocket-valve design (atmospheric intake valve above pushrod exhaust valve) had worked well enough on the single, but the twin's crankcase pressure pulses were at odds with the valves. The twin design went back to Bill Harley's drafting table.

BELOW: *By 1909 the Harley-Davidson was a thoroughly modern motorcycle. Throttle and spark control wires were enclosed in the handlebar, and riders had the choice of battery or magneto ignition. The fuel tank, now carried between the new frame's twin top tubes, had compartments for fuel and oil. With a more powerful engine and higher speeds, the longer wheelbase aided stability. The compartment in the rear frame section held tools and extra gear.*

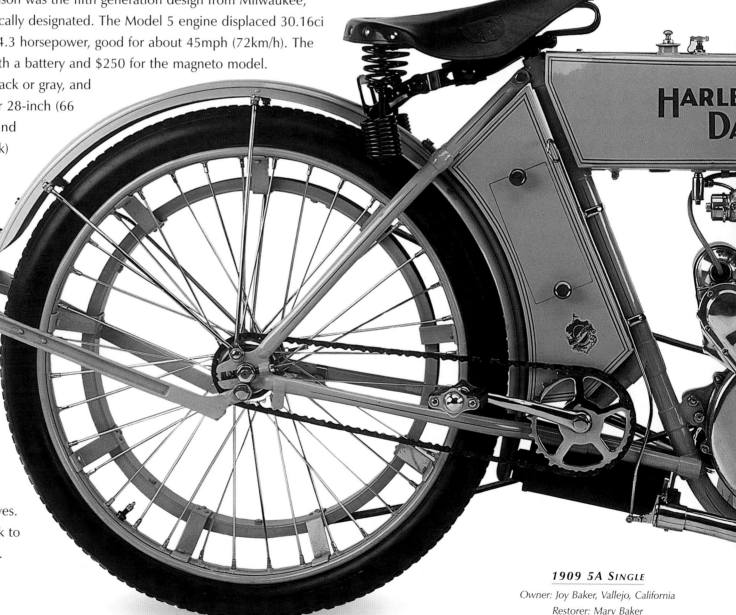

1909 5A SINGLE
Owner: Joy Baker, Vallejo, California
Restorer: Marv Baker

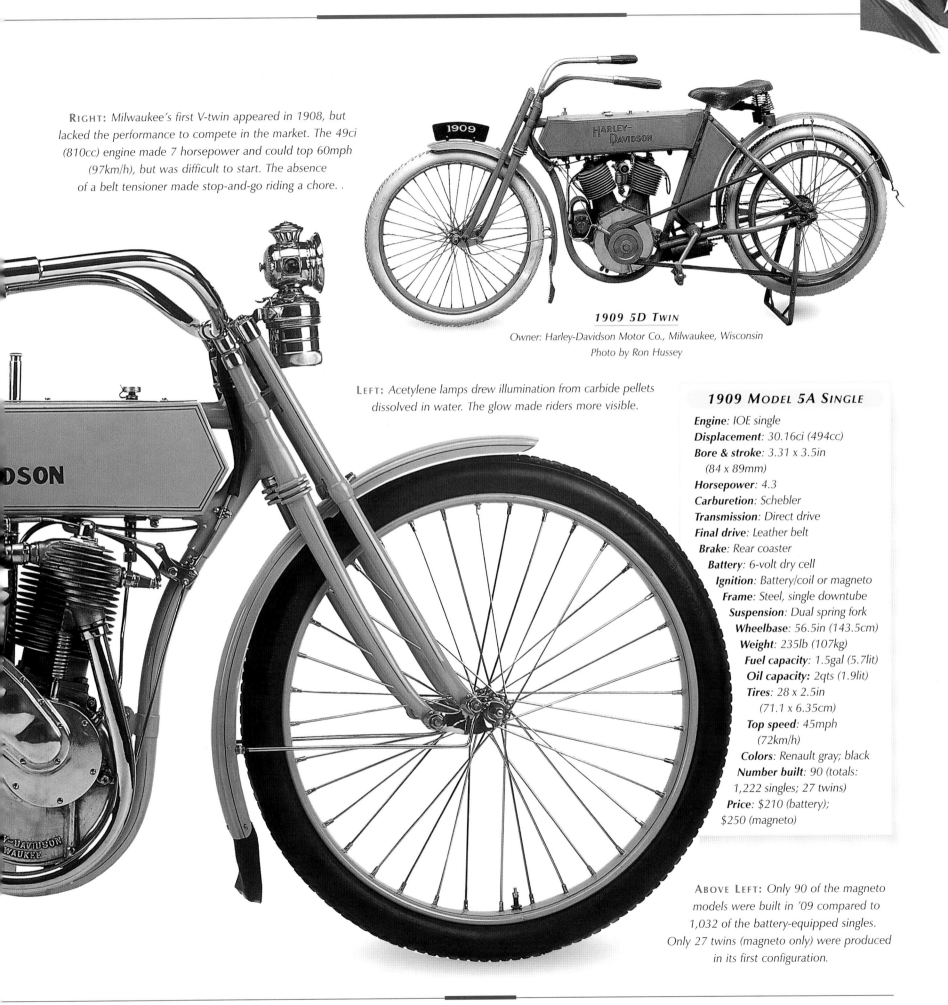

RIGHT: Milwaukee's first V-twin appeared in 1908, but lacked the performance to compete in the market. The 49ci (810cc) engine made 7 horsepower and could top 60mph (97km/h), but was difficult to start. The absence of a belt tensioner made stop-and-go riding a chore. .

1909 5D TWIN
Owner: Harley-Davidson Motor Co., Milwaukee, Wisconsin
Photo by Ron Hussey

LEFT: Acetylene lamps drew illumination from carbide pellets dissolved in water. The glow made riders more visible.

1909 MODEL 5A SINGLE

Engine: IOE single
Displacement: 30.16ci (494cc)
Bore & stroke: 3.31 x 3.5in
(84 x 89mm)
Horsepower: 4.3
Carburetion: Schebler
Transmission: Direct drive
Final drive: Leather belt
Brake: Rear coaster
Battery: 6-volt dry cell
Ignition: Battery/coil or magneto
Frame: Steel, single downtube
Suspension: Dual spring fork
Wheelbase: 56.5in (143.5cm)
Weight: 235lb (107kg)
Fuel capacity: 1.5gal (5.7lit)
Oil capacity: 2qts (1.9lit)
Tires: 28 x 2.5in
(71.1 x 6.35cm)
Top speed: 45mph
(72km/h)
Colors: Renault gray; black
Number built: 90 (totals:
1,222 singles; 27 twins)
Price: $210 (battery);
$250 (magneto)

ABOVE LEFT: Only 90 of the magneto models were built in '09 compared to 1,032 of the battery-equipped singles. Only 27 twins (magneto only) were produced in its first configuration.

living the dream

"[The Harley-Davidson] is a machine the very appearance of which suggests substantiability and power."

BICYCLING WORLD AND MOTORCYCLE REVIEW, APRIL 1908

Motorcycling at the turn of the century was a challenging affair, physically and socially. The majority of the early machines were merely bicycles with motors attached. Most of the roads outside the cities were rough, unpaved paths created by horse-drawn wagons. The two foremost means of personal transport at the time were horses and bicycles and neither horseman nor pedalers were generally pleased to share the byways with these noisy, smoke-belching machines.

So motorcyclists were at a disadvantage in the American transportation mix. In Europe the horse was superseded by the motorcycle, since most people couldn't afford cars. Henry Ford changed that scenario in the United States, and effectively relegated the self-propelled two-wheelers to the recreational category. Nonetheless, for the century's first decade, motorcycle manufacturers would pursue the market for practical transport.

The situation was defined by 1901, in this excerpt from the *Cycle and Automobile Trade Journal*, written by pioneer manufacturer George Holley:

"The successful motor cycle must present a symmetrical appearance, be reliable, free from vibration and disagreeable noise. The latter two have been accomplished, but the two former have been by no means so easily done, the reason being principally that up to date the makers of motor cycles have restricted themselves to bolting a motor to a bicycle, and in the majority of cases simply to an ordinary wheel. They have not attempted to design a complete motor cycle with the motor an integral part of the frame, but have built first the bicycle, then the motor."

Bill Harley and Art Davidson either didn't read the article, or decided on the trial-and-error approach common at the time. Their first two were unsatisfactory, but with the assistance of older brother Walter Davidson, the third one was a success. And it conformed exactly to Holley's description.

Within three years, the Harley-Davidson Motor Company had become a real manufacturing business. And its reputation grew quickly, characterized, as legend has it, by the question a motorcyclist on another brand asked his companion, "Who was that chap on the silent gray fellow?"

Harley and the Davidson brothers introduced social responsibility to motorcycling, and the standards of sturdy, durable construction and honest value for the dollar. Their methods would come to define the American motorcycle.

ABOVE: *Harley-Davidson went postal early on, competing with Indian for U.S. Post Office contracts. The advent of rural free delivery gave motorcycles an advantage on the dirt roads of remote towns and farms.*

ABOVE: *This photo is inscribed "To Police Commissioner Fred W. Smith, June 30, 1909." Fred is most likely the senior-looking gent on the right, who also happens to have the most well-equipped motorcycle of the lineup.*

ABOVE: *Arthur Davidson was a pioneer in the use of national advertising in the motorcycle business, featuring primarily original art.*

By 1908 the motorcycle industry was crowded with competitors. More than 200 companies had suddenly sprung up in the rush of excitement over personal motorized travel.

Art Davidson had basic technical skills, but his contribution to The Motor Company would be his management and marketing talents. He realized that extensive advertising, and the pursuit of fleet contracts, would be keys to the company's growth. Arthur was tireless in promoting Harley-Davidson in magazine and newspaper ads, and cultivating relationships with police departments and post offices in all the major cities. His first advertising slogan was, "The Harley-Davidson Makes Good Because it is Made Good."

1911–20: Growing to War

decade design evolution

"Our claims that the Harley-Davidson is the cleanest, most silent, most comfortable and the most economical motorcycle made are rather broad, but can easily be verified. Its extreme cleanliness is due to the fact that all moving parts requiring oil are enclosed. As for silence, the Harley-Davidson is known everywhere as the 'Silent Gray Fellow.'" 1912

Milwaukee's motorcycle production had tripled again in 1909 and 1910. Although the first V-twin failed to meet its performance goals, the single continued to improve each year. The cylinder and head remained a single casting, but in 1911 the head's cooling fins were vertical rather than horizontal to improve cooling.

A large measure of Milwaukee's need for a V-twin derived from the racing successes and popularity of Indian motorcycles. Harley-Davidson had thus far avoided direct factory participation in contests of speed and daring, but the drama and notoriety of racing had made it a marketing necessity. So the 49.48ci (810cc) V-twin of 1911 was the first Harley fitted with mechanical intake valves, and the straight front downtube added strength to the chassis. In 1912 the model 8D was a Sixty-one incher, and the 1000cc twin

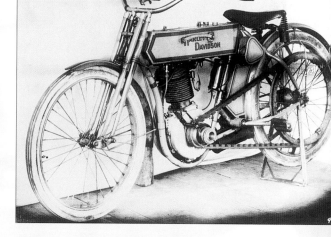

ABOVE: *In 1910 H-D experimented with a clutch on the belt-drive pulley, incorporating a notched belt. Proving unsatisfactory, a clutch was later fitted in the rear hub.*

can rightfully be considered Harley's first high-performance motorcycle.

The boom in board track racing, and the publicity (and sales) generated for Indian, Excelsior, Merkel and Cyclone, could no longer be ignored. Bill Harley put the styling sketches on a shelf and went looking for a racing director, which he found in William Ottaway, then an engineer with Thor Motorcycles.

By 1914 Harley and Ottoway had built a handful of racing motorcycles, in which competition exposed the problems of overheating (lubrication), valve-train reliability and chain and sprocket life. In the Georgia 300-mile (483km) national championship, Harley team rider Irving Janke finished third to Indian and Excelsior riders, and the battle was on. In 1915 Harley-Davidson teammates Otto Walker and Red Parkhurst finished 1-2 in the Venice, California 300-mile

1,097,315.

Patented May 19, 1914.

LEFT: *William S. Harley filed numerous patents on engine designs in the early days. This V-twin drawing was submitted on July 1913 and the patent was awarded a patent the following year on May 19.*

ABOVE: *The 5-horsepower 1913 single was offered with either magneto (shown) or battery ignition.*

LEFT: *The big end on the 1912 twin had roller bearings, to withstand the forces of 8 horsepower. Lever at right controlled the clutch in the rear hub.*

roadrace, announcing the arrival of the Milwaukee Wrecking Crew.

Indian had built and sold an overhead eight-valve twin racer for three years, and Harley was compelled to do the same. The first three appeared in 1916, one with a hand oil pump, one with a mechanical pump and one with both. The keystone frame used the engine as a stressed member; a single four-lobe cam lifted the valves, compression was about 6:1 and the engine made between 15 and 20 horsepower. The machine weighed 275 pounds (125kg), the wheelbase was 51.5 inches (131cm) and top speed was over 100mph (161km/h).

With the United States' entry into World War I, the racing program was supplanted by the demand for military hardware. By 1917 the intake valves were enclosed and the four-lobe cam developed for the eight-valve racer was used in the pocket-valve twins. Valve clearances and timing were increased for higher performance, and everything on the outside, including the engine and transmission cases, was painted olive green. In 1918 Milwaukee upgraded the electrical system on the twins, as well as the valve covers, clutch and chainguard.

In 1919 Harley-Davidson introduced the Model W Sport Twin, a 36ci (584cc) opposed twin based on the British Douglas. The six-horsepower lightweight was outsold by the Indian Scout, and was distributed mostly as an export model.

LEFT: *In 1914 Harley-Davidson introduced two-speed transmissions, generating "the largest advance sale" of any model it had made.*

RIGHT: *As the customer gained technical acumen, the advertising was more engineering oriented. "5-35" refered to horsepower-cubic inches.*

Harley-Davidson Two-Speed

With Exclusive Shuttle-Shift
(PATENTED)

Not Simply Noiseless—It is SOUNDLESS

It has—

no spur planetary gears to howl
no idler gears to rattle or wear
no expanding clutch to grab or wear
no planetary bands to squeal or wear
no cone clutches to jerk or to adjust
no brass, bronze or babbit bushings
no excessive weight
no oil to leak out

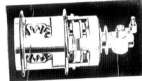

Harley-Davidson Two-Speed Hub with section cut away

The Harley-Davidson Two-Speed

is the strongest, the simplest, and at the same time the lightest two-speed made. It is provided with a safety factor in excess of 200% of the strains it is subjected to on the 8 horsepower model. Its simplicity has been worked out almost to the point of absurdity.

One part has been made to do the work of three, so that this remarkable two-speed adds but six pounds to the weight of the Harley-Davidson.

Note comparison of the coil construction of the Harley-Davidson hub, brake, clutch and two-speed

More Harley-Davidson two-speed twins will be manufactured in 1914 than all other Harley-Davidson models combined. To date this model has had the largest advance sale of any the Harley-Davidson Company has ever announced.

Quality Counts

DYNAMOMETER TEST CHART
HARLEY-DAVIDSON MOTOR CO.
MILWAUKEE, WIS.

The "5-35" motor actually develops 35% more power than the 4 H.P. at 40 miles per hour.

The "5-35" develops 48% more power at 30 miles per hour.

The "5-35" develops 80% more power at 20 miles per hour.

The "5-35" develops 105% more power at 15 miles per hour.

The "5-35" develops 145% more power at 10 miles per hour.

The "5-35" develops 166% more power at 5 miles per hour.

H.P. | Revolutions per Minute

An Actual Reproduction of Dynamometer Test Chart

The Most Powerful Single Cylinder Motorcycle Made and Why

It has been conclusively proven time and time again that the Harley-Davidson "5-35" is the most powerful single cylinder motorcycle made. The most accurate means of testing the power of a gasoline engine is by dynamometer. Above is reproduced an actual dynamometer test chart showing power produced by the "5-35" (black line) and that produced by our former popular 4 H.P. model (dotted line), which was acknowledged to be the most powerful single in the world.

Note the tremendous increase in power developed by the new "5-35." Note that it develops 166% more power at five miles an hour, 145% more power at ten miles an hour and 35% more power at forty miles an hour. Do you know that this means that hills that would stall the ordinary single cylinder motorcycle, the "5-35" will take with ease? The Harley-Davidson "5-35" will "pick-up" to forty miles an hour in 190 feet from a standing start. Its wonderful power development has made the

HARLEY-

1911 Model 7

In 1910 black paint was discontinued, making all the silent fellows gray. Harley-Davidson maintained its non-racing posture in terms of direct factory support, but now offered the model 6E "stock racer" for $275. The standard models were fitted with an idler arm, allowing the engine to tick over without disengaging the belt. Production had nearly tripled for an output of 3,168 motorcycles.

The big news from Milwaukee in 1911 was the reappearance of the Harley V-twin, now with mechanical intake valves, displacement of 49.48ci (810cc) and a conservative 6.5-horsepower rating. The new twin had no parts in common with the 1909 engine, and the new frame featured a straight rather than curved front downtube. The twin, model 7D, magneto ignition only, weighed 295 pounds (134kg) and was good for 60mph (97km/h).

Finning on the cylinder heads was now vertical rather than horizontal to improve engine cooling. The new twin, mechanically superior to its predecessor and bolted to an improved frame, represented a

1911 MODEL 7	
Engine: IOE single	**Frame**: Steel, single downtube
Displacement: 30.16ci (494cc)	**Suspension**: Dual spring fork
Bore & stroke: 3.31 x 3.5in (84 x 89mm)	**Wheelbase**: 56.5in (143.5cm)
Horsepower: 4.3	**Weight**: 235lb (107kg)
Carburetion: Schebler	**Fuel capacity**: 1.5gal (5.7lit)
Transmission: Direct drive	**Oil capacity**: 2qts (1.9lit)
Final drive: Leather belt	**Tires**: 28 x 2.5in (71.1 x 6.35cm)
Brake: Rear coaster	**Top speed**: 45mph (72km/h)
Battery: 6-volt dry cell	**Color**: Renault gray
Ignition: Battery/coil or magneto	**Number built**: 5,625 (all models)
	Price: $225

BELOW: *Long tiller-style handlebars prevailed until test riders determined that better control was afforded by moving the seat and rider closer to the middle of the motorcycle.*

RIGHT: *Luggage racks and tandem seats were among the first motorcycle accessories offered by the factory.*

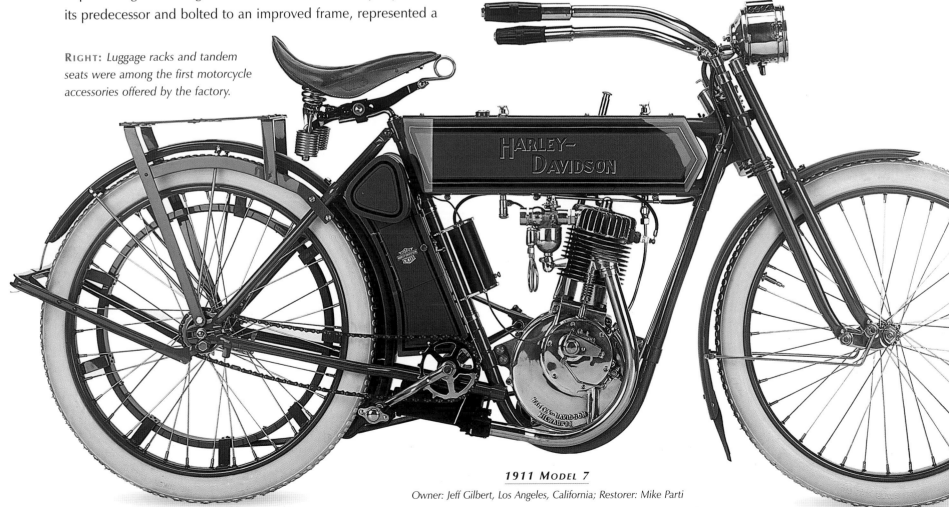

1911 MODEL 7
Owner: Jeff Gilbert, Los Angeles, California; Restorer: Mike Parti

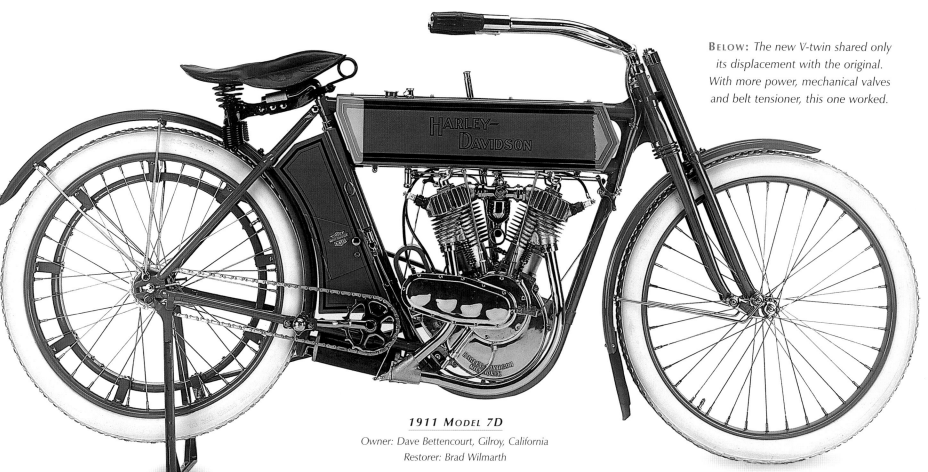

BELOW: *The new V-twin shared only its displacement with the original. With more power, mechanical valves and belt tensioner, this one worked.*

1911 MODEL 7D

Owner: Dave Bettencourt, Gilroy, California
Restorer: Brad Wilmarth

significant improvement in performance. But its price of $300 put the twin at a disadvantage against less costly competitors, most of which had chain rather than belt drive.

When staunch opponent Indian posted a 1-2-3 victory sweep in the prestigious Isle of Man race, the conviction in Milwaukee to stay out of racing began to waver. This suited Bill Harley just fine, since he and William Davidson had been urging their partners to take a more active stance in professional competition.

RIGHT: *Like the singles, the belt-tensioner pulley had moved closer to the drive pulley and was more efficient. The magneto had moved from the front to the rear of the engine.*

1911 MODEL 7D

Engine: IOE 45° V-twin
Displacement: 49.48ci (810cc)
Bore & stroke: 3 x 3.5in
 (76 x 89mm)
Horsepower: 6.5
Carburetion: Schebler
Transmission: Direct drive
Final drive: 1.75in (44mm)
 leather belt
Brake: Rear coaster
Ignition: Bosch magneto
Frame: Steel, single downtube
Suspension: Dual spring fork
Wheelbase: 56.5in (143.5cm)
Weight: 295lb (134kg)
Fuel capacity: 2.5gal (9.5lit)
Oil capacity: 1gal (3.8lit)
Tires: 28 x 2.5in (71.1 x 6.35cm)
Top speed: 60mph (97km/h)
Color: Renault gray
Number built: Unknown
Price: $300

1912 Models 8 & X8E

High performance made its first appearance at Harley-Davidson in 1912. The twin was joined by a big-bore 60.32ci (989cc) version, chain drive was an option, a new frame lowered the riding position and the spring-suspension seat made rough roads smoother. The rear fender was skirted to keep mud and debris off the rider's boots and chain or belt adjustment was now made at the pedal crank, eliminating the need to move the rear wheel.

The new twin also featured a clutch developed by Bill Harley and associate Henry Melk. Operated by a hand lever on the left side, the clutch was fitted within the rear wheel hub; the X designation noted the clutch model. The big twin had self-aligning ball bearings carrying the crankshaft and roller bearings at the connecting rods, and a crankcase breather routed to a chain oiler. Both twins were now equipped with hand oil pumps to complement the drip-feed oiler and reduce engine temperatures.

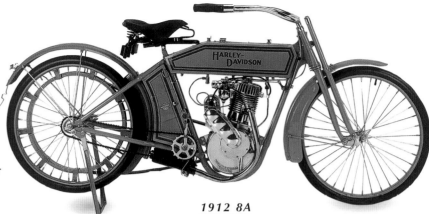

1912 8A

Owner: Otis Chandler, Ojai, California; Restorer: Jerry Sewell

ABOVE: *The condition of early sparkplugs could be checked easily by inspection through the glass insulator. Choosing the proper heat range would slowly become a more exact science.*

1912 MODEL X8E

Engine: IOE 45° V-twin
Displacement: 60.32ci (989cc)
Bore & stroke: 3.5 x 3.3125in (89 x 84mm)
Horsepower: 8
Carburetion: Schebler
Transmission: Direct drive
Clutch: Rear hub
Final drive: Chain (X8D: Belt)
Brake: Rear coaster
Ignition: Bosch magneto

Frame: Steel, single downtube
Suspension: Dual spring fork
Wheelbase: 56.5in (143.5cm)
Weight: 312lb (141.5kg)
Fuel capacity: 2.5gal (9.5lit)
Oil capacity: 1gal (3.8lit)
Tires: 28 x 2.5in (71 x 6.35cm)
Top speed: 65mph (105km/h)
Color: Renault gray
Number built: 1,616
Price: $285

LEFT: *Three models of the V-twin were offered in 1912, belt drive with or without clutch, and the big-bore, eight-horsepower E model, all at a lower price.*

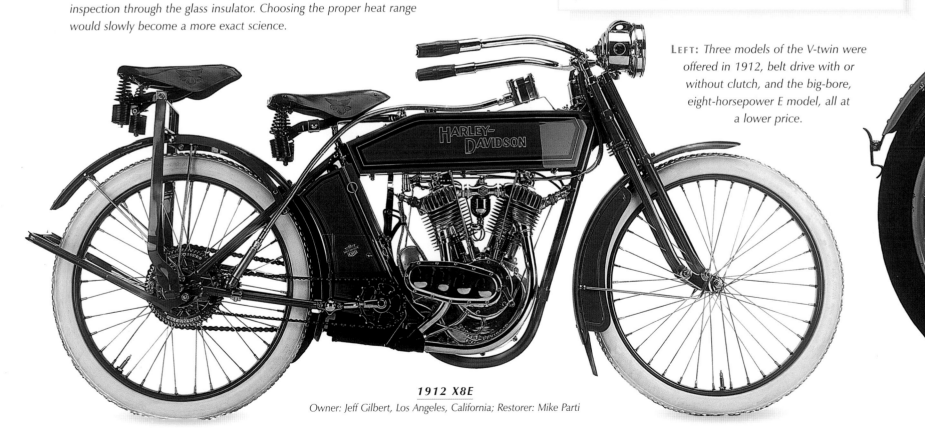

1912 X8E

Owner: Jeff Gilbert, Los Angeles, California; Restorer: Mike Parti

1913 Model 9A

In 1913 the single got the mechanically operated intake valve and a longer stroke, making it a 35ci (565cc) engine with 5 horsepower; thus the designation of "5-35" motor. An alloy piston, balanced with the crank and rod assembly, contributed to a smoother running single, and the 5-35 was soon showing good results in amateur races around the country.

Harley-Davidson had obviously grown more serious about going racing.

LEFT: *But for color changes, the Harley-Davidson logo had remained unchanged since the beginning. The letters were often larger in ad photos.*

BELOW: *The Ful-Floteing seat, introduced in 1912, employed a spring in the seat post which provided 4 inches (10cm) of suspension travel.*

1913 MODEL 9A	
Engine: IOE single	**Frame**: Steel, single downtube
Displacement: 34.47ci (564.89cc)	**Suspension**: Dual spring fork
Bore & stroke: 3.31 x 4in (84 x 102mm)	**Wheelbase**: 56.5in (143.5cm)
	Weight: 316lb (143kg)
Horsepower: 4.5	**Fuel capacity**: 1.5gal (5.7lit)
Carburetion: Schebler	**Oil capacity**: 3.5qts (3.3lit)
Transmission: Direct drive	**Tires**: 28 x 2.75in (71.1 x 7cm)
Final drive: Belt (9B: Chain)	**Top speed**: 50mph (80km/h)
Brake: Rear coaster	**Color**: Renault gray
Ignition: Bosch magneto	**Number built**: 1,510
	Price: $290

BELOW: *Tire sizes grew steadily in the first years, as designers discovered that more rubber on the road was an asset to both comfort and safety. While tire diameters varied little, their widths grew as motorcycles got heavier and faster. Tire technology moved beyond the bicycle stage.*

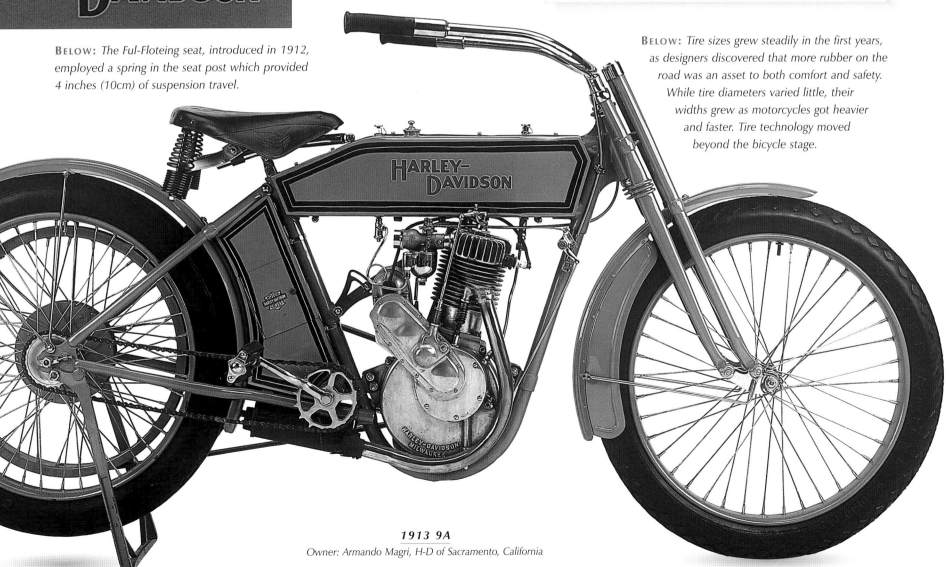

1913 9A
Owner: Armando Magri, H-D of Sacramento, California

1914 Model 10F; 1915 11K Racer; 1916 Model 16F

In 1914 the new Harleys had a step-starter linked to the pedals, eliminating the need to start the engine with the bike on the wheelstand. The single, still offered with belt or chain drive, and the twin both had the option of a two-speed transmission, valve springs were now enclosed and the new models were fitted with footboards for the first time. Milwaukee was out to make motorcycling easier in the hope of attracting a wider audience.

Another way to accomplish that goal, as Indian had demonstrated, was to win races. So the first Harley factory racer, the K model, appeared officially in 1914 though it didn't appear on the order blank until the following year. The "stripped stock racer" was based on the E model (direct drive) and was code-named Lightning. The racing department was now in operation, with Bill Harley in charge.

LEFT: *In 1915 Harley-Davidson for the first time offered electrical lighting as an option to acetylene lamps. The gas system soon faded to history.*

1914 MODEL 10F

Engine: F-head 45°V-twin
Displacement: 49.48ci (810.83cc)
Bore & stroke: 3 x 3.5in (76.2 x 89mm)
Compression ratio: n/a
Horsepower: 6.5
Transmission: 2-speed
Primary drive: Chain
Final drive: Chain
Brake: Rear coaster
Ignition: Magneto

Frame: Steel, single downtube
Suspension: F. Dual spring fork
Wheelbase: 56.5in (143.5cm)
Weight: 310lb (140.6kg)
Fuel capacity: 2.5gal (9.46lit)
Oil capacity: 4 qts (3.79lit)
Tires: 28 x 3in (71.1 x 7.62cm)
Top speed: 65mph (105km/h)
Color: Harley-Davidson gray
Number built: 7,956
Price: $285

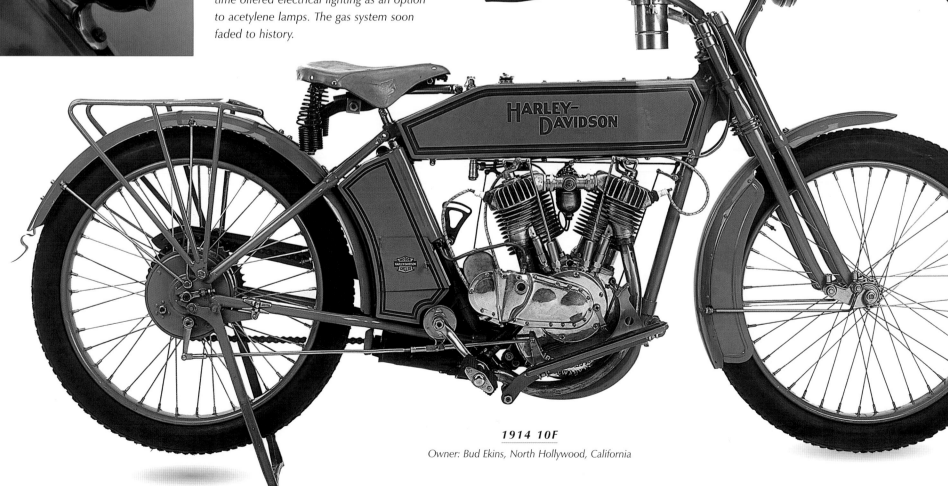

1914 10F
Owner: Bud Ekins, North Hollywood, California

In 1916 the company conformed model designations with the year of production, so the sequence went from the 1915 Model 11F to 16F the next year. The popularity of sidecars continued to grow, especially in Harley-Davidson's export markets. A three-speed transmission was introduced in 1915, and electric lighting was first offered as an option. Milwaukee produced more than 16,000 motorcycles each year from 1914 through 1916.

The tribe in Springfield, Massachusetts had built nearly 32,000 machines in 1913, but by 1916 their output dropped to 22,000. The gap was closing.

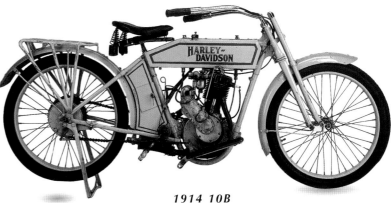

1914 10B
Owner: Trev Deeley Museum, Vancouver, British Columbia

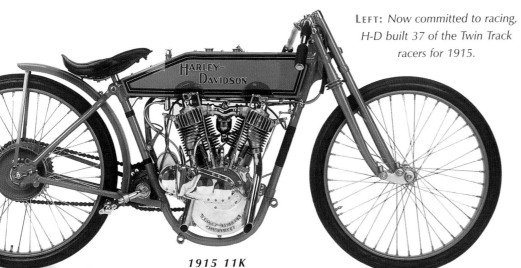

LEFT: *Now committed to racing, H-D built 37 of the Twin Track racers for 1915.*

1915 11K
Owner: Daniel Statnekov, Tesuque, New Mexico

1916 MODEL 16F

Engine: F-head 45° V-twin	**Frame**: Steel, single downtube
Displacement: 60.33ci (987.67cc)	**Suspension**: F. Leading link spring fork
Bore & stroke: 3.31 x 3.5in (84 x 89mm)	**Wheelbase**: 59.5in (151.1cm)
Horsepower: 11 @ 3,000rpm	**Weight**: 325lb (147.4kg)
Carburetion: Schebler	**Fuel capacity**: 2.75gal (10.4lit)
Transmission: 3-speed	**Oil capacity**: 5pts (2.4lit)
Primary drive: Chain	**Tires**: 28 x 3in (71.1 x 7.62cm)
Final drive: Chain	**Top speed**: 60mph (97km/h)
Brake: Rear drum	**Color**: Harley-Davidson gray
Battery: 6-volt	**Number built**: 5,898
Ignition: Coil/points	**Price**: $295

BELOW: *In 1916 the sidecar profile was lower and the fuel tank more rounded.*

1916 16F
Owner/restorer: Mike Parti, North Hollywood, California

1917 Model J; 1919 Model W; 1920 FCA Racer

Silent gray yielded to olive green in 1917, with war in Europe and the U.S. straddling the fence while still making preparations. German Bosch magnetos, no longer available, were replaced by American-made units. The four-lobe cam designed for the eight-valve racer was incorporated in the new J model, as the twin continued to eclipse the single cylinder. Fewer than 800 singles were built in 1917, compared to nearly 19,000 twins.

With the conclusion of the world's first mechanized war, peacetime motorcycle production shifted to new models and engineering innovation. Based on the British Douglas longitudinal opposed twin, Harley's 1919 Model W departed entirely from Milwaukee's past designs. But predictions of a strong interest in lightweight motorcycles after the war proved merely speculation. Although the Sport Twin was in production for four years, fewer than 10,000 were built and most of them exported.

American twins, apparently, were supposed to be V-shaped.

Motorcycle racing resumed in earnest after the war, and Harley-Davidson maintained its factory team. Jim Davis won the big Dodge City race in 1920 on the Harley pocket-valve FCA, and teammate Ray Weishaar took the victory in the 200-miler (322km) at Marion, Indiana. In 1921, members of the Harley-Davidson "Wrecking Crew" won every national championship event on the calendar.

1917 MODEL J
Owner: Harold Mathews,
Mathews Harley-Davidson, Fresno, California

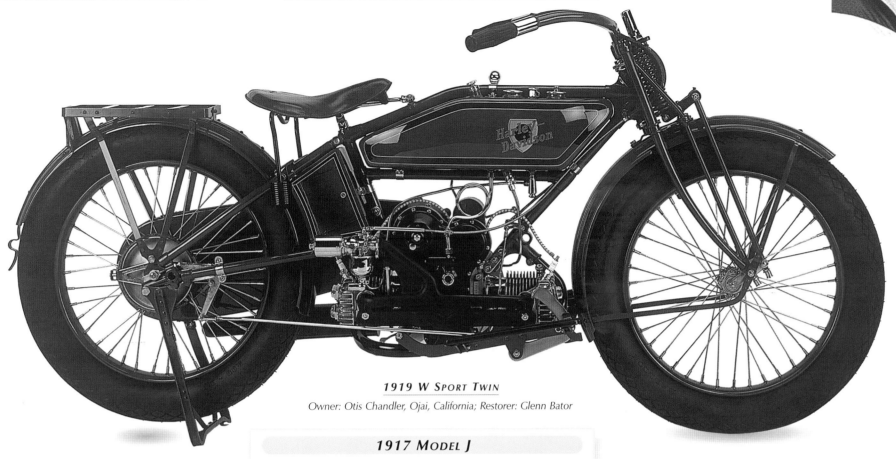

1919 W SPORT TWIN

Owner: Otis Chandler, Ojai, California; Restorer: Glenn Bator

LEFT: *Rumors of war: olive green replaced gray. Intake valves were enclosed.*

1917 MODEL J

Engine: F-head 45° V-twin
Displacement: 60.33ci (987.67cc)
Bore & stroke: 3.31 x 3.5in (84 x 89mm)
Horsepower: 16 @ 3,000rpm
Carburetion: Schebler
Transmission: 3-speed
Primary drive: Chain
Final drive: Chain
   Brake: Rear expanding band
    Battery: 6-volt
     Ignition: Coil/points

Frame: Steel, single downtube
Suspension: F. Leading link spring fork
Wheelbase: 59.5in (151cm)
Weight: 325lb (147.4kg)
Fuel capacity: 2.75gal (10.4lit)
Oil capacity: 5pts (2.36lit)
Tires: 28 x 3in (71.1 x 7.62cm)
Top speed: 65mph (105km/h)
Color: Olive green
Number built: 9,180
Price: $310

ABOVE: *Patterned on the British Douglas, the Sport Twin was one of the best Harley-Davidsons not to achieve domestic success. The six-horsepower opposed twin had little appeal to riders interested in powerful twins.*

BELOW: *The short-stroke two-cam, housed in a keystone racing frame, proved to be one of the most formidable racing machines of the era. Only a tick slower than its eight-valve sibling, the pocket valve held the edge in endurance in the long-distance races.*

1920 FCA RACER

Owner: Daniel Statnekov, Tesuque, New Mexico

living the dream

American motorcycling was a thriving enterprise by 1910, and although Harley-Davidson production was about 50 percent that of Indian's, the margin was beginning to shrink.

Milwaukee, despite the entreaties of racing enthusiasts, remained steadfast in not supporting professional competition. Both Walter Davidson, company president and general manager, and his brother Arthur, secretary and sales manager, saw scant benefit in having a factory team. The company's reputation had been built on reliable, durable machines; personal transportation and commercial applications took priority, and had established continued growth.

That perception and policy held sway in Milwaukee until 1913, when it was apparent that Indian, Excelsior, Merkel and Thor were widely popular. The reason, Bill Harley

Official Program
Saturday Eve., Aug. 30th, 1913
Races Every Saturday, Sunday and Wednesday at 8:30 P. M.

Program
., July 6th, 1913
nday and Wednesday at 8:30 P. M.

Milwaukee
Motordrome
Oakland and Newton Avenues
SEASON 1913
PRICE FIVE CENTS

LEFT: *Board track racing was on the verge of decline by 1913, just about the time Harley-Davidson took real interest in racing.*

BELOW: *The stuff of legends: (L–R) Ralph Hepburn, Shrimp Burns, Red Parkhurst, William Ottaway and Otto Walker. The Harley Wrecking Crew came to dominate pro racing.*

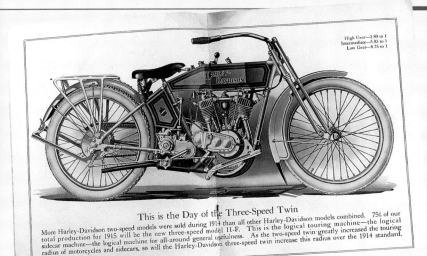

This is the Day of the Three-Speed Twin

More Harley-Davidson two-speed models were sold during 1914 than all other Harley-Davidson models combined. 75% of our total production for 1915 will be the new three-speed model 11-F. This is the logical touring machine—the logical sidecar machine—the logical machine for all-around general usefulness. As the two-speed twin greatly increased the touring radius of motorcycles and sidecars, so will the Harley-Davidson three-speed twin increase this radius over the 1914 standard.

High Gear—3.89 to 1
Intermediate—5.83 to 1
Low Gear—8.75 to 1

ABOVE: *This two-page ad for the 1915 twin touted the addition of a third gear. The price was $275.*

BELOW: *Adventure and romance on two wheels: this 1916 poster features a stylish couple on the open road. Note the passenger's side-saddle position.*

RIGHT: *If some pictures are worth a thousand words, this one contains a novel. Is Virgil miffed that Martha chose to go to town, and now he can't open it up? Does she not trust him to go alone, or is she really a thrill seeker? Oh, the story possibilities…*

RIGHT: *The Motorcycle Equipment Company of Hammondsport, New York issued its first accessory catalog in 1904.*

argued to his thrifty Scots partners, was professional racing. Indian riders Don Johns, Jake DeRosier, Maldwyn Jones and Shrimp Burns were household names among enthusiasts across the nation, and were lauded in the motorcycle press and general-interest newspapers. The daredevil young men racing on the "Wall of Death" were big news, and they sold motorcycles.

At this point Arthur Davidson was pushing economy and reliability in the company's advertising, as in this 1912 testimonial from the Home Telephone Company, Portland, Indiana: "Used our Harley-Davidson Motorcycle in the Trouble Department for two months, doing the work of three horses. It has traveled 2,400 miles [3,862km], has given entire satisfaction and the expense of gasoline and oil is so small as to hardly be worth consideration."

When Henry Ford began the mass production of cars on an assembly line, and raised the pay of factory workers to $5 a day (twice the prevailing wage), the American motorcycle industry took a triple hit. Cars would be less expensive, more people could afford them and motorcycles would cost more to produce, since the wages of all factory workers would rise.

Thus began the shift from motorcycles as transportation and utility vehicles to recreational and sporting devices, and consequently Harley-Davidson's slide into professional racing.

"The time is coming when no man can be in the middle of the road. He must either be for America or against America, and the sooner we get together on this question, the better able we will be to win this war."

ARTHUR DAVIDSON

Once Harley-Davidson got into the racing game, they took to the task with serious intent. Working together, Bill Harley and William Ottaway, former racing engineer for Thor, improved both the reliability and power output of the pocket-valve engine, and set to work on an overhead-valve version to match Indian's OHV model. Following a year of development in 1914, with a few good results including Irving Janke's third place in the 300-mile (483km) National at Savannah, Georgia, the Harley-Davidson Racing Team was set to go.

By March, 1915 both Indian and Excelsior knew they were in for a real scrap, and that Milwaukee had found the speed to match their established reliability. The premier showdown came at Venice, California, where former racer Paul "Daredevil" Derkum had put together a street course incorporating sections of board track. The best of the best were on hand: Don Johns on the blazing Cyclone, Excelsior star Bob Perry and factory teams from Indian, Thor and Pope. But after 300 miles (483km), it was Harley riders Otto Walker and Red Parkhurst in first and second, followed by the Excelsiors of Carl Goudy and Bob Perry.

ABOVE: The Harley-Davidson Enthusiast *was first published in 1916; this is issue number 4. The title was later shortened to* The Enthusiast.

RIGHT AND FAR RIGHT: *Harley-Davidson devoted a third of its 1918 production to military models. The cover of the November 3, 1917 issue of* The Literary Digest *shows an army dispatch rider in action.*

LEFT: *A 1916 ad from the* Illustrated London News. *The accompanying copy reads: "A soldier bluff with a little bit of fluff on a winter afternoon," credited to "The Bystander," November 10, 1915.*

RIGHT AND BELOW: *British lady rider, perhaps a nurse, and injured soldiers. Two American farm girls ready for a break from the chores.*

In June, at a 100-mile (161km) dirt track event in Detroit, a new name appeared in the winner's circle. Jim Davis, 18, of Columbus, Ohio rode an Indian to beat factory riders from Harley-Davidson and Excelsior. Otto Walker went on to win the prestigious 300-mile (483km) Dodge City National, and in 1916 the victory went to Irving Janke on the new Harley eight-valve built by Ottaway. The team manager also introduced strict training for the riders and efficient pit stops, which other teams had neglected.

But the first golden age of American motorcycle racing between the big three factories would soon conclude with the effects of World War I. Although the United States had chosen to remain neutral in the conflict for more than two years, nearly half of Milwaukee's 1916 production went for military use. The factories agreed to suspend racing activities in 1917, as the prospects of U.S. involvement in the war gained probability.

Woodrow Wilson was re-elected to the U.S. presidency in 1916 on a strong wave of anti-war sentiment. The war in Europe, now well into its third year, held little interest for most Americans, many of whom had recently emigrated from there and others old enough to recall the bloody toll of the American Civil War. The isolationist policy, and often pro-German sentiment, prevailed until 1917 when Wilson's attempt to negotiate peace had failed and German ambitions appeared to be global.

RIGHT: *In the mid-teens, Harley-Davidson was still emphasizing the practical aspects of sidecars. Detailed illustration in advertising soon yielded to photography.*

BELOW: *The editor of* The Literary Digest *obviously appreciated motorcycles. This is the edition of August 23, 1919.*

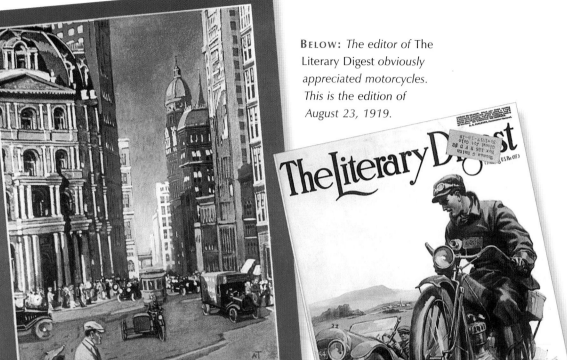

ABOVE: *For either going to the city or escaping from it, the Harley with a sidecar was the means to the sporting life.*

RIGHT: *Motorcycle commercial delivery vehicles were popular in the 1910s and '20s. The forecar (shown) and side-mount parcel car were both economical and easier to park than trucks.*

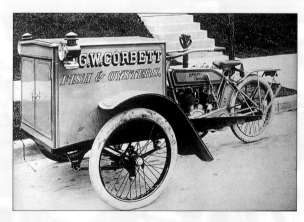

Indian, whose co-founders had left the company, was in a weakened financial condition. Management decided to devote nearly all Indian production to military contracts, while Harley-Davidson consigned about half its output to the war effort. At this point the two companies were roughly even in terms of production, but Milwaukee would draw ahead from here on.

The three-speed twins now accounted for the bulk of Harley-Davidson's market, and substantial numbers were exported to Great Britain, which had suspended production of civilian machines for the duration of the war. A photo in the May 18, 1916 issue of *Motor Cycle Illustrated* showed a dozen motorcyclists with sidecars motoring beside the Thames River. The caption read: "Party of British sidecarists taking convalescent soldiers for daily rides on England's magnificent roads. This is but one of many ways in which motorcyclists in Britain aid the various branches of the army."

At home *The Enthusiast* kept Harley-Davidson owners informed on the company's contribution to the war effort,

ABOVE: *A photo from the* Illustrated London News, *September 4, 1915, shows a group of Birmingham Harley riders at Shakespeare's Stratford-on-Avon birthplace.*

RIGHT: *Harley ad shot of 1914 shows a sporting couple pausing on a country bridge. Tank lettering in early ads was enlarged for maximum brand identification.*

BELOW: *Harley-Davidson bicycles, made by the Davis Sewing Machine Company, lasted only a few years.*

including photos of soldiers apparently in combat situations. These were training photos staged for publication, since motorcycles rarely figured in real battles. The machines, with and without sidecars, were employed mostly for military police duties and dispatch work, as shown in the illustration on page 49 used on the cover of *The Literary Digest*. Bill Harley did design a machine-gun mount for the sidecar, which found limited use for scouting duties when self-defense seemed an appropriate measure.

Of the military motorcycles built by Harley-Davidson (14,000) and Indian (41,000), the majority stayed in the United States for training purposes and post duties. Many of them remained in use until the beginning of World War II. The surplus machines on hand when the war ended in 1918 were auctioned on the civilian market and refitted for road use by dealers.

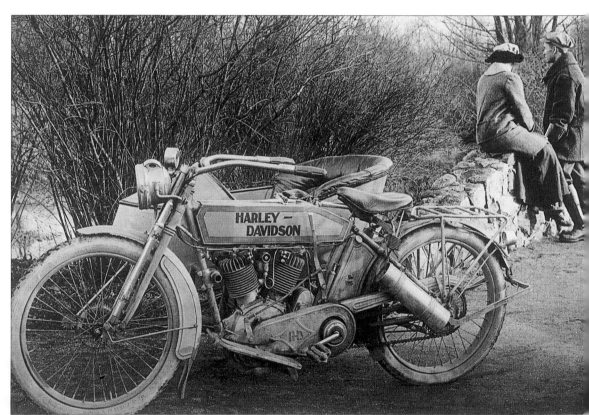

The Harley-Davidson Service School was instituted in 1917 to train military personnel in the maintenance and repair of motorcycles. After the war the school shifted to the training of civilian mechanics, but would return to military activity some two decades down the road.

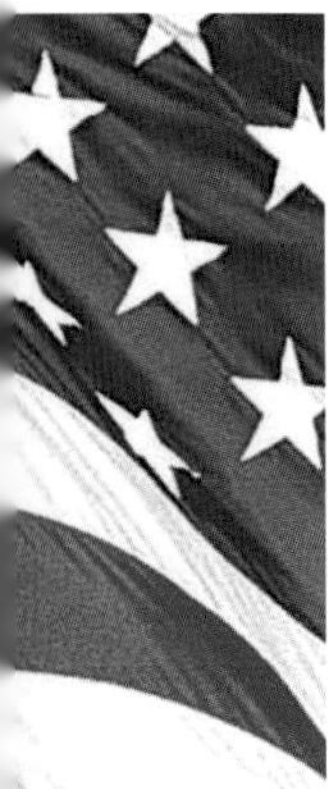

1921—30: Post-War Prosperity

decade design evolution

"We found that instead of racing activities consuming a small portion of the time of the engineering department, the demands had gradually increased until it was out of all proportion to the results obtained. With the new arrangement, the entire engineering department will be devoted to the solving of problems connected with the standard production mounts and the purchaser will benefit accordingly."

WILLIAM S. HARLEY

The prospects for a flourishing motorcycle market after the war were promising at first. Pressed to compete with Indian's biggest twin, and the four-cylinder models of Henderson and Ace, Harley's new JD Seventy-four (1200cc) had bore and stroke of 3.42 x 4 inches (87 x 101.6mm) and new silicon-chrome steel exhaust valves. The carburetor throat was upped to 1.25 inches (32mm).

The Seventy-four also ran solid flywheels, new pistons, connecting rods and crankcase. Harley-Davidson had introduced their own generator the previous year, replacing the occasionally troublesome Remy unit. The 18-horsepower twin was advertised as the perfect match for Harley's new two-passenger sidecar. The JDS (sidecar) engine had compression shims for lower-rpm urge and two fewer teeth on the countershaft sprocket compared to the solo engine.

But the optimism for a booming market was short-lived. Leftover military models, and another reduction of automobile prices by Henry Ford, put the motorcycle business in the dumps. In the hope of appealing to the economy market, Harley-Davidson revived the single in 1921. Even at the claimed 80 miles per gallon (28km per liter), the 37ci (600cc) model CD found few buyers at $430, only $20 below the standard 61ci (1000cc) model F twin. Prices were cut drastically across the model line for 1922, and the single sold for $315.

Darker Brewster green with gold striping replaced the military olive hue in 1922, and the single was dropped at the end of the year. The twins had compression ratios reduced in the interest of economy, and new crankcases and gearbox appeared. Both the Seventy-four and Sixty-one twins now had solid flywheels, and an improved oil pump was

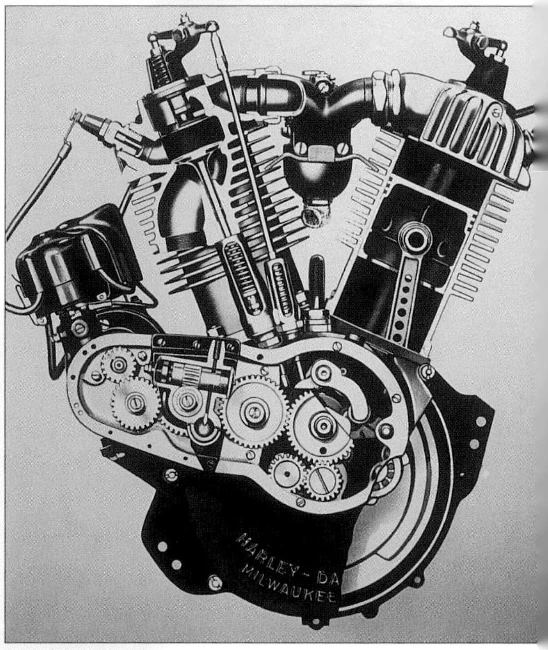

ABOVE: *The JD engine (74ci/1200cc) was introduced in 1921. This cutaway of a 1924 model shows drilled connecting rods and aluminum pistons inherited from the racing models.*

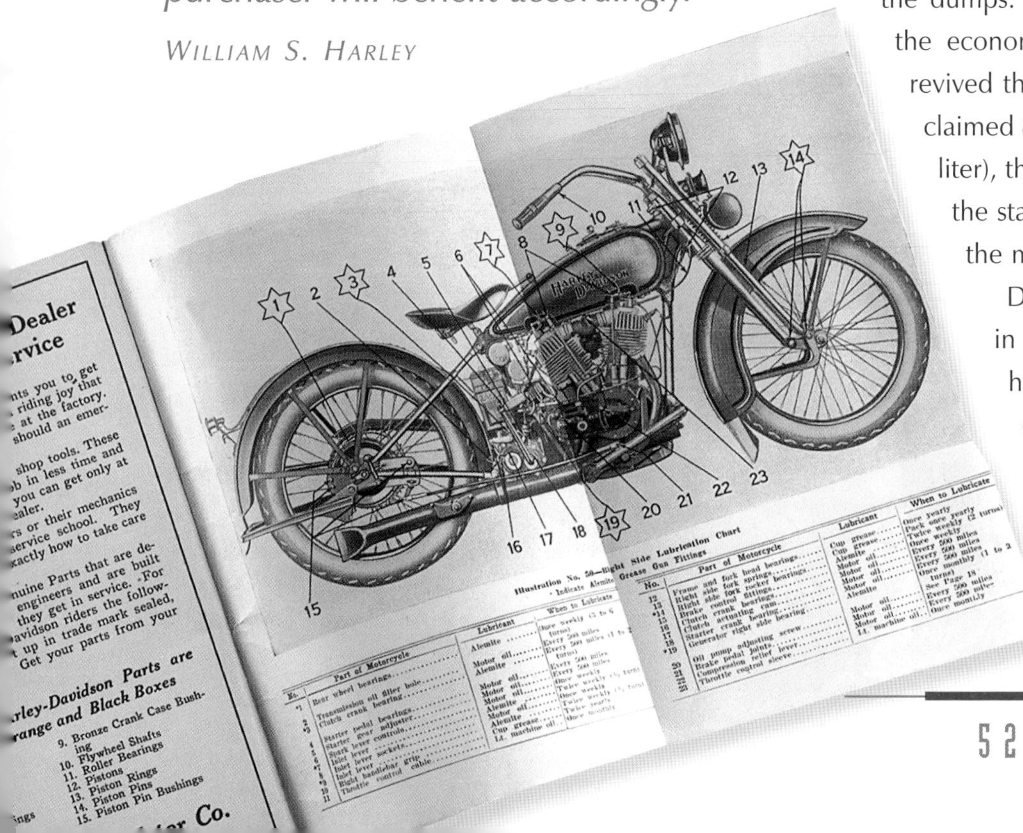

LEFT: *Harley-Davidson produced some of the most detailed handbooks in the industry. This 1924 edition includes a lubrication chart calling out the grease fitting locations, types of lubricants and maintenance schedule.*

RIGHT: *The 1927 Sporting Single with overhead valves was produced in limited numbers (524) compared to the basic flathead version (4,155). Only six of the magneto-equipped Racing Singles were built.*

BELOW: *Economic conditions improved in the late 1920s, and Harley advertising expanded in proportion. Mechanical features inherited from racing received greater emphasis in print.*

introduced late in the year. The front fork design was unchanged, but had strengthened components throughout.

The racing program also fell victim to the stalled economy. Harley-Davidson had dominated professional competition for six years, developing in the process a reliable machine and an efficient team of racers and crew.

The national economy improved gradually in 1923 and '24, when Harley introduced new iron-alloy pistons, an even more stout front fork and grease fittings on the running gear. Milwaukee's desire to make motorcycling easier for the general public led to a new, lower frame in 1925. With smaller wheel diameter, seat height was dropped by three inches (7.6cm), and the frame positioned the rider closer to the handlebars. And streamlined styling arrived in the larger, teardrop fuel tank.

The single was back in 1926 with the 21ci (350cc) side-valve model A and a limited production overhead-valve version for racing. Priced at only $210, the single featured detachable Ricardo cylinder heads, three-speed transmission, external contracting rear brake and the "Ful-Floteing" sprung seat. Most of the singles were exported to Great Britain, Europe and Australia.

The single's detachable heads forecast the end of the pocket-valve era in Milwaukee, and the ensuing debate over the choice between an overhead or side-valve design. The success of Indian's flatheads was the single largest factor in Bill Harley's decision to go with the side-valve configuration; that and their economy of manufacture. The appearance of the 45ci (750cc) R model in 1929, and the side-valve Seventy-four a year later, signaled the end for the pocket-valve engine, now retired after decades of commendable service.

The V series side-valve Seventy-fours, introduced in 1930, were fundamentally enlarged Forty-fives. The engine made slightly more power than the Two-cam JD, but the motorcycle was considerably heavier, so top speed was about the same. Despite some problems with the early side-valve engines, once sorted out they proved more durable than the IOE engine. The new flathead had detachable heads, a broader torque spread than its predecessor and the primary chain was lubricated automatically. The V model was rated at 28 horsepower; the high-compression VL at 30.

Production in Milwaukee had gradually increased to match the pre-war figures, but the period of prosperity was about to end with the advent of the Great Depression.

1921 Models J & JD; 1923 8-Valve Racer

The trusty 61-inch (1000cc) J model was joined in 1921 by a 74-inch (1200cc) engine designated the JD, but known thereafter simply as the Seventy-four. Lower-compression versions, the JS and JDS, were sold for sidecar duty. Both twins had new fenders, the front cover with a more deeply valenced contour. With electrics the big twin sold for $520, and the magneto version was priced at $485. Only one single, the 37ci (600cc) CD model, remained in production.

Harley-Davidson was now the world's largest motorcycle company, with dealers in 67 countries around the world and production of more than 27,000 machines in 1920. Unfortunately most of those motorcycles represented overproduction from the war years, leaving Milwaukee with excess inventory. Output for 1921 fell to 11,460.

BELOW: *The accessory catalog grew larger in the 1920s. The luggage carrier was a $6 item.*

In February that year, Harley rider Otto Walker on an eight-valve factory racer won the one-mile (1.6km) time trial at the Fresno, California board track at 107.78mph (173.45km/h). Walker also took the 15- and 50-mile (24 and 80.5km) events at over 100mph (161km/h). At the final Dodge City 300-miler (483km), Ralph Hepburn broke the 100-, 200- and 300-mile (161, 322 and 483km) records on another Harley eight-valve racer.

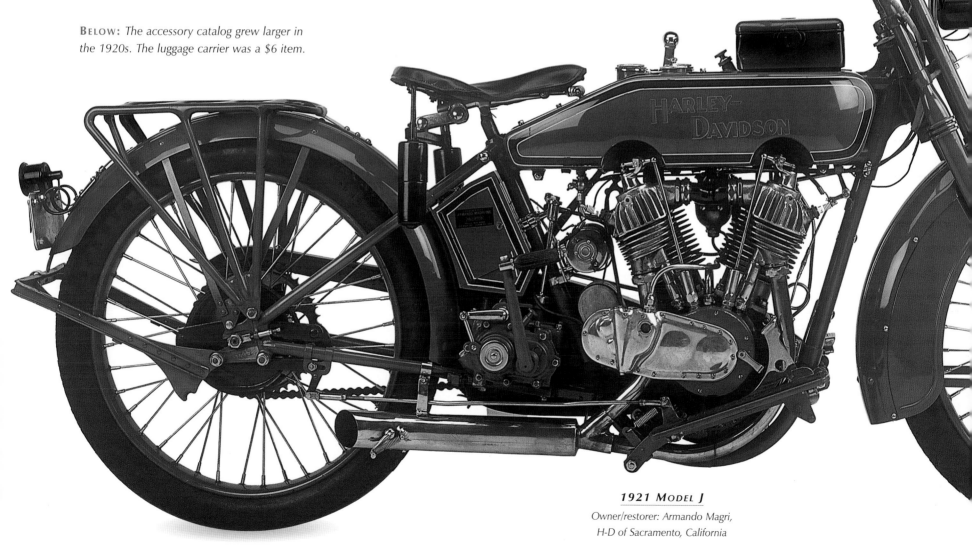

1921 MODEL J
Owner/restorer: Armando Magri,
H-D of Sacramento, California

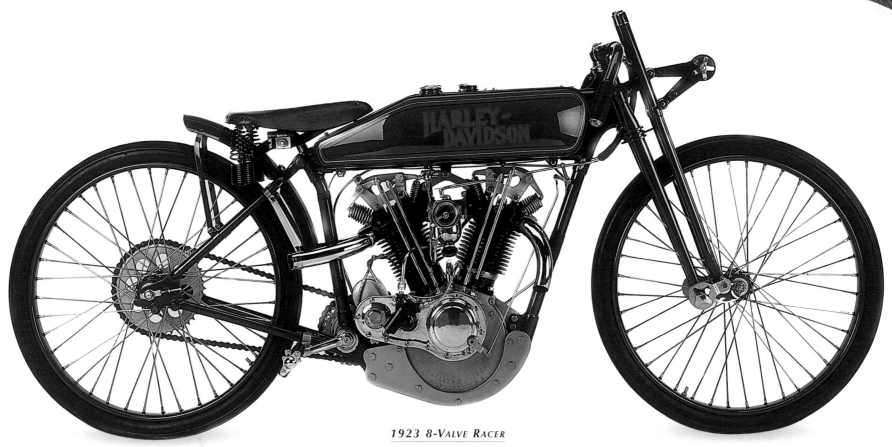

1923 8-VALVE RACER

Owner: Daniel Statnekov, Tesuque, New Mexico; Restorer: Brad Wilmarth

1921 MODEL J

Engine: F-head 45° V-twin
Displacement: 60.33ci (987.67cc)
Bore & stroke: 3.31 x 3.5in
  (84 x 89mm)
Horsepower: 16 @ 3,000rpm
Carburetion: 1in (25mm) Schebler
Transmission: 3-speed
Primary drive: Chain
Final drive: Chain
Brake: Rear drum
Battery: 6-volt
Ignition: Coil/points
Frame: Steel, single downtube
Suspension: F. Leading link
  spring fork
Wheelbase: 59.5 in (151cm)
Weight: 365lb (165.6kg)
Fuel capacity: 2.75gal (10.4lit)
Oil capacity: 4pts (1.9lit)
Tires: 28 x 3in (71.1 x 7.62cm)
Top speed: 70mph (113km/h)
Color: Olive green
Number built: 4,526
  (V-twin total: 9,477)
Price: $485

ABOVE: *The eight-valve racer, first offered in 1916 in response to Indian's model, was priced at $1,500 to discourage privateers.*

8-VALVE RACER

Engine: OHV 45° V-twin	**Ignition**: Magneto
Displacement: 60.33ci (987.67cc)	**Frame**: Steel, single downtube
Bore & stroke: 3.31 x 3.5in (84 x 89mm)	**Suspension**: F. Leading link spring fork
Compression ratio: Approx. 6:1	**Wheelbase**: 51.5in (130.8cm)
Horsepower: Approx. 20	**Weight**: 275lb (124.7kg)
Carburetion: Schebler	**Fuel capacity**: 1.43gal (5.4lit)
Transmission: Direct drive	**Oil capacity**: 5pts (2.4lit)
Primary drive: Chain	**Tires**: 28 x 3in (71 x 7.62cm)
Final drive: Chain	**Top speed**: 105–115mph (170–185km/h)
Brake: None	**Color**: Olive green
Battery: None	**Number built**: Approx. 30–50
	Price: $1,500

Introduced in 1916 to compete with Indian's similar overhead-valve racing engine, the Harley eight-valve and its four-valve single counterpart won many races in the States and abroad. Harley-Davidson withdrew its factory team in 1922, having made their point.

1926 Model JD; 1926 A & B Singles; 1926 FHAC

After two years of lowered production, Milwaukee's output rose again in 1923–24. By 1925 Harley-Davidson was back on form with a host of new and improved features in both form and function. The motorcycles were built on new frames with a single downtube and lowered seat height, which improved handling. The streamlined teardrop fuel tank debuted in '25, and the twins got wider rims and tires, a better fork and a more comfortable seat with longer spring travel.

Few changes were made to the twins for 1926. The fenders were slightly wider, and although Milwaukee had yet to exhaust the supply of olive green paint, cream and white were offered as optional colors. The 61-inch (1000cc) J model sold for $315 and the Seventy-four was $335. Accessories included a luggage carrier, jiffy stand, ammeter and either a Corbin Brown or Johns-Manville speedometer.

In 1926 the A (magneto) and B (battery) 21ci (350cc) singles were available in both side-valve and overhead valve ("sporting single") editions. The OHV engine was rated at 12 horsepower and the side-valve at 8. The racing version of the single, nicknamed the "Peashooter" for its exhaust note, was good for almost 85mph (137km/h) on a dirt track.

BELOW: *The JD moved to the forefront of sport performance. Racing did improve the breed.*

1926 MODEL JD

Engine: F-head 45° V-twin
Displacement: 74.66ci (1207.11cc)
Bore & stroke: 3.44 x 4in (87 x 102mm)
Horsepower: 24
Carburetion: 1.25in (32mm) Schebler
Transmission: 3-speed
Primary drive: Chain
Final drive: Chain
Brake: Rear drum
Battery: 6-volt
Ignition: Coil/points
Frame: Steel, single downtube
Suspension: F. Leading link spring fork
Wheelbase: 59.5in (151.1cm)
Weight: 405lb (184kg)
Fuel capacity: 11.5pts (5.44lit)
Oil capacity: 5pts (2.36lit)
Tires: 27 x 3.85in (68.6 x 9.78cm)
Top speed: 75mph (121km/h)
Colors: Olive green (options: white; cream)
Number built: 9,544
Price: $335

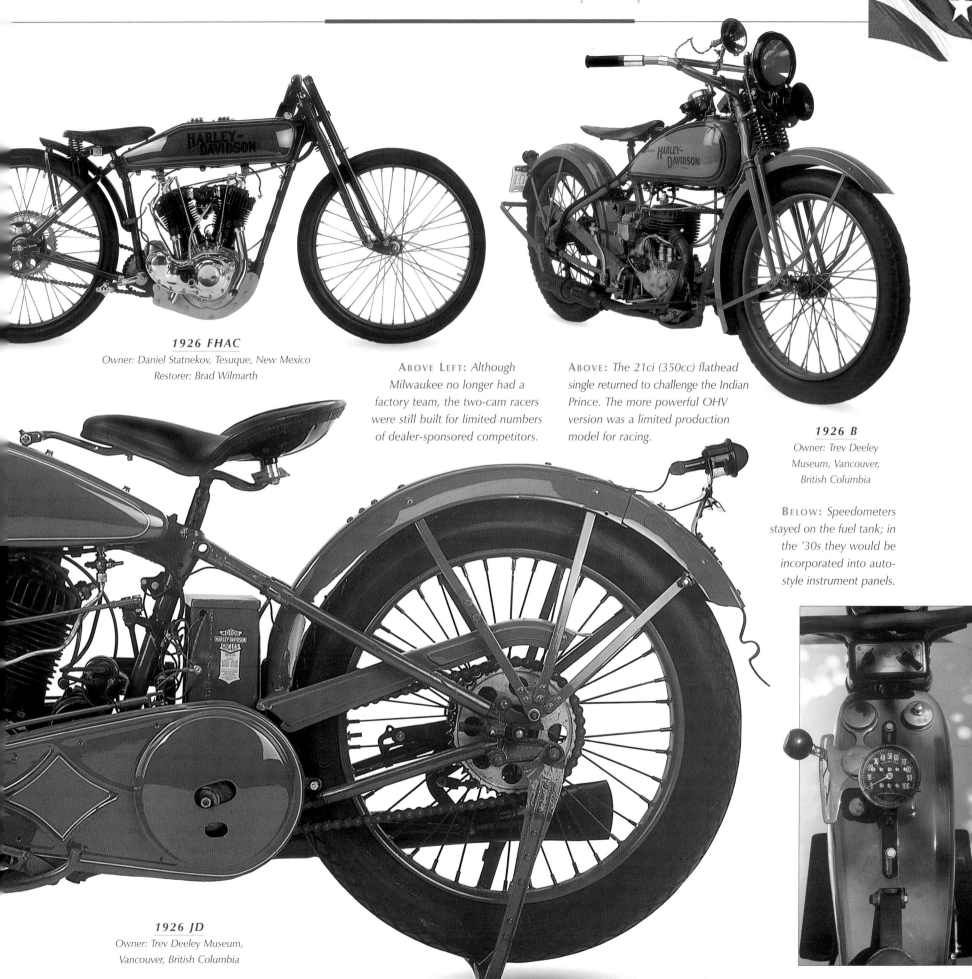

1926 FHAC
Owner: Daniel Statnekov, Tesuque, New Mexico
Restorer: Brad Wilmarth

ABOVE LEFT: *Although Milwaukee no longer had a factory team, the two-cam racers were still built for limited numbers of dealer-sponsored competitors.*

ABOVE: *The 21ci (350cc) flathead single returned to challenge the Indian Prince. The more powerful OHV version was a limited production model for racing.*

1926 B
Owner: Trev Deeley Museum, Vancouver, British Columbia

BELOW: *Speedometers stayed on the fuel tank; in the '30s they would be incorporated into auto-style instrument panels.*

1926 JD
Owner: Trev Deeley Museum, Vancouver, British Columbia

1926 Model AA & BA

Indian had introduced their 21ci (350cc) side-valve single in 1925, followed by an overhead-valve rendition the following year. Designer Charles Franklin remained convinced that lightweight motorcycles would sell in the U.S., and they made swell racing bikes. Milwaukee was more or less forced to agree, and built quite similar machines. Unlike the twins, the singles had detachable cylinder heads based on the design of British engineer Harry Ricardo.

The singles weighed about 265 pounds (120kg), while the racing version was some 30 pounds (13.5kg) lighter. Harley-Davidson riders took six of the national championship races in 1926, with eight falling to Indian.

LEFT: *The tank-mounted gearshift gate would remain for decades to come. The design would outlive the shared compartments for fuel and oil, when lubrication fluid eventually got its own container nearer the engine's moving parts.*

1927 MODEL BA

Engine: Overhead valve single
Displacement: 21.10ci (345.73cc)
Bore & stroke: 2.875 x 3.25in (73 x 82.5mm)
Horsepower: 12 @ 4,000rpm
Carburetion: Schebler
Transmission: 3-speed
Primary drive: Chain
Final drive: Chain
Brake: Rear contracting band
Ignition: Battery/coil

Frame: Steel, single downtube
Suspension: Leading link spring fork
Wheelbase: 56.5in (146.3cm)
Weight: 263lb (119.3kg)
Fuel capacity: 3gal (11.36lit)
Oil capacity: 3qts (2.84lit)
Tires: 26 x 3.3in (66 x 8.38cm)
Top speed: 60mph (97km/h)
Color: Olive green
Number built: 524
Price: $275

BELOW: *Although most of the OHV singles were built for competition duty, some did see service as road models. Overheads were produced in the hundreds, flatheads in the thousands.*

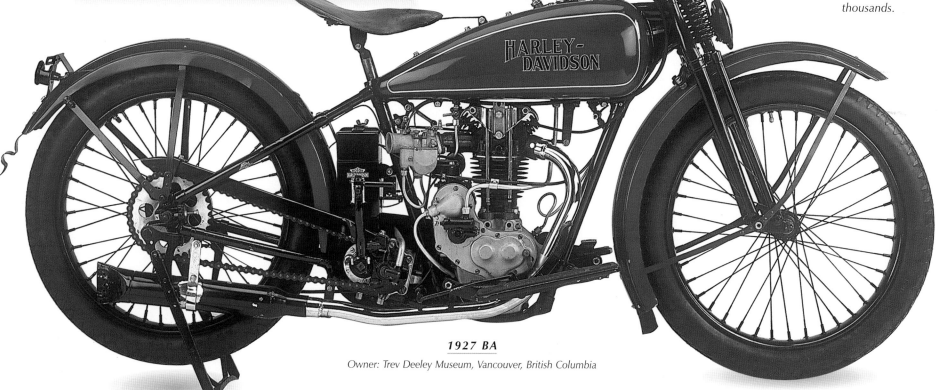

1927 BA
Owner: Trev Deeley Museum, Vancouver, British Columbia

1929 Model JDH

T he JDH—also known as the Two-cam—came to market in 1928. The Sixty-one and Seventy-four J models had smaller diameter wheels, narrowed fuel tank and—for the first time from Milwaukee—a front brake. Fears that riders would pitch themselves headlong into harm's way proved nearly as weak as the brakes themselves.

The Two-cam was based on Harley's well-developed pocket-valve racing engine, and in 1929 the twins were given minor mechanical improvements, a four-tube muffler and dual "bullet" headlights. Olive green remained the standard color, but cream, blue, orange, maroon and gray were now options. The JDH made about 30 horsepower in stock trim, and was good for 50 in the hands of an astute tuner. But the pocket-valve engine was headed for history.

LEFT: *The ammeter occupied the center of the instrument panel, flanked by switches for ignition and lights. Charging current for the battery was regulated by a lever on the generator.*

1929 JDH
Owner: Otis Chandler, Ojai, California
Restorer: Glenn Bator

1929 MODEL JDH

Engine: IOE 45° V-twin
Displacement: 74ci (1200cc)
Bore & stroke: 3.4 x 4in (87 x 101.6mm)
Compression ratio: 6.5:1
Horsepower: 29 @ 4,000rpm
Carburetion: Schebler
Transmission: 3-speed
Primary drive: Chain
Final drive: Chain
Brakes: F. & R. Drum
Battery: 6-volt
Ignition: Coil/points
Frame: Steel, single downtube
Suspension: F. Double spring fork
Wheelbase: 59.5in (151.1cm)
Weight: 408lb (185kg)
Fuel capacity: 4.75gal (18lit)
Oil capacity: 4qts (3.79lit)
Tires: 18 x 3.85in (45.7 x 9.78cm)
Top speed: 85mph (137km/h)
Colors: Olive green (options: azure blue; police blue; fawn gray; cream; maroon; orange)
Number built: JDH: unknown; JD: 10,182
Price: $370

1929 Model D; 1930 Model C

Indian had won all the national championship events in 1928 and did it again in '29; Harley-Davidson was intent on preventing that happening again. Thus the appearance of the D model in 1929; a 45ci (750cc) flathead, 45-degree V-twin and the high-compression engine DL. The new Forty-five was a direct challenge to Indian's 101 Scout, which it would meet regularly on dirt tracks for the next 25 years.

Of course the Forty-five also served as a sportbike, transportation, mail carrier, police bike and three-wheeled delivery vehicle. The flathead Forty-five would carry on through generations of redesigned big twins, and as lady luck would have it, remained in production for 45 years.

Milwaukee added a bigger single to the roster in 1930, the 30.50ci (500cc) C model which came to be called the Thirty-fifty. The single shared the frame of the Forty-five, made a bit more than 10 horsepower and had a three-speed gearbox. Of course the all-purpose single was also drafted for racing.

Jim Davis rode the Thirty-fifty to one national win at Syracuse, New York in 1931, but Indian riders dominated most of the events. Springfield built both flathead and overhead 30.50ci (500cc) track machines. Motorcycle racers were now free agents who owed allegiance to no single factory. Joe Petrali of San Francisco rode the Harley Peashooter in short track events, the Excelsior twin on the mile (1.6km) and the Harley Sixty-one for board track.

BELOW: *Harley's first flathead Forty-five had a vertical generator mounted at the left side of the engine. Low-compression D (4.3:1) was rated at 15 horse-power, standard DL (5:1) at 18.5 ponies and high-compression DLD at 20.*

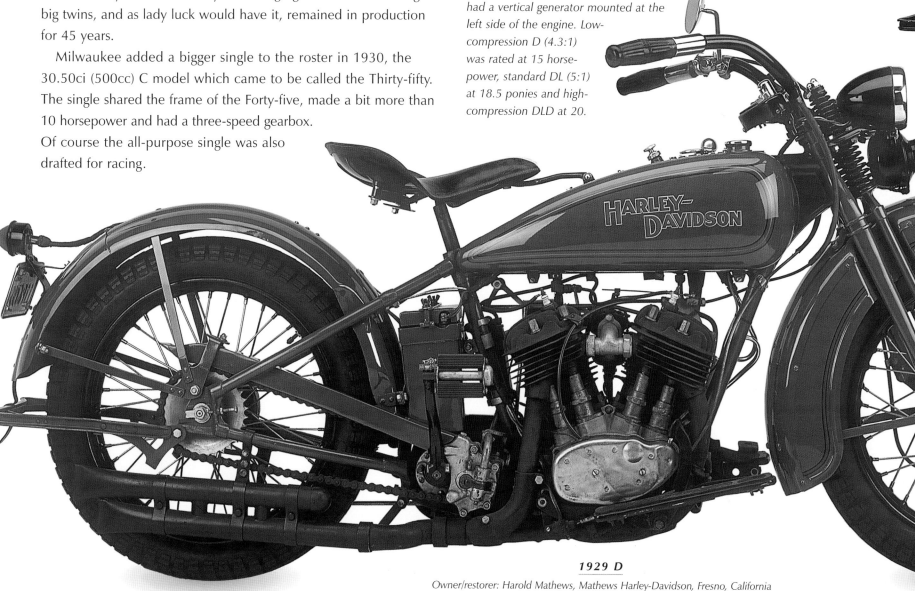

1929 D
Owner/restorer: Harold Mathews, Mathews Harley-Davidson, Fresno, California

BELOW: *The Thirty-fifty (30.50ci/500cc) was the next single conceived in both overhead and flathead configurations. The OHV version never got past the prototype stage, but the flathead went into production and shared the Forty-five chassis.*

1930 C
Owner/restorer: Armando Magri, H-D of Sacramento, California

LEFT: *The first Forty-fives didn't quite match the Indian in the handling department, but within a few years the Harley was more than equal to the task. The flathead twin was destined to become Milwaukee's longest-running model.*

1929 MODEL DL

Engine: Flathead 45° V-twin
Displacement: 45.32ci (746.33cc)
Bore & stroke: 2.75 x 3.81in (70 x 97mm)
Compression ratio: 5:1
Horsepower: 18.5 @ 4,000rpm
Carburetion: Schebler Deluxe
Transmission: 3-speed
Primary drive: Duplex chain
Final drive: Chain
Brakes: F. Expanding shoe; R. Contracting band
Battery: 6-volt
Ignition: Coil/points
Frame: Steel, single downtube
Suspension: F. Leading link spring fork
Wheelbase: 57.5in (146cm)
Weight: 390lb (177kg)
Fuel capacity: 3.75gal (14.2lit)
Oil capacity: 7.5pts (3.55lit)
Tires: 4 x 18in (10.16 x 45.72cm)
Top speed: 70mph (113km/h)
Colors: Olive green (options: black; maroon; gray; blue; cream)
Number built: 6,856 (D, DL) in 1929
Price: $290

1930 MODEL C

Engine: Flathead single
Displacement: 30.1ci (493.28cc)
Bore & stroke: 3.09 x 4in (78.6 x 101.6mm)
Horsepower: 10.4 @ 3,600rpm
Carburetion: Schebler Deluxe
Transmission: 3-speed
Primary drive: Duplex chain
Final drive: Chain
Brakes: F. Expanding shoe; R. Contracting band
Battery: 6-volt
Ignition: Coil/points
Frame: Steel, single downtube
Suspension: F. Leading link spring fork
Wheelbase: 57.5in (146cm)
Weight: 340lb (154.2kg)
Fuel capacity: 3.75gal (14.2lit)
Oil capacity: 7.5pts (3.55lit)
Tires: 4 x 18in (10.16 x 45.72cm)
Top speed: 60mph (97km/h)
Colors: Olive green (options: maroon; black; blue; gray; cream)
Number built: 1,629 (C, CM, CR)
Price: $260

WHILE THE FORTY-FIVE TWIN was just embarking on a long chapter in Harley history, the singles were approaching their twilight in the framework of American motorcycling. It's ironic that the most economical machines wouldn't survive the Depression, but American riders had voted almost unanimously for the V-twin and would continue to do so.

1930 Model VL; 1932 Model DAH 750

New side-valve Seventy-fours, the V and VL, were introduced in 1929 to an eager market for the big-bore twin. But the first V models, built to compete with the Indian Chief, were plagued with numerous mechanical problems. By 1930 most of the defects were sorted out, but the expensive new model had arrived with the advent of the Great Depression. Suddenly the market for a $340 motorcycle dropped sharply.

Milwaukee's production dropped from 24,000 in 1929 to 18,000 for 1930, and plunged to 10,400 in 1931 when the Depression had firmly set in. Still, the technological refinements to the twins were in place before the financial dilemma arrived. All the engines now had Ricardo detachable heads, interchangeable wheels, better brakes and a forged front fork. The motorcycles were stronger all around than the J models, and considerably more reliable.

Harley-Davidson scored a promotional boost in 1930 when Bill Davidson, son of founder William, won the Michigan's 420-mile (676km) Jack Pine Tour on a Forty-five. Both the small and big twin flatheads continued to win fans, despite the economic conditions

that prevailed. Under these constraints, the Harley/Indian battle shifted from the race track to the contests for commercial fleet and police contracts. And despite the staggered economy, Milwaukee maintained a strong advertising program.

RIGHT: *The sidecar offered an economical alternative to cars during the Depression. The three wheels were interchangeable, and the third wheel had an integrated brake.*

BELOW: *Even during times of severe economic hardship, the sport of hillclimbing withstood the hard times. The overhead-valve 750 was one of the most formidable competitors.*

1932 DAH 750
Owner: Daniel Statnekov, Tesuque, New Mexico

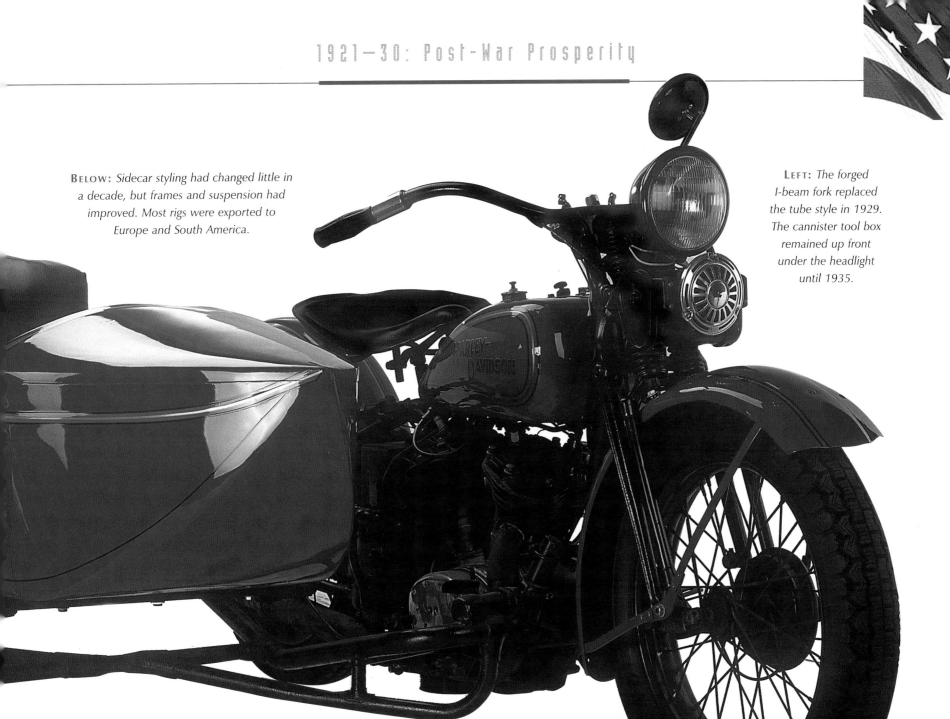

BELOW: *Sidecar styling had changed little in a decade, but frames and suspension had improved. Most rigs were exported to Europe and South America.*

LEFT: *The forged I-beam fork replaced the tube style in 1929. The cannister tool box remained up front under the headlight until 1935.*

1930 MODEL VL

Engine: Flathead 45° V-twin
Displacement: 73.73ci (1208.19cc)
Bore & stroke: 3.44 x 4in (87.3 x 101.6mm)
Compression ratio: 4.5:1
Horsepower: 30 @ 4,000rpm
Carburetion: 1.25in (32mm) Schebler
Transmission: 3-speed
Primary drive: Duplex chain
Final drive: Chain
Brakes: F. & R. Drum
Battery: 6-volt/22-amp
Ignition: Coil/points

Frame: Steel, single downtube
Suspension: F. Leading link spring fork
Wheelbase: 60in (152.4cm)
Weight: 529lb (240kg)
Fuel capacity: 4gal (15.14lit)
Oil capacity: 1gal (3.79lit)
Tires: 4 x 18in (10.16 x 45.72cm)
Top speed: 85mph (137km/h)
Colors: Olive green (options: black; gray; blue; maroon; coach green; cream)
Number built: 3,246
Price: $340

1930 VL

Owner/restorer: Dave Royal, Nipomo, California

ABOVE: *The new flathead big twins were well-suited to sidecar chores since they produced a better torque spread throughout the power range. Milwaukee stressed the economic advantages of fuel economy compared to cars.*

AS THE EFFECTS OF THE DEPRESSION spread throughout all industries in the country, motorcycle sales and production dropped drastically. Walter Davidson wrote to the board of directors: "Our foreign business has shown a very great decrease in the last several years, and it would almost seem that is going to be a very small part of our business in the future."

living the dream

The post-war celebration, now that the world had been made safe for democracy, was underway with some enthusiasm when the U.S. Congress, over the president's veto, passed the Prohibition Act. So the Roaring Twenties began with the election of Warren G. Harding as President of the United States, and the sale of alcoholic beverages was illegal.

Initially the outlook for a wonderful return to civilian motorcycling was quite rosy. The Harley-Davidson racing team was back in action, more powerful than ever, but the country which had mobilized so quickly for war did not shift seamlessly to a peacetime economy. Inflation created higher prices but wages were rising even faster. Henry Ford, faced with an over-supply of cars, dropped the retail price, which rendered motorcycles less

BELOW: *One way to compete with low-cost automobiles in the 1920s was to emphasize the spirit of fun and adventure. Motorcycling was, after all, an outdoor sport.*

RIGHT: *While stylish beachwear may not have been the best riding gear, motorcycles were the easiest way down to the shoreline.*

BELOW: *From early on, Milwaukee provided customers with a handbook of helpful hints on maintenance and safety.*

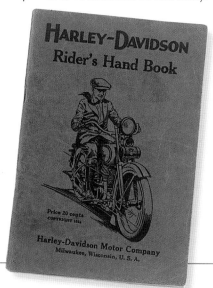

ABOVE: *The new trend of installment buying was adopted by Arthur Davidson to show the affordability of motorcycles.*

RIGHT: *Milwaukee furnished dealers with cardboard window signage and enameled steel exterior signs in orange and black.*

"When we go fishing, Walter rows the boat. Walter's surplus energy is fine stuff around the factory, and in the Harley-Davidson bowling club, but when we go fishing the only way we can use it is to have him furnish the motive power."

BILL HARLEY

appealing as common transportation. Plus, Harley-Davidson, expecting a post-war boom in sales, had borrowed heavily for plant expansion and new tooling.

The work force in Milwaukee was cut by half and the company dropped the bicycle line. The racing budget, reportedly about $250,000, was eliminated at the end of the 1921 season. But Harley-Davidson, unlike its major competitors Indian and Excelsior, was still a family business, and its owners now wealthy men. Their own funds would see the company through the slow times.

Arthur Davidson now undertook a comprehensive program of advertising and public relations designed to express the enjoyment and the economy of motorcycling. In addition to enthusiast publications, hunting and fishing magazines were included in the campaign. Among the founders, only Walter was a non-fisherman.

RIGHT: *The Harley-Davidson bar-and-shield logo became one of the most recognized commercial symbols in motoring, and would remain in use into the next century—by authorized dealers only.*

As the American economy stabilized in the mid-1920s, motorcycling flourished in kind. The slow yet steady rising sales trend was bolstered by the company's direct mail advertising. The mailing campaign added the personal touch of Arthur Davidson, explaining the wonderful advantages of the pay-as-you-ride program. Walter Davidson and Bill Harley appeared in many of the flyers and magazines, which included a signed message from the president of the company. Milwaukee also intensified the effort to enlist dealers in staging local events for riders.

Although motorcycles were now a distinct minority in the American transportation mix (about 150,000 on the road, compared to 20 million cars), the even smaller faction of two-wheeled hell-raisers drew a disproportionate share of public attention. The Motorcycling and Allied Trades Association and the American Motorcycle Association (AMA), which regulated organized racing, joined forces to help minimize the hooligan effect. While the AMA was designed to function as a member-supported organization to work on behalf of riders,

LEFT: *Milwaukee revived the single in 1926, responding to the Indian Prince. Combining the appeals of economical operation, safety, comfort and low price, the 21ci (350cc) flatheads sold well.*

LEFT AND BELOW: *The 30.50in (500cc) B model was another member of the singles revival. The letter to Mr. Cleaves reveals Harley's advertising approach, and highlights the new single's appeal to first-time buyers.*

RIGHT: *As board track racing began receding into history, dirt track events gained popularity. Most races were held at local fairgrounds.*

ABOVE: *Harley team rider Ralph Hepburn won the Dodge City 300 in 1921.*

RIGHT: *Speedway racing on dirt and cinder tracks was most popular in Europe, Australia and New Zealand. Here, Harley rider Frank Arthur accepts his trophy at the Harringay track in North London, England.*

financial weakness soon led to its control by the motorcycle industry. Business and political machinations would dilute its functions for decades to come.

While the 21ci (350cc) single never approached the commercial success of the V-twin, now firmly established as the American motorcycle engine of choice, it did serve to help keep professional racing alive. And it offered amateur riders a relatively economical means to compete as well. Overhead-valve versions of the thumper, from both Harley-Davidson and Indian, were capable of speeds over 80mph (129km/h) and provided exciting competition.

Of course the V-twins were still the big show, even though Milwaukee no longer had an official team. In his long career, Jim Davis rode for both Indian and Harley Davidson. "I'll tell ya, they were both good machines," he recalled at the age of 98.

LEFT: *Harley-Davidson began producing its own sidecar bodies in 1925, when former supplier Rogers suspended operation. Sidecar classes remained popular in racing events.*

RIGHT: *A fleet of 1930 Harleys destined for California Highway Patrol duty, freshly serviced at Frank Murray's dealership in Sacramento.*

BELOW: *Arthur Davidson recognized early the importance of serving motorcyclists with a comprehensive catalog of accessories.*

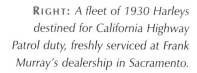

BELOW: *The company steadily expanded their offerings in the accessory catalogs. Shown here are some cold weather items.*

"In '26, on the board track at Altoona, I beat the Harleys on an Indian. The next year I rode a Harley and beat the Indians. I'd say it has more to do with the rider than the bike." Another rider who switched between Indian and Harley was the irrepressible Albert "Shrimp" Burns. "He was a real good rider," Davis recalled. "And he was the only one who came up to see me that time I was laid up in California. But he took more chances on the track than I ever did."

Prosperity and prohibition co-existed through the Republican presidencies of Calvin Coolidge and Herbert Hoover. The graft and corruption of the Harding administration, which sent some top officials to prison, were at least temporarily relegated to history. Taxes and the national debt were down, motorcycle production and sales were up.

The AMA, besides sanctioning racing events, chartered road riding clubs that held regular events, promoted safety and the rights of motorcyclists. The Gypsy Tours, enjoying a growth in popularity following World War I, were expanded by the AMA, which produced commemorative souvenirs for each event. Members of AMA clubs gathered for organized rides to various

RIGHT: *Technical innovation, safety, economy and social responsibility all figured in 1928 ads. The new front brake, easy-pay plan and quiet mufflers were featured.*

BELOW: *The J model series came to an end in 1929, much to the dismay of sport riders and racers who were pleased with the powerful new Two-cam engine.*

The Popular Police Model 74 Twin

RIGHT: *Sidecars were still being featured in ads for 1929, but most were in fact exported.*

locations around the country, and some events included field meets with friendly non-speed contests of riding skill. Some gatherings included dirt track races, hillclimbs and TT scrambles, and the themes of responsible riding, camaraderie and fellowship helped enhance the positive image of the motorcycle sport.

With the transatlantic solo flight of Charles Lindbergh, also a motorcyclist, the American spirit of achievement, adventure and technological accomplishment infused the country. Both Harley-Davidson and Indian were enjoying their most rewarding seasons in years, and Indian had recaptured the winner's circle in national championship races. In 1929 a second generation of Davidsons, Walter C., Gordon and Alan, made a transcontinental promotional tour on the new D model Forty-fives.

But soon the combined effects of the Great Depression and high import tariffs imposed by President Hoover would cripple the motorcycle industry once again. Milwaukee's substantial export market dried up when other countries followed with tariff increases, and cars suddenly became cheaper than motorcycles.

Nonetheless, from 1929 to 1931, motorcycle racing remained a popular sport and entertainment around the country. Both Harley and Indian produced 21ci (350cc) and 30.50ci (500cc) singles, 45ci (750cc) and 61ci (1000cc) twins, which all had designated AMA class divisions, and the least expensive sport to organize and contest—hillclimb—enjoyed renewed interest. It seemed that no matter what shape the economy might be in, and with or without factory support, motorcycle racers were going to race.

ABOVE: *Motorcycle competition was back in full swing by the early '20s. Hillclimb, both amateur and pro, was a popular and economical format, and drew sizeable crowds.*

1931—40: Riding Out the Depression

decade design evolution

"An outstanding characteristic ... is that one color dominates the entire motorcycle ... The striping along the edge of the crown of the fenders ... makes the motorcycle look like a million dollars."

1937 DEALER ORDER FORM

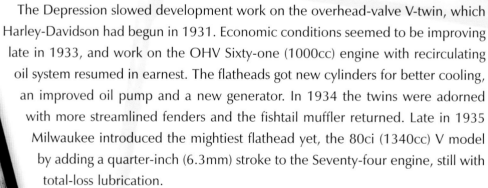

The effects of the stock market crash were not felt immediately in Milwaukee, but by 1933 output had plummeted from 24,000 motorcycles in 1929 to 3,700. Nonetheless, design and engineering advances made before the economy crashed still found their way into production.

The four-tube mufflers on the V series side-valve Seventy-fours, which debuted in 1930, were replaced by single-tube units in 1931. The main fork members were now drop-forged rather than tubular units, the wheels were interchangeable, the riding position was lower by 2 inches (5cm) and the rear brake was an internal expanding type. Slowly and steadily, Harley-Davidson was making motorcycling more comfortable, less intimidating to neophytes and simpler in terms of maintenance.

The 30.50ci (500cc) side-valve single, which was also introduced in 1930, was housed in the Forty-five chassis and both got the new rear brake in '31. The single got stuck with the remaining double-tube mufflers. In 1932, responding quickly to Indian's instant success with the Dispatch-Tow, Milwaukee issued the Servi-Car, a Forty-five (750cc) powered three-wheeler for police and commercial duties.

The Depression slowed development work on the overhead-valve V-twin, which Harley-Davidson had begun in 1931. Economic conditions seemed to be improving late in 1933, and work on the OHV Sixty-one (1000cc) engine with recirculating oil system resumed in earnest. The flatheads got new cylinders for better cooling, an improved oil pump and a new generator. In 1934 the twins were adorned with more streamlined fenders and the fishtail muffler returned. Late in 1935 Milwaukee introduced the mightiest flathead yet, the 80ci (1340cc) V model by adding a quarter-inch (6.3mm) stroke to the Seventy-four engine, still with total-loss lubrication.

The high-compression (7:1) EL made nearly 40 horsepower and was good for almost 100mph (161km/h). Tightly packed into the twin-downtube cradle frame, with its stout front fork, 18-inch (45.7cm) wheels and teardrop tank, the Knucklehead broadcast its power and speed even at a standstill. Its polished rocker boxes and pushrod tubes, and tank-mounted instrument panel all ensured the new Harley's instant appeal to sporting riders around the world.

LEFT: *Shop Dope didn't refer to dummies or mechanics on drugs. Dope was the true inside info, in this case the Forty-five transmission with reverse gear, as used on the Servi-Car.*

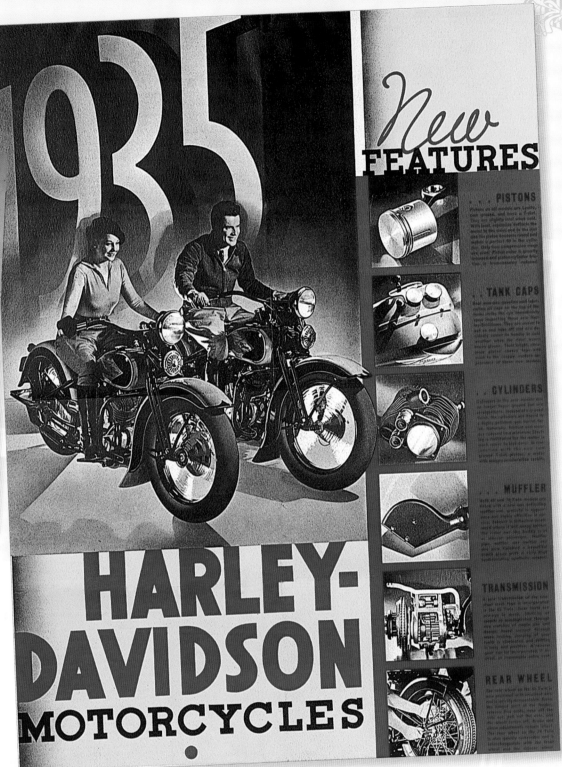

RIGHT: *1935 advertising reflected emergence from the Depression and more artistic layouts and lighting. The Art Deco influence had arrived.*

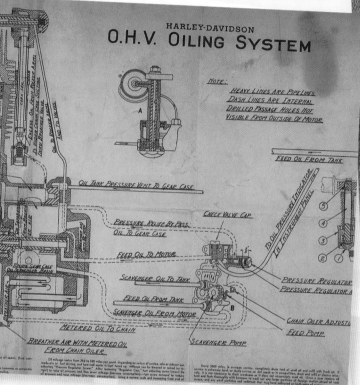

ABOVE: *The first Harley-Davidson recirculating oil system appeared in the 1936 OHV 61 dry-sump engine, which came to be called the Knucklehead.*

BELOW: *Motorcycles got prettier in the 1930s; this '34 design is shown on optional silver and seafoam blue paint.*

With its recirculating oil system and constant-mesh four-speed transmission, the Knucklehead was a thoroughly modern motorcycle. The same features and styling transfered to the side-valve twins the following year. In 1939 the overhead engines were refined with improved oiling systems and stronger valve springs, and all models got self-aligning upper and lower steering head bearings.

Military prototypes of the OHV Sixty-one and the side-valve Forty-five had been in development for over a year, and once again Harley-Davidson was gearing up for war.

1932 Model VL

<table>
<tr><td colspan="2">1932 MODEL VL</td></tr>
<tr><td>Engine: Flathead 45° V-twin</td><td>Frame: Steel, single downtube</td></tr>
<tr><td>Displacement: 73.73ci (1208.19cc)</td><td>Suspension: F. Leading link spring fork</td></tr>
<tr><td>Bore & stroke: 3.44 x 4in (87.3 x 101.6mm)</td><td>Wheelbase: 60in (152.4cm)</td></tr>
<tr><td>Compression ratio: 4.5:1</td><td>Weight: 529lb (240kg)</td></tr>
<tr><td>Horsepower: 30 @ 4,000rpm</td><td>Fuel capacity: 4gal (15.14lit)</td></tr>
<tr><td>Carburetion: 1.25in (32mm) Schebler</td><td>Oil capacity: 1gal (3.79lit)</td></tr>
<tr><td>Transmission: 3-speed</td><td>Tires: 4 x 18in (10.16 x 45.72cm)</td></tr>
<tr><td>Primary drive: Duplex chain</td><td>Top speed: 85mph (137km/h)</td></tr>
<tr><td>Final drive: Chain</td><td>Colors: Olive green (options: black; gray; blue; maroon; coach green; cream)</td></tr>
<tr><td>Brakes: F. & R. Drum</td><td></td></tr>
<tr><td>Battery: 6-volt/22-amp</td><td>Number built: 2,684</td></tr>
<tr><td>Ignition: Coil/points</td><td>Price: $320</td></tr>
</table>

By 1932 the Depression had sunk roots, and Harley-Davidson production was trimmed again. By mid-year the Milwaukee plant was forced to cut expenditures in every department, most employees were put on a two-day work week and production figures for the following year were cut severely. Output for '32 fell to 7,218.

But despite the economic situation, Harley products continued the phased engineering developments created before the crash. The VL, introduced in 1929 as a 1930 model, was sorted out with improved engine and running gear, and the three-wheeled Servi-Car Forty-five was presented late in '31 for the following model year. Both flatheads, and the Twenty-one and Thirty-fifty singles, took price cuts in 1932 and again in '33. The twin headlights were gone and the double mufflers supplanted by single silencers in 1931. The wheels on the VL, including the sidecar, were now interchangeable.

BELOW: *The first big twins were plagued with engine and running gear problems, which forced production delays until new parts were made available. In 1932 a stronger front fork and transmission enhanced reliability. A tool cannister is fitted below the headlight.*

1932 MODEL VL
Owner: Trev Deeley Museum, Vancouver, British Columbia

2222222222222222222222

1934 VLD & CB Single; 1935 RL

In 1933, either because or in spite of the Depression, Harley introduced new streamlined fenders and Art Deco graphics. The VLD Special Sport Solo had a new intake manifold and carburetor, for a 15 percent power increase and a $10 higher price. In 1934 the CB single (a Thirty-fifty engine in a Twenty-one frame) was the last one-cylinder model on the Milwaukee roster. The RL Forty-five twin, which sold for $295 in 1935, was offered in teak red/black, venetian blue/silver, egyptian ivory/brown, verdant green/black and olive green/black.

BELOW: In 1935 the Forty-fives were granted the constant-mesh transmission, internal expanding rear brake and the return of the fishtail muffler.

1934 CB SINGLE
Owner/restorer: Harold Mathews, Mathews Harley-Davidson, Fresno, California

ABOVE: The 1934 Twenty-one (350cc) and Thirty-fifty (500cc) singles would be Harley's last one-cylinder machines for years to come; also the last of the twin-tube mufflers.

1935 RL
Owner: Trev Deeley Museum, Vancouver, British Columbia

1934 VLD
Owner: Mike Lady, Arroyo Grande, California
Restorer: Scott Ashley

RIGHT: Skirted and flared fenders and Airflow taillight appeared in 1934. The tool box remained under the headlight until the following year when it moved behind the engine. The upswept tailpipe would be gone as well.

1936 EL 61 OHV

As the American economy improved, Harley pushed ahead with finalizing a design begun five years earlier. The 61-inch overhead-valve twin was scheduled as a 1935 model, but the lingering Depression postponed its release until the following year.

Dubbed the Knucklehead for its bulging rocker arm covers, the new 1000cc engine signaled both the end of the Depression and the dawn of a new high-performance era in Milwaukee. Devotees of the 61-inch JD model had been disappointed with the 74-inch (1200cc) flathead, and performance enthusiasts approved the Knuckle's hemispherical combustion chambers, dry clutch and constant-mesh four-speed gearbox. The EL was the first Harley-Davidson with a recirculating oil system, and the single-cam engine was quieter than its two- and four-cam predecessors.

And not only was the Knucklehead fast, it looked rapid sitting still. The teardrop fuel tank, with its artful comet design, and streamlined fenders gave the EL its profile of style and speed; and the aircraft-style engine bits added the final touches of muscularity. The Knucklehead was an instant success among sporting riders, and gave Milwaukee just the marketing edge it needed over Indian, which decided to stick with the flathead design.

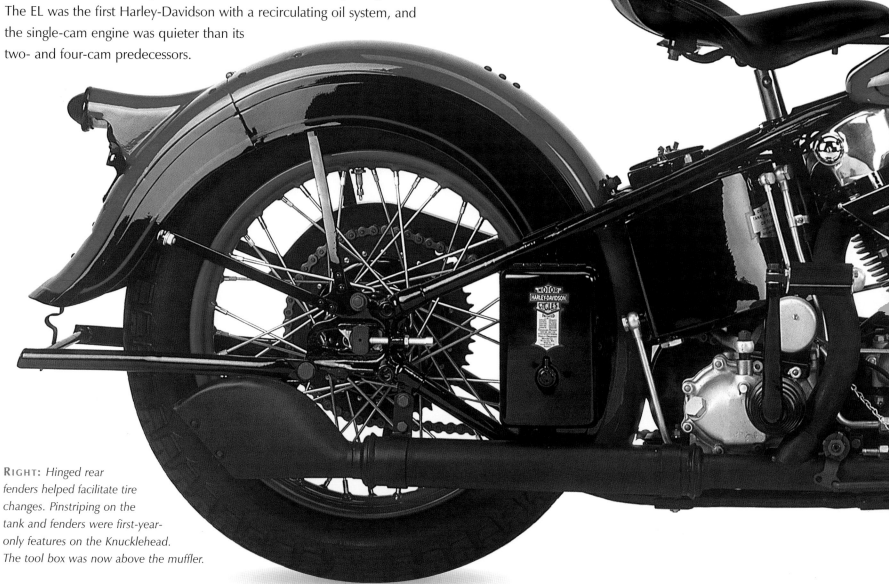

RIGHT: *Hinged rear fenders helped facilitate tire changes. Pinstriping on the tank and fenders were first-year-only features on the Knucklehead. The tool box was now above the muffler.*

The Knucklehead was a benchmark in the integration of motorcycle engineering and design. Although production of the OHV model would be limited for the first few years, it would eventually supersede the flathead after World War II.

1936 EL

Engine: OHV 45° V-twin
Displacement: 60.33ci (988.56cc)
Bore & stroke: 3.31 x 3.5in (84 x 89mm)
Compression ratio: E 6.5:1; EL 7:1
Horsepower: E 37, EL 40 @ 4,800rpm
Carburetion: 1.25in (32mm) Linkert
Transmission: 4-speed
Primary drive: Duplex chain
Final drive: Chain
Brakes: F. & R. Drum
Battery: 6-volt

Ignition: Coil/points
Frame: Steel, double downtube
Suspension: F. Spring fork
Wheelbase: 59.5in (151.1cm)
Weight: 565lb (256kg)
Fuel capacity: 3.75gal (14.2lit)
Oil capacity: 4qts (3.79lit)
Tires: 4.5 x 18in (11.4 x 45.7cm)
Top speed: 95mph (153km/h)
Colors: Sherwood green/silver; teak red/black; dusk gray/buff; venetian blue/croydon cream; maroon/nile green
Number built: 1,526
Price: $380

1936 EL
Owner: Otis Chandler,
Ojai, California
Restorers: Carman & Eldon Brown

1936 VLH; 1938 U Series; 1938 WLDR

While the Knucklehead had generated considerable hoopla in the motorcycle press, the venerable V-series flatheads remained Harley's bread-and-butter machines. Nearly 5,500 V models were built in 1936, compared to only 1,700 of the overheads.

In 1935 the flatheads were offered in both 74-inch (1200cc) and 80-inch (1340cc) versions, designated VLD and VLH respectively. The big twins wouldn't be granted the recirculating oil system until 1937, but options for '36 included a three- or four-speed transmission. The Eighty VHS, with lower compression and gearing for sidecar use, was a popular choice among the tri-wheelers.

The twin frames were reinforced for 1938, and the former V series became the U model flatheads fitted with stronger transmissions,

clutches and brakes. The Seventy-four shared a common stroke with the Eighty and the same bore as the Sixty-one, so the two smaller twins could use the same pistons. New finning on the flathead cylinders was employed against overheating.

The inaugural Daytona 200 race was run in 1937, with the victory going to Indian rider Ed Kretz. Harley's championship rider Joe Petrali rode a specially prepared Knucklehead to a new world record of 136mph (219km/h) at Daytona Beach. Five weeks later William A. Davidson, founder and factory manager, died in Milwaukee at age 66.

1936 VLH
Owner/restorer: Dave Royal, Nipomo, California

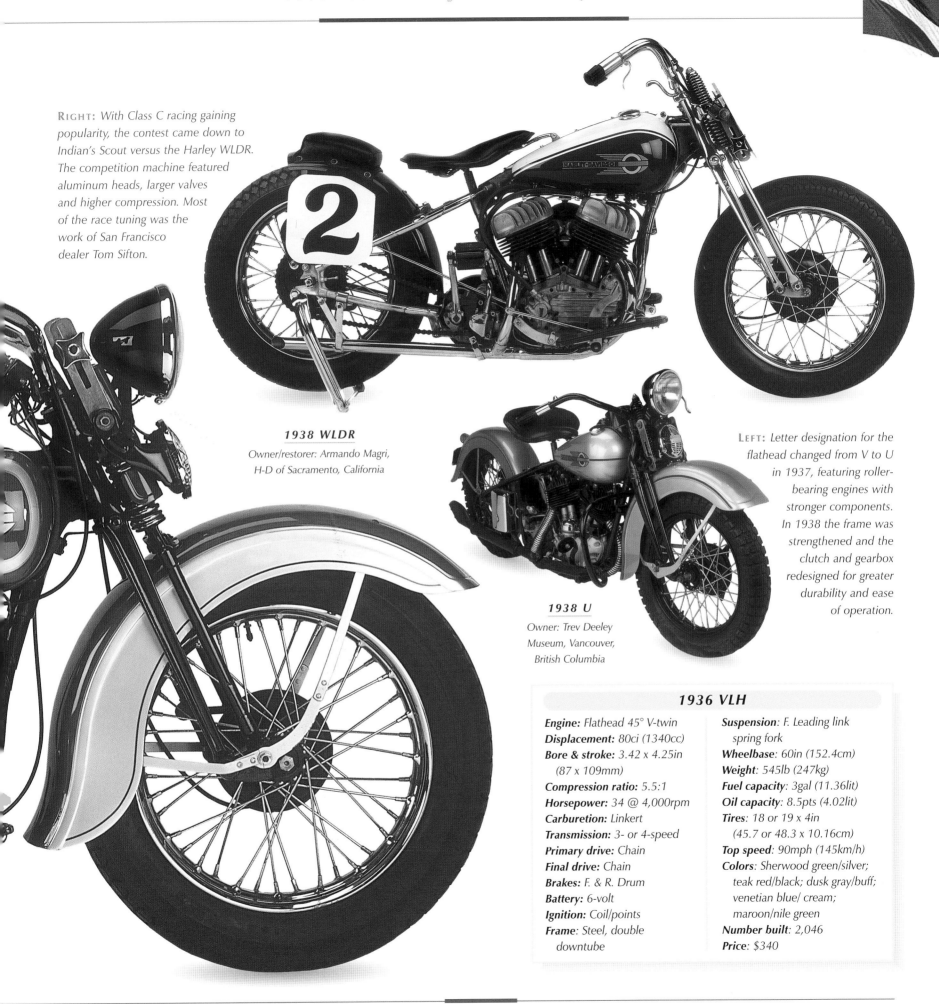

RIGHT: *With Class C racing gaining popularity, the contest came down to Indian's Scout versus the Harley WLDR. The competition machine featured aluminum heads, larger valves and higher compression. Most of the race tuning was the work of San Francisco dealer Tom Sifton.*

1938 WLDR

Owner/restorer: Armando Magri, H-D of Sacramento, California

1938 U

Owner: Trev Deeley Museum, Vancouver, British Columbia

LEFT: *Letter designation for the flathead changed from V to U in 1937, featuring roller-bearing engines with stronger components. In 1938 the frame was strengthened and the clutch and gearbox redesigned for greater durability and ease of operation.*

1936 VLH

Engine: *Flathead 45° V-twin*
Displacement: *80ci (1340cc)*
Bore & stroke: *3.42 x 4.25in (87 x 109mm)*
Compression ratio: *5.5:1*
Horsepower: *34 @ 4,000rpm*
Carburetion: *Linkert*
Transmission: *3- or 4-speed*
Primary drive: *Chain*
Final drive: *Chain*
Brakes: *F. & R. Drum*
Battery: *6-volt*
Ignition: *Coil/points*
Frame: *Steel, double downtube*

Suspension: *F. Leading link spring fork*
Wheelbase: *60in (152.4cm)*
Weight: *545lb (247kg)*
Fuel capacity: *3gal (11.36lit)*
Oil capacity: *8.5pts (4.02lit)*
Tires: *18 or 19 x 4in (45.7 or 48.3 x 10.16cm)*
Top speed: *90mph (145km/h)*
Colors: *Sherwood green/silver; teak red/black; dusk gray/buff; venetian blue/ cream; maroon/nile green*
Number built: *2,046*
Price: *$340*

1939 EL

More refinement came to the lusty Knucklehead in 1939. Improvements in the transmission, valve springs, pistons and lubrication system elevated the reliability factor, and the valve train had been completely enclosed a year earlier. Steering integrity on the big twins was enhanced by self-aligning upper and lower steering head bearings.

Motorcycle styling also continued to receive more attention in Milwaukee. The color-matched instrument panels now featured warning lights rather than oil and amp gauges, in what would become known as the "cat's-eye" design. Stainless steel strips replaced the painted stripes on the fenders and the old Airflow taillight was replaced by what came to be called the "beehive" light with license plate bracket above it. The rectangular tool box in the rear frame section would be replaced by a rounded container the following year.

BELOW: *The Knucklehead roster now included two rather than three models, with the standard medium-compression E version dropped in favor of the ES with sidecar gearing. The sport sidecar sold for $125. Color choices were down to three, and Harley later deleted the two-tone schemes.*

1939 EL

Engine: *OHV 45° V-twin*
Displacement: *60.33ci (988.56cc)*
Bore & stroke: *3.31 x 3.5in (84 x 89mm)*
Compression ratio: *E 6.5:1; EL 7:1*
Horsepower: *E 37, EL 40 @ 4,800rpm*
Carburetion: *1.25in (32mm) Linkert*
Transmission: *4-speed*
Primary drive: *Duplex chain*
Final drive: *Chain*
Brakes: *F. & R. Drum*
Battery: *6-volt*
Ignition: *Coil/points*
Frame: *Steel, double downtube*
Suspension: *F. Spring fork*
Wheelbase: *59.5in (151.1cm)*
Weight: *565lb (256kg)*
Fuel capacity: *3.75gal (14.2lit)*
Oil capacity: *4qts (3.79lit)*
Tires: *4.5 x 18in (11.4 x 45.7cm)*
Top speed: *95mph (153km/h)*
Colors: *teak red/black; airway blue/white; black/ivory*
Number built: *2,909*
Price: *$435*

Testing was underway for overhead-valve versions of the Forty-five and Seventy-four, but preparations for war in Europe soon eclipsed plans for new civilian models. The small twin was shelved but work continued on the 74-inch (1200cc) model and several military prototypes. The U.S. Army had used the Forty-fives for courier and reconnaissance work for many years, along with Seventy-fours equipped with sidecars and armaments.

The Knucklehead was now reaching production parity with the flathead; 2,909 EL models were made in 1939, against 3,317 Eighty and Seventy-four U models.

LEFT: A fender lamp featured in the standard solo group, which included front safety guard (crash bar), odometer, jiffy stand and four-ply tires. The fork springs were originally painted black.

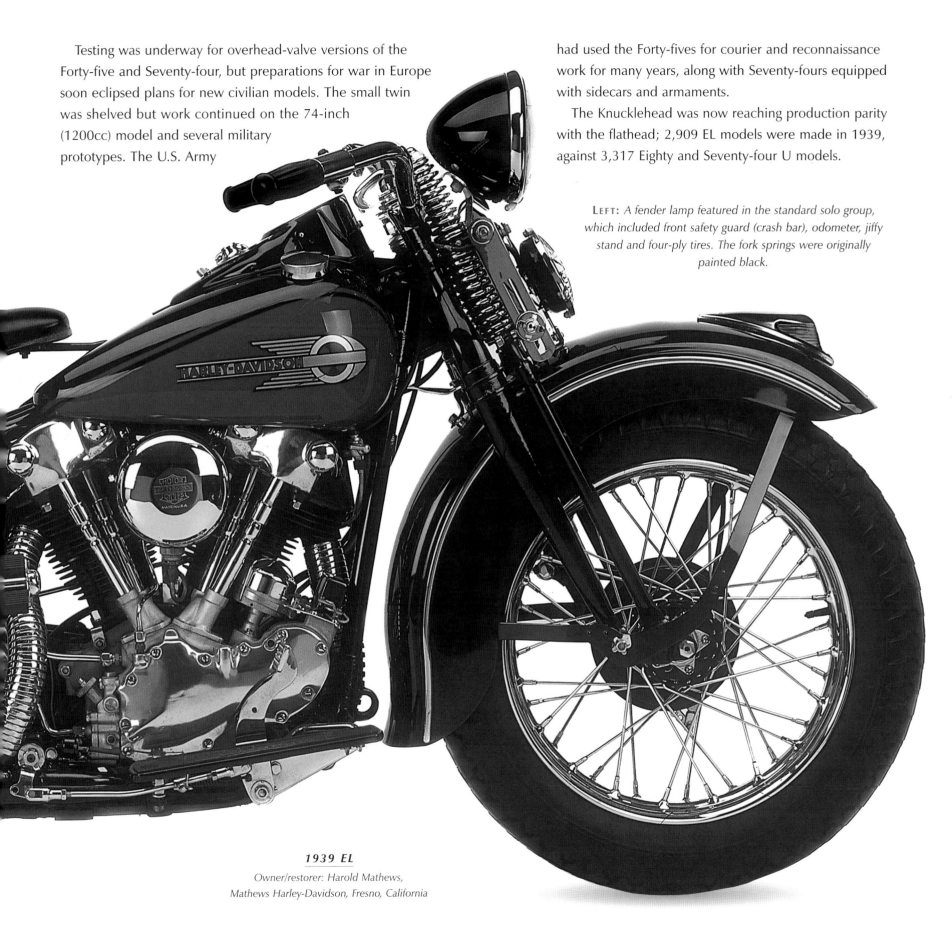

1939 EL

Owner/restorer: Harold Mathews,
Mathews Harley-Davidson, Fresno, California

living the dream

FAR RIGHT: Perhaps the most reprinted Harley-Davidson poster of all time, "the greatest sport" theme sought to reinforce public interest in motorcycling early in the Depression years.

With production falling sharply and the single being dropped from the line in 1933, Harley-Davidson's advertising budget was cut to the bone. But Milwaukee could not afford to allow its name recognition to fall completely out of public view. Elaborate color advertising spreads in major publications were no longer feasible; even dealer advertising materials were scaled down to black-and-white layouts.

Few riders were trading in their motorcycles for new ones during the Depression, and the market for new riders was all but absent. Harley-Davidson thus redoubled its efforts to keep the commercial accounts they had, and do what they could to find new business markets. Some small businesses could no longer afford to maintain truck services and switched to the Servi-Car for light deliveries and automobile repair work. Police departments likewise were under budget constraints, and motorcycles saw increasing use in lieu of patrol cars. Harley-Davidson and Indian were drawn into a fierce struggle for these contracts, with each factory trying to undercut the other on price.

Organized motorcycle racing naturally dwindled during the Depression, but the basic format of hillclimbing still served to gather enthusiasts together for a day of fun and games. Nearly every locale with a sufficient incline held at least one event each year, and attracted "slant artists" from throughout the region. These occasions were well attended by not only motorcyclists but by cars full of families out for a picnic and a day's entertainment.

Many of the racing engines built by both Indian and Harley-Davidson were put to use in hillclimbers when the board track era slid into history. Some of these were overhead-valve V-twins built for high-speed contests and

LEFT: Evidence of the economic situation was apparent in 1932 when Harley-Davidson dropped prices on all their models, which they would do again in 1933.

ABOVE: *Minneapolis dealer Guy Webb's display at the 1931 Minnesota State Fair. The new Servi-Car (right) with fixed tow bar attracted interest.*

BELOW: *Another sign of the depressed market was the banner on the 1932 catalog: "prices greatly reduced."*

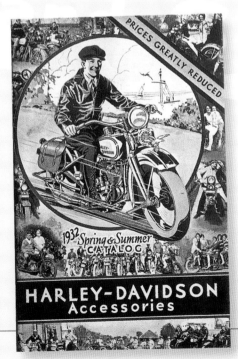

produced significant horsepower. Controlling that thrust with the throttle, while maintaining balance and momentum on a steep hill with changing surface conditions, was a matter of some challenge and ability. San Francisco Harley dealer Dud Perkins was one of the era's top hillclimb riders, as was Joe Petrali, Howard Mitzell on the Indian and Excelsior Super X rider Gene Rhyne.

Excelsior-Henderson, owned by the Schwinn Bicycle Company, was the smallest of the big three manufacturers, but produced some of the most advanced machines of the period. The 45ci (750cc) Super X matched the performance of Harley and Indian's 61ci (1000cc) machines, and OHV versions captured the national hillclimb championships in 1929 and '30. But Excelsior-Henderson closed its doors in 1931, no longer able to compete in the diminished motorcycle market. Some 300 manufacturers had come and gone in the past 30 years, and now only Indian and Harley-Davidson remained.

In addition to the Gypsy Tours, the American Motorcycle Association initiated an annual AMA club activity competition to boost attendance and diminishing membership rosters. Clubs gained points by adding new members, cultivating the appearance of the riders and accumulating mileage by the membership. The first national contest was won by the Fritzie Roamers Club of Springfield, Massachusetts in 1934.

The first Class C racing championship was also held in '34, at Jacksonville, Florida, and won by Georgian Bremen Sykes on a Harley-Davidson. The AMA required racers to be

"[The motorcycle's] appeal lies to the young man between 18 and 25, and forms a rapid means of transport and exhilarating sports."

WILLIAM S. HARLEY

members to participate in sanctioned events, and "participation by AMA members in non-sanctioned (or 'outlaw') events was strictly forbidden. The role of the AMA as the controlling body for competition was to implement and review rules that would promote safety, fairness and spectator appeal." Each of these issues would create sticking points among riders, promoters and AMA personnel over the years, and still do.

Another competition that returned to prominence in the 1930s was the cross-country record dash. In the heyday of these heroic sprints in the teens and '20s, Erwin "Cannonball" Baker achieved fame aboard an Indian. Walter Davidson reportedly solicited Baker to ride for Milwaukee, but wouldn't agree to Baker's appearance fee.

When Roosevelt was re-elected overwhelmingly to the presidency in 1936, the country's climb back to prosperity was well underway. The New Deal was working; the

LEFT: *In the limited civilian market, competition between Harley-Davidson and Indian for police contracts became even more critical. Both firms pitched directly to municipalities.*

BELOW: *Daredevil stunts grew more spectacular in the 1930s. This heroic rider dashes through a tunnel of fire at the Minnesota State Fair in 1937.*

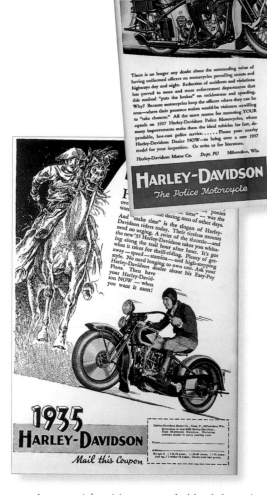

ABOVE: *Advertising was scaled back from the elaborate full-color spreads of the '20s. Ad budgets were cut severely but not eliminated.*

RIGHT: *Graphics and two-tone paint schemes were the focus of Harley-Davidson advertising efforts in 1935.*

LEFT AND BELOW: *Milwaukee continued its long-standing appeal to women riders. Dot Robinson (pictured below) became the first lady of the sport and co-founder of the famous Motor Maids.*

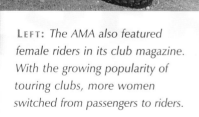

LEFT: *The AMA also featured female riders in its club magazine. With the growing popularity of touring clubs, more women switched from passengers to riders.*

public works segment initiated bridge and road building on a national scale, which meant more people buying motorcycles and riding them on the new roads. But a recession in 1937, followed by the military activities of Mussolini and Hitler in Europe, would revise American plans for economic recovery and stability.

The achievements of Dot Robinson attracted more women to the sport of motorcycling in the '30s, which would serve the country well during the impending war. Another notable female motorcyclist of the era was speedboat racer Florence Burnham, who road a spiffy '36 Knucklehead with chromed wheels and fuel tank. The advent of adventurous women also had its downside, when news came that Amelia Earhart was lost on her attempted flight around the world.

American motorcycling had settled more or less comfortably into its minority role in transportation and sport. Harley-Davidson's production had climbed back to about 10,000 machines a year, the AMA slowly but steadily increased its membership and production-based Class C racing gradually established its credentials.

In addition to oval dirt track events, Class C included TT racing, derived from the annual Isle of Man Tourist Trophy event. From the 1933 AMA rules: "The course should be irregular insofar as possible, so that both right- and left-hand turns have to be negotiated. It is advised to include, if possible, a hill that will necessitate gear changing so that the entire motorcycle is made to perform its regular road functions." The Class C concept led to the birth of an American motorcycle racing classic in 1937, the Daytona 200. It had two 1.5-mile (2.4km) straights, one on a paved road, the other on the Florida beach, connected at each end by a 180-degree turn.

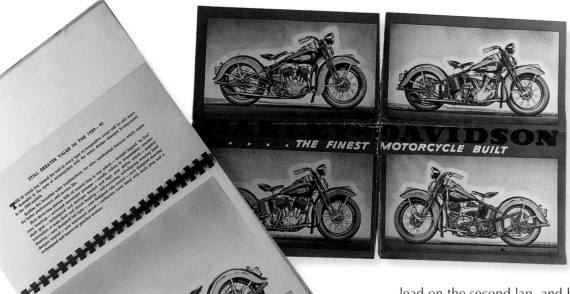

. . . . THE FINEST MOTORCYCLE BUILT

The traditional season opener had formerly been held in Savannah, Georgia on the Vanderbilt Cup course, site of the first 300-mile (483km) race in 1913. Indian rider Ed Kretz won the final Georgia race in 1936, and came to the inaugural Daytona event with his winning Sport Scout. His competitors included other accomplished Indian pilots Lester Hillbish, Archie Sprague and Howard Mitzell. After 200 miles (322km), Ed Kretz took the checkered flag, followed by the Norton of Clark Trumbull and Ellis Pearce on a Harley-Davidson. Ed Kretz took over the lead on the second lap, and by the end of the race he had lapped the entire field. In 1938 he won the Laconia Classic TT, its first year as a national championship, and was known thereafter as "Iron Man" Kretz, going on to a long and illustrious racing career. His feats of strength and endurance pushed Harley-Davidson riders and tuners to new efforts.

ABOVE: *The spiral-bound booklet contained the Harley-Davidson model roster for 1935. Prices had begun to rise as economic conditions improved. The high-compression RL Forty-five sold for $295, while the RLDR competition special was priced at $322. The Eighty was $347.*

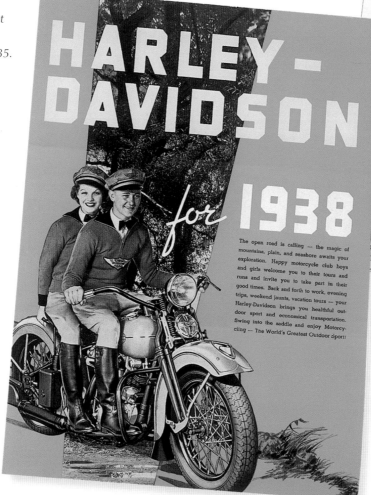

HARLEY-DAVIDSON for 1938

The open road is calling — the magic of mountains, plain, and seashore awaits your exploration. Happy motorcycle club boys and girls welcome you to their tours and runs and invite you to take part in their good times. Back and forth to work, evening trips, weekend jaunts, vacation tours — your Harley-Davidson brings you healthful out-door sport and economical transportation. Swing into the saddle and enjoy Motorcycling — The World's Greatest Outdoor Sport!

RIGHT: *This 1938 brochure featured a happy couple in matching outfits on a Knucklehead. Other pages covered more utilitarian models such as the Servi-Car, Package Truck and Sidecar.*

ABOVE: *Michigan's Earl Robinson is congratulated by Los Angeles dealer Rich Budelier and AMA referee Al Koogler. He rode the Forty-five from New York in 77 hours, 53 minutes.*

RIGHT: *Clark Gable, seen here in 1938, was one of the many Hollywood motion picture stars who rode motorcycles regularly; usually Harleys.*

ABOVE: *Embossed steel, baked enamel dealer signs, such as this 1939 Oklahoma sign, have become valued collectibles.*

With the successes of the Daytona and Laconia races, the AMA had the foundation for a series of major annual races that would attract the nation's top riders. These events grew in status over the years, incorporating support races, motorcycle trade shows and assorted activities and entertainment. All of which attracted growing crowds of motorcyclists from around the country.

The success of the Knucklehead, which was received enthusiastically by the motoring press at home and abroad, had put Harley-Davidson a step ahead of Indian in the heavyweight division. The flathead Seventy-four and Indian's similar Chief were running about even in sales, and the contest between the two companies' Forty-fives continued on and off the track. Overall motorcycle sales were still running at about half their pre-Depression levels. Used motorcycles were cheap, but used cars were cheaper.

Earl Robinson had knocked 37 hours off the previous cross-country record aboard his Harley RLD Forty-five. Perhaps even more remarkable was the sidecar record set the same year by Earl and his wife, Dot Robinson. The pair crossed the United States in just under 90 hours, only about 12 hours longer than Earl's solo ride.

But records were made, as they say, to be broken, and in 1936 Fred Dauria and Bill Connelly did it in style. With a Harley Eighty and a sidecar, the enterprising lads added a 15-gallon (56.8lit) fuel tank, extra oil tank and plenty of spare parts. Fully loaded the rig weighed nearly 1,800 pounds (816.5kg) and had a top speed of just over 60mph (96.5km/h). In three days they reached the Nevada desert, where the temperature was so high that the Harley's top speed was 30mph (48.3km/h). But that afternoon they rolled into Los Angeles, having covered 3,104 miles (4,995km) in 69 hours and 46 minutes, beating the current solo record by two hours. And they did it in October.

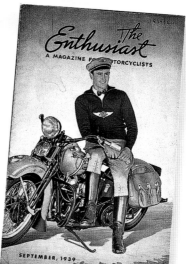

ABOVE: *The standard riding gear of the period retained the quasi-military look. Helmets were just for racers.*

1941—50: Still Greater Wars

The 45 S

The 61 O.H.V.

decade design evolution

"The employees of Harley-Davidson are working long, hard hours. We're buying war bonds and accepting shortages. Most of us are staying on the job ... often working on days when we aren't well. That's the way we are dealing blows to our enemies."

LEONARD HACKERT, LOCAL 209 PRESIDENT

The U.S. military services had utilized the side-valve Seventy-four, usually fitted with a sidecar, for dispatch and police duties. But for combat conditions, a lighter and more maneuverable machine was in order. The army requirements included a top speed of at least 65mph (105km/h) and an engine that would not overheat under continuous low-speed operation. Both Harley and Indian offered their side-valve Forty-fives, outfitted for rugged terrain and low-maintenance conditions.

Designated WLA, the military Forty-five featured an exhaust cutout for use when noise wasn't a problem, and unskirted fenders to avoid mud build-up. New aluminum heads, developed in 1939, were 4 pounds (1.8kg) lighter than their cast-iron counterparts and had more finning area for better heat dissipation. With a compression ratio of 5:1, the engine was rated for 23 horsepower at 4,600rpm. Both the clutch and transmission were upgraded for durability, and an oil bath air filter fitted to aid engine life under dusty and muddy conditions. The WLA used the new tubular-style front fork, lengthened by 2.4 inches (6cm) for added ground clearance.

Harley-Davidson also built, at government request, a copy of the BMW opposed twin as a military model. The 45ci (750cc) flathead featured shaft drive, foot shift, four-speed transmission and plunger rear suspension. A lengthened WLA fork was fitted to meet the military's requirement for 8 inches (20.3cm) of ground clearance. This was the first Harley with foot shift and telescopic fork. Designated the XA model, the horizontal cylinders did offer engine temperatures some 100 degrees F (55 degrees C) less than the V-twin, but production plans were dropped because the machine was far more expensive than the WLA. A sidecar version with a driven third wheel was also suspended with the military's adoption of the Jeep.

Few design or engineering changes were made to any models during the war. The OHV Seventy-four had been introduced in 1941, but saw only limited production mostly for military and police use.

LEFT: *Specifications and technical information on the WLA Forty-five military model. The framework on the front fender is for a submachine gun scabbard.*

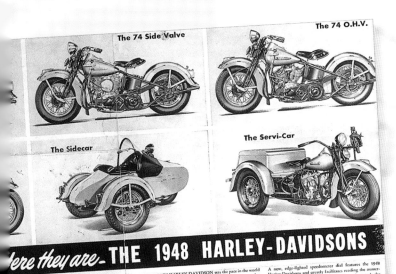

Here they are— **THE 1948 HARLEY-DAVIDSONS**

HARLEY-DAVIDSON MOTOR CO., MILWAUKEE 1, WIS., U.S.A.

Reprinted from November 1947 issue of American Motorcycling Magazine.

ABOVE: *The November 1947 issue of* American Motorcycling *carried this spread featuring the Harley lineup, with emphasis on the new Panhead engine. The 125 two-stroke was introduced later in the model year.*

Although civilian production had resumed completely, the only colors available in 1947 were gray and red. The Ride-Control friction damper on the fork was replaced by a Monroe shock absorber. The cat's eye instrument panel made its final appearance, and the airplane-style speedometer was introduced in three two-tone color combinations. Early models had no stainless steel fender trim, and the tank badges were painted rather than chromed until mid-year. The "beehive" taillight, introduced in 1939, was another last-year item, supplanted in '47 by a squared zinc-alloy housing called the "tombstone" lamp, incorporating the license plate bracket.

The Knucklehead engine also made its last appearance in 1947. The instrument panel was a new design with warning lights in a common panel, and a new tank badge that came to be called the "speedball" design premiered. With the arrival of the Panhead engine in '48, Milwaukee entered the second phase of overhead-

FAR RIGHT: *The first Panhead (1948) featured bowed front downtubes to accommodate the taller engine. The springer front fork, originally painted black, would be replaced in 1949 by the Hydra-Glide fork.*

The Mighty **HARLEY-DAVIDSON O. H. V. MOTOR**

...Heart of the 61" and 74" O. H. V. Models — World's Most Popular Motorcycles

RIGHT: *The first OHV 74 arrived in 1941. It shared production parity with the 61, but the output dropped sharply with military production of the WLA Forty-five.*

valve design and engineering. The FL engine incorporated its oil lines inside, and hydraulic lifters addressed the problems of frequent valve adjustment and overheating.

A new frame accommodated the taller engine, and included a steering head lock and mounting plate for crash bars. The first Panhead was also the last springer fork model, supplanted by a telescopic fork in 1949. Seamless, more deeply skirted fenders adorned the new model, complementing the Hydra-Glide fork.

1941 GA Servi-Car

The Servi-Car, built in response to Indian's similar Dispatch Tow three-wheeler, first appeared in late 1931 as a '32 model. Sidecar rigs had previously been modified for various commercial applications, but the Forty-five powered trike was a better multi-purpose machine in most respects.

Both manufacturers offered optional tow bars with the three-wheelers, which automotive service shops found useful for picking up and returning cars due for service. A single employee could ride to the client's site, tow the Servi-Car back to the shop, return the car, unhook the trike and ride back. The three-wheelers also found wide use as light-duty delivery vehicles and parking enforcement conveyances for city police departments.

1941 GA SERVI-CAR	
Engine: Flathead 45° V-twin	**Suspension**: F. Leading link spring/shock fork; R. Coil springs
Displacement: 45.32ci (742.65cc)	
Bore & stroke: 2.75 x 3.81in (70 x 97mm)	**Wheelbase**: 61in (155cm)
	Track: 42in (106.7cm)
Compression ratio: 4.75:1	**Weight**: 1,360lb (619kg)
Horsepower: 22 @ 4,500rpm	**Fuel capacity**: 3.4gal (12.9lit)
Carburetion: Linkert	**Oil capacity**: 3.5qts (3.31lit)
Transmission: 3-speed w/reverse	**Tires**: 5 x 16in (12.7 x 40.6cm)
	Top speed: 50mph (80km/h)
Primary drive: Duplex chain	**Colors**: Skyway blue; cruiser green; flight red; brilliant black
Final drive: Gear differential	
Brakes: F. & R. Drum	
Battery: 6-volt	**Number built**: 1,159 (all models)
Ignition: Coil/points	
Frame: Steel, single downtube	**Price**: $510

ABOVE: *For commercial applications, Servi-Cars were equipped with a tow bar for an additional $15. A chromed rear bumper was available for $5 and fender "Ad" skirts at $3.50 the pair.*

1941 FL 74 OHV; 1941 WLDR

Another Seventy-four, the 1200cc overhead-valve FL, appeared in 1941. With both larger bore and stroke than the Sixty-one, the new big twin was rated at 48 horsepower. Military tests of a three-wheeled version were less than successful, so the big Knucklehead was reserved for civilian use.

1941 FL

Engine: OHV 45° V-twin
Displacement: 73.73ci (1208.19cc)
Bore & stroke: 3.43 x 3.5in (87 x 101.6mm)
Compression ratio: F 6.6:1; FL 7:1
Horsepower: 48 @ 5,000rpm
Carburetion: 1.31in (33.3mm) Linkert
Transmission: 4-speed
Primary drive: Chain
Final drive: Chain
Brakes: F. & R. Drum
Battery: 6-volt

Ignition: Coil/points
Frame: Steel, double downtube
Suspension: F. Spring fork
Wheelbase: 59.5in (151.1cm)
Weight: 575lb (261kg)
Fuel capacity: 3.75gal (14.2lit)
Oil capacity: 4qts (3.79lit)
Tires: 5 x 16in (12.7 x 40.6cm)
Top speed: 95mph (153km/h)
Colors: Clipper blue; flight red; cruiser green; black; olive green (export)
Number built: 2,452
Price: $465

The Forty-five engine got a stronger clutch and transmission in '41. This was the last year for the WLDR, which became the WLD Sport Special. Racing versions, the WR and WRTT, featured high-performance engines to compete with the popular Indian Sport Scout in the growing arena of Class C racing.

1942 WLA; 1942 XA

Preparations for war had begun in 1937, when the U.S. War Department went scouting manufacturers for military vehicles. Indian, Harley-Davidson and the Delco Corporation were later invited to submit motorcycles for testing at Fort Knox, Kentucky. The Army stipulated machines that would be able to ford streams, would not overheat and be capable of 65mph (105km/h).

Both Indian and Harley received military contracts for their Forty-five twins, but the Milwaukee version prevailed. The WLA accounted for nearly half of Harley's production (53,000) in 1942, while Indian's output was less than half that and most of them non-civilian models. The Harley-Davidson army flathead was fitted with a longer fork to increase ground clearance, footboards, skid plate, cargo rack and saddlebags. While it was superseded by the Jeep for actual combat use, the WLA proved a worthy instrument for dispatch and reconnaissance work. Milwaukee also supplied the armed forces of Great Britain, South Africa, China and Russia, building in five years some 88,000 motorcycles for military use.

1942 WLA	
Engine: Flathead 45° V-twin	**Frame**: Steel, single downtube
Displacement: 45.12ci (739.38cc)	**Suspension**: F. Leading link spring fork
Bore & stroke: 2.75 x 3.81in (70 x 97mm)	**Wheelbase**: 57.5in (146cm)
Compression ratio: 5:1	**Weight**: 540lb (250kg)
Horsepower: 23.5 @ 4,600rpm	**Fuel capacity**: 3.375gal (12.8lit)
Carburetion: Linkert	**Oil capacity**: 7.5pts (3.55lit)
Transmission: 3-speed	**Tires**: 4 x 18in (10.16 x 45.7cm)
Primary drive: Duplex chain	**Top speed**: 65mph (105km/h)
Final drive: Chain	**Color**: Olive drab
Brake: F. & R. Drum	**Number built**: 13,051
Battery: 6-volt	**Price**: $380
Ignition: Coil/points	

1942 WLA
Owner: Trev Deeley Museum, Vancouver, British Columbia

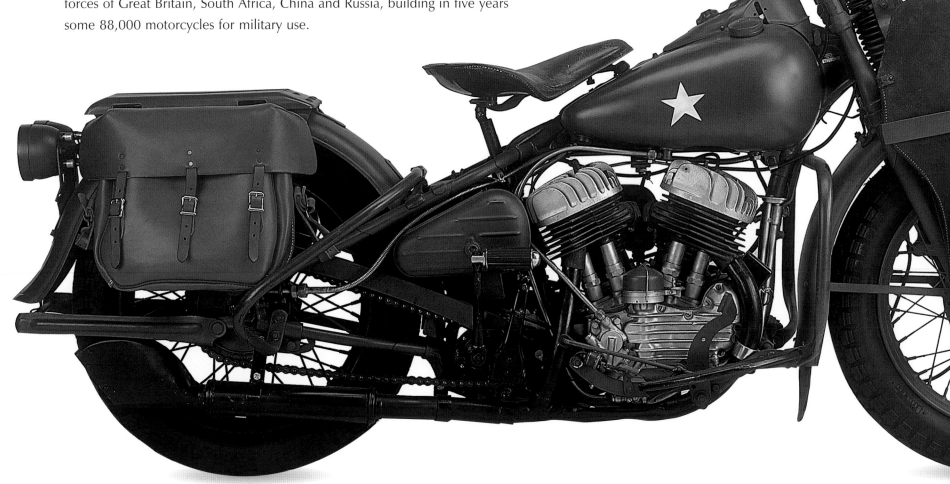

BELOW: *The shaft-drive opposed twin was a project that Bill Harley accepted with reluctance. The wet-sump engine did run cooler than the V-twin and service life was extended in kind, but the XA was expensive to build. Harley's first foot-shift model, the XA was configured at the Army's request with the throttle and handbrake on the left handlebar and clutch on the right.*

1942 XA
Owner/restorer: Fred Lange, Santa Maria, California

Less successful was the XA model, a BMW clone built at the request of the U.S. Army. Military strategists had been impressed with the performance of the German opposed twins in the African desert, and reasoned that a similar mount would also serve the Allied cause. But the shaft-drive twin was expensive to build, the desert war was effectively over and the Jeep had made the project redundant. Only about 1,000 of the boxers were built.

LEFT: *The military Forty-five introduced thousands of soldiers to motorcycling, and made many of them Harley riders after the war. Wheel interchangeability was achieved by using the front wheel and brake from the big twin. The tube steel luggage rack was replaced by a stronger square-section unit to meet the Army's requirement of a 40-pound (18kg) carrying capacity. Aluminum heads were later painted black.*

1942 XA

Engine: Flathead opposed twin	**Frame**: Steel, double downtube
Displacement: 45.04ci (738cc)	
Bore & stroke: 3.125 x 3.125 (78 x 78mm)	**Suspension**: F. Leading link spring fork; R. Plunger
Compression ratio: 5.7:1	**Wheelbase**: 58.75in (149.2cm)
Horsepower: 23 @ 4,600rpm	
Carburetion: 2 Linkert	**Fuel capacity**: 4.1gal (15.5lit)
Transmission: 4-speed	**Oil capacity**: 2qts (1.89lit)
Primary drive: Gear	**Tires**: 4 x 18in (10.16 x 45.7cm)
Final drive: Shaft	
Brakes: F. & R. Drum	**Top speed**: 65mph (105km/h)
Battery: 6-volt	**Color**: Olive drab
Ignition: Coil/points	**Number built**: 1,000
Weight: 538lb (244kg)	**Price**: $870.35

1945 WL; 1946 F & FL

As the war wound down, Milwaukee began the process of conversion to civilian production. With military orders dwindling, surplus Forty-fives were made available to both Harley dealerships and auto dealers around the country. Harley-Davidson was well prepared for the post-war sales boom, while Indian had neglected its domestic market and faced serious financial problems.

In 1945 the middleweight flathead was back to the WL designation, with either iron heads at $396 or, for an extra $7, aluminum lids. The shift to civilian machines was effective in November, and most of the more than 8,000 WLA models intended for the military were converted for public sale and offered at discount rates. Although national championship racing wouldn't resume until 1946, some Harley Forty-fives returned to local events in late '45.

Milwaukee's output of big twins, flatheads and overheads combined was 2,715 in 1945. For 1946 the figure rose to more than 11,000, with the FL Seventy-four accounting for about 4,000 machines. This was the debut of the 30-degree steering head called the "bull neck," and the new shock absorber between the fork springs. Gray and red were the only color options at first, with blue added later in the year.

1945 WLD	
Engine: Flathead 45° V-twin	**Frame:** Steel, single downtube
Displacement: 45.12ci (739.38cc)	**Suspension:** F. Leading link spring fork
Bore & stroke: 2.75 x 3.81in (70 x 97mm)	**Wheelbase:** 57.5in (146cm)
Compression ratio: 5:1	**Weight:** 540lb (250kg)
Horsepower: 23.5 @ 4,600rpm	**Fuel capacity:** 3.375gal (12.8lit)
Carburetion: Linkert	**Oil capacity:** 7.5pts (3.55lit)
Transmission: 3-speed	**Tires:** 4 x 18in (10.16 x 45.7cm)
Primary drive: Duplex chain	**Top speed:** 65mph (105km/h)
Final drive: Chain	**Color:** Gray
Brake: F. & R. Drum	**Number built:** 1,357
Battery: 6-volt	**Price:** $396
Ignition: Coil/points	

BELOW: Surplus military Forty-fives were converted for civilian use after World War II. The WLD featured aluminum heads, which cost $7 extra.

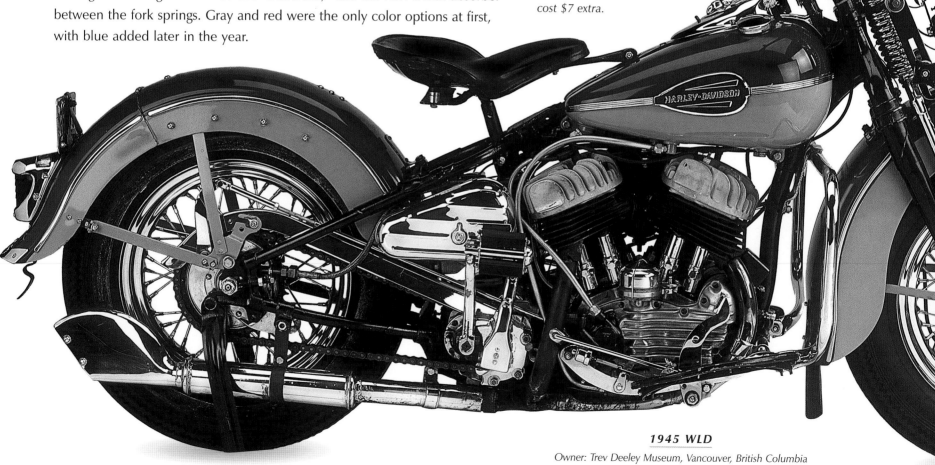

1945 WLD

Owner: Trev Deeley Museum, Vancouver, British Columbia

1946 FL

Engine: OHV 45° V-twin
Displacement: 73.73ci (1208.19cc)
Bore & stroke: 3.43 x 3.5in
   (87 x 101.6mm)
Compression ratio: F 6.6:1; FL 7:1
Horsepower: 48 @ 5,000rpm
Carburetion: 1.31in (33.3mm) Linkert
Transmission: 4-speed
Primary drive: Chain
Final drive: Chain
Brakes: F. & R. Drum
Battery: 6-volt
Ignition: Coil/points
Frame: Steel, double downtube
Suspension: F. Spring fork
Wheelbase: 59.5in (151.1cm)
Weight: 575lb (261kg)
Fuel capacity: 3.75gal (14.2lit)
Oil capacity: 4qts (3.79lit)
Tires: 5 x 16in (12.7 x 40.6cm)
Top speed: 95mph (153km/h)
Colors: Gray; red
Number built: 3,986
Price: $465

1946 FL
Owner: Oliver Shokouh,
Glendale Harley-Davidson,
Glendale, California

LEFT: The cat's eye
instrument panel was
fitted from 1939–46. The
airplane-style speedometer
was offered in three two-
tone color schemes:
green/cream, black/silver
and gray/white.

ABOVE: The post-war price of the FL
remained at $435, but would take a
sizeable jump in 1947. Subsequent
designs moved away from the Art
Deco style, though it would return
even later.

BELOW: The new front
shock absorber is visible
behind the horn. The solid
color scheme is correct
for 1946, though most
of the chromed parts
were originally
painted black.

1946 F
Owner/restorer: Ken Lang, Oakville, Ontario, Canada

1947 FL; 1948 125 Model S

Harley-Davidson returned to full civilian production in 1947, which would be the final year for the fabled Knucklehead. Total production of Sixty-one and Seventy-four model overheads for the year was 11,648. Several features distinguished the final Knucklehead from its predecessors. The new tank badge ("speedball") and taillight ("tombstone") were introduced in '47; the fuel tank and instrument panel were new and stainless steel fender trim and front fender lamps returned. Post-war inflation accounted for the single biggest change for the FL when the price jumped from $465 to $605, a 30 percent increase in one year.

Mechanical revisions to the 12th and last-edition Knuckles included a new shifter mechanism, reversed shift pattern, new circuit breaker and auto-style foot clutch. Rubber hand grips and starter pedal replaced the plastic items, and fender braces were wider on all models. This was the final year for the frame with straight front downtubes.

Post-war predictions for a growing market in lightweight machines were addressed in Milwaukee by the 125 S model two-stroke. One reward of the allied victory in Europe was the right to build German DKW motorcycles in the U.S. and England. Harley-Davidson shared the spoils with BSA, and Milwaukee hoped the entry-level tiddler would prime younger riders for larger machines.

While the three-horsepower 125 was never a major seller, it did introduce many youngsters to motor-cycling and evolved into larger two-stroke models over the years.

1947 FL

Engine: OHV 45° V-twin
Displacement: 73.73ci (1208.19cc)
Bore & stroke: 3.43 x 3.5in
  (87 x 101.6mm)
Compression ratio: F 6.6:1; FL 7:1
Horsepower: 48 @ 5,000rpm
Carburetion: 1.31in (33.3mm)
  Linkert
Transmission: 4-speed
Primary drive: Chain
Final drive: Chain
Brakes: F. & R. Drum
Battery: 6-volt
Ignition: Coil/points
Frame: Steel, double downtube
Suspension: F. Spring fork
Wheelbase: 59.5in (151.1cm)
Weight: 575lb (261kg)
Fuel capacity: 3.75gal (14.2lit)
Oil capacity: 4qts (3.79lit)
Tires: 5 x 16in (12.7 x 40.6cm)
Top speed: 95mph (153km/h)
Colors: Skyway blue; flight red; black
Number built: 6,893
Price: $605

BELOW: *The final Knucklehead, with its streamlined tank badge designed by auto stylist Brooks Stevens, which would carry through 1950. One-year-only features included the speedometer face and adjustable tool box above the muffler.*

1948 125 MODEL S
Owner/restorer: Fred Lange, Santa Maria, California

1947 FL
Owner: Trev Deeley Museum, Vancouver, British Columbia

1948 FL

The first Panhead was a transitional model, introducing riders to forthcoming changes in the engineering, manufacture and style of motorcycles. The technical advances generated by the war were quickly transposed to peacetime automotive and motorcycle production.

With its saucepan-style valve covers, the Panhead signaled the coverage of more mechanical bits and pieces. Function was easing ahead of form once again, which effectively de-emphasized the mechanical components of the machine. But while the new FL may have been visually less interesting than the Knucklehead, its

hydraulic valve lifters and aluminum heads promised fewer valve adjustments and lower operating temperatures, thus longer engine life. Milwaukee was out to make motorcycling easier. The new oil pump and self-contained lubrication system contributed to sustained operation at speed. Horsepower was only slightly higher than the

Knucklehead, and though the Panhead was slightly lighter, performance was roughly equal. The new frame, dubbed the "wishbone" for its bowed front downtubes, had a fork lock and crash bar mounts.

This was the last year of production for the flathead Seventy-four. The first Panhead also became the last girder/spring fork model, with a telescopic fork in place the following year. Harley was now moving decisively ahead of Indian in the market; production in 1948 rose to 29,612, and more than 40 percent were Panheads.

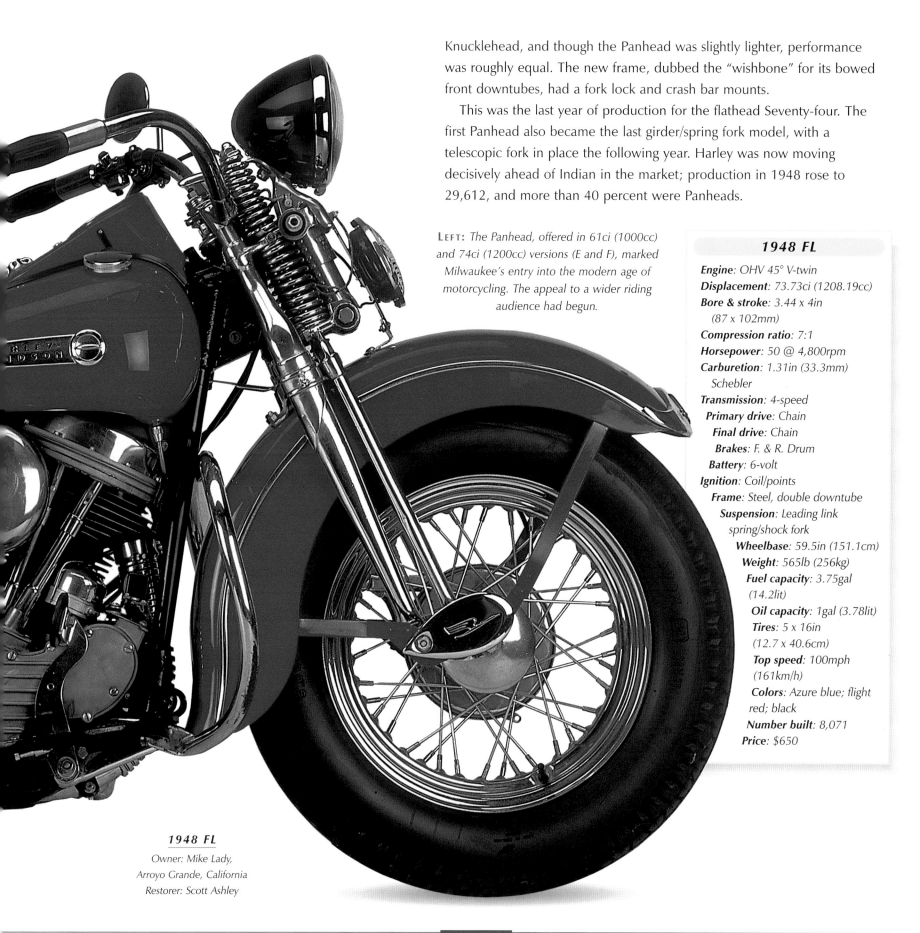

LEFT: *The Panhead, offered in 61ci (1000cc) and 74ci (1200cc) versions (E and F), marked Milwaukee's entry into the modern age of motorcycling. The appeal to a wider riding audience had begun.*

1948 FL

Owner: Mike Lady,
Arroyo Grande, California
Restorer: Scott Ashley

1948 FL

Engine: OHV 45° V-twin
Displacement: 73.73ci (1208.19cc)
Bore & stroke: 3.44 x 4in
 (87 x 102mm)
Compression ratio: 7:1
Horsepower: 50 @ 4,800rpm
Carburetion: 1.31in (33.3mm)
 Schebler
Transmission: 4-speed
Primary drive: Chain
Final drive: Chain
Brakes: F. & R. Drum
Battery: 6-volt
Ignition: Coil/points
Frame: Steel, double downtube
Suspension: Leading link
 spring/shock fork
Wheelbase: 59.5in (151.1cm)
Weight: 565lb (256kg)
Fuel capacity: 3.75gal
 (14.2lit)
Oil capacity: 1gal (3.78lit)
Tires: 5 x 16in
 (12.7 x 40.6cm)
Top speed: 100mph
 (161km/h)
Colors: Azure blue; flight
 red; black
Number built: 8,071
Price: $650

1950 EL

The Hydra-Glide fork appeared on the Panhead in 1949, and subsequently provided the first official model name in Milwaukee. The letter/number designations would remain, but Harleys henceforth would get their own monikers.

Rubber-mounted handlebars helped damp out some of the big twin's characteristic vibration, and Harley offered more accessories to entice touring riders. A slowing economy brought manufacturing reductions for the second year running, and few modifications were made to the motorcycles. In 1950 the finned muffler was replaced by a straight Mellow-Tone silencer, and the Hydra-Glide fork could be adjusted to change handling characteristics for sidecar use.

As part of Harley's concern for engine longevity, a new remote oil filter was fitted in 1950, and the steel exhaust valve guides were replaced by bronze sleeves. New cylinder heads had larger intake ports for a moderate power increase, which brought the Seventy-four (FL) a rating of 55 horsepower. The only slightly less powerful Sixty-one (EL) sold for $15 less.

Another distinction for the Hydra-Glide was the change to seamless, automotive-style fenders. The "airflow" mudguards were

RIGHT: *The second-generation Panhead, in addition to its telescopic fork, got "mellow-tone" mufflers and the official Hydra-Glide model name embossed on the fork cover. The front fender braces were gone and the rear fender had three stripes.*

more contemporary and complemented the contours of the fork and engine. The Hydra-Glide established the distinctive Harley look that would characterize the big twins from here on.

1950 EL

Engine: OHV 45° V-twin
Displacement: 60.33ci (988.56cc)
Bore & stroke: 3.31 x 3.5in (84 x 89mm)
Compression ratio: 7:1
Horsepower: 50 @ 5,000rpm
Carburetion: 1.25in (32mm) Schebler
Transmission: 4-speed
Primary dive: Chain
Final drive: Chain
Brakes: F. & R. Drum
Battery: 6-volt
Ignition: Coil/points

Frame: Steel, double downtube
Suspension: Leading link spring/shock fork
Wheelbase: 59.5in (151.1cm)
Weight: 580lb (263kg)
Fuel capacity: 3.75gal (14.2lit)
Oil capacity: 1gal (3.78lit)
Tires: 5 x 16in (12.7 x 40.6cm)
Top speed: 95mph (153km/h)
Colors: Black; red; blue (options: metallic green; flight red; azure blue; white)
Number built: 2,046
Price: $735

1950 EL

Owner: Trev Deeley Museum,
Vancouver, British Columbia

living the dream

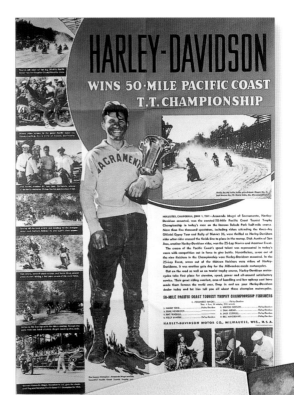

By 1942 World War II had reordered the priorities of everyone in the United States, and motorized recreation was subordinated by more pressing matters. Civilian defense volunteers in the U.S. and Great Britain worked as air-raid wardens and medical aides, often using motorcycles in their duties.

The American Office of Civil Defense was formed in May, 1941, and within the next 18 months had established some 12,000 local defense councils around the nation, with a roster of about 12 million volunteers. A block plan was created in urban areas to facilitate quick mobilization of civilians in case of enemy attack, which would organize the creation of emergency medical centers, planning for protection of civilians and possible evacuation procedures.

Many women were introduced to motorcycle riding in this period, when their husbands and boyfriends left for military service. Women also filled many of the factory jobs that had to be vacated by men who volunteered for active duty. John Harley, son of founder William S., was a lieutenant in the U.S. Army Signal Corps, where he put his motorcycle experience to work.

With the adoption of the Jeep, fewer motorcycles would be employed in Europe compared to World War I, but riders were still to serve in specialized missions in Europe and North Africa.

ABOVE LEFT: *Armando Magri won the Hollister TT title in '41, owned Sacramento H-D from 1950–83 and still rode in his mid-eighties.*

BELOW: *Bound copies of* The Enthusiast *show Milwaukee's support of the war effort.*

So 1941 was to be the last unrestricted riding season that many motorcyclists would enjoy for years to come. And of course for some, the last ever.

Harley-Davidson went to Daytona in March with a three-win run in hand and a new machine, the purpose-built WRTT, constructed just for Class C competition. The engine incorporated tuner Tom Sifton's developments in valve size, cam profiles and improved lubrication. But both Harley and Indian came away grumbling that year, when the checkered flag fell to Norton rider Billy of Mathews of Canada, riding a 500cc OHV single. The 50 percent displacement disadvantage confered by AMA rules was more than outweighed by the Norton's powerful, durable engine, foot shift, four-speed transmission and rear suspension.

Harley riders filled the next nine positions at Daytona in 1941, but the Milwaukee management was more than a bit miffed at the victory of a "foreign" bike and rider. Following the attack on Pearl Harbor, the 1942 Daytona race was canceled. In the words of AMA President E.C. Smith, "We have

HARLEY-DAVIDSON
Motorcycling Accessories

EVERYTHING TO MAKE YOU HAPPY

I AM YOUR HARLEY-DAVIDSON DEALER — AT YOUR SERVICE

SCHOTT MOTORCYCLE SUPPLY
HARLEY-DAVIDSON SALES & SERVICE
3 STRAWBERRY AVE.
LEWISTON   MAINE

MILWAUKEE, WIS., U.S.A. ALL DUTIES,
EXTRA. PRICES SUBJECT TO CHANGE

HARLEY-DAVIDSON MOTOR COMPANY
MILWAUKEE 1, WISCONSIN, U.S.A.

LEFT: *The advertising campaigns and accessory catalogs for 1941 maintained the happiness theme, although by summer of that year the prospects for domestic tranquility had dimmed.*

HARLEY-DAVIDSON
Motorcycling's Pace-setter for 1941

BRILLIANTLY ENGINEERED
FOR GREATER PERFORM-
ANCE AND VALUE . . . .

* Centrifugally-Controlled Oil Pump on All Models * New Design Clutch on All Models * Improved Transmission on 45 Twins and Servi-Cars * Improved 45 Twin and Servi-Car Clutch Releasing Mechanism * New, Quiet Big Twin Muffler * Airplane-Style Speedometer Dial * Improved 45 Twin Brakes * Positive-Grip Hand Brake Lever * Restyled Big Twin Clutch Foot Lever Assembly * Giant Air Cleaner * Oxide-Coated Piston Rings * Hardened Gear Shifter Lovers * New 45 Twin Tool Box * New Front Wheel on Servi-Cars * Relocated Police Radio Carrier * Cleaner Summer Sport Shield * A New Model—The 74 OHV * Beautiful Color Options * Lower Prices on 61 OHV and 45 WLDR.

by Hap Hayes

WELL—WELL—WELL! Here we are again folks. Howdy Greetings! and hello— from your ol' boy friend Hap Hayes, the head-hunter-scoops, (gotta cut down on those horror stories I've been reading) I mean headline hunter. And what a headline story I've got to tell. It's the hottest news story of the motorcycling year. So just bend your quivering ears in this direction while I give you all the interesting details on the 1941 line of Harley-Davidsons — the finest motorcycles

ABOVE: *Milwaukee had always included women in its advertising spreads, both as passengers and riders. Always smartly attired.*

LEFT: *Nestled snugly in the Harley's Buddy Seat, two AMA club members pause during a ride on the Mohawk Trail in the Berkshire Hills of Massachusetts. Touring riders formed the backbone of the AMA.*

"That 61 OHV Harley-Davidson that I rode surely did its share for our Middle East forces and aided materially in helping eventually drive the enemy completely out of Africa."

EDWARD DUNCAN

a more important job to do right now, and after we have finished that job to the satisfaction of humanity, we can have a lot of Daytona races in the years to come."

Although most military motorcyclists were not involved in front-line combat, the story of Edward Duncan bears mention. Stationed in Egypt as part of the British Long Range Desert Group, Duncan rode a Knucklehead Sixty-one and reported his tale in *The Enthusiast*. After riding hundreds of miles of desert in Libya and Egypt, he was sent to Greece.

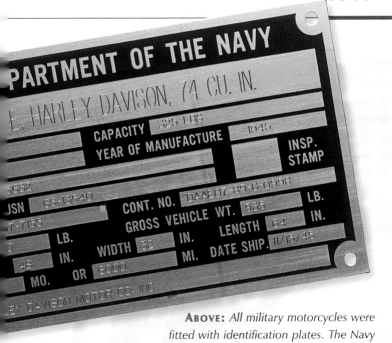

ABOVE: *All military motorcycles were fitted with identification plates. The Navy used bikes primarily for police duties.*

"I rode through a railroad town called Trikkala, which at that time was occupied by the Germans. I never discovered it until I was halfway through. Without warning, the German motorcyclists got after me in a hurry. I made up my mind not to be captured, although my map showed that I would have to ride through a mile-high pass near Metsovo, in and across the Pindus Mountains along a rough Greek road. A blinding snowstorm was raging at the time. How far the Germans followed me, I do not know because I soon lost them. But I am sure they must have sent a radio message to other German motorcyclists near the pass.

"As I arrived at the pass, I noticed the road sloped downward in the direction I was going, so I shut off the motor of my Harley-Davidson and was nearly through the pass when the Germans got after me again. By their uniforms, I could see they belonged to the Adolf Hitler Division of the Elite Guards. They were on motorcycles and immediately it became a battle of motorcycles. A few shots were fired at me

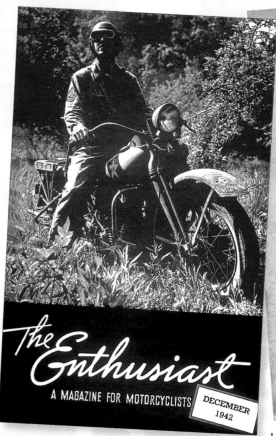

ABOVE THREE: *As the war continued, The Enthusiast expanded military coverage. Fort Knox was the primary training center.*

LEFT: *During the war, armored divisions used motorcycle reconnaissance units to scout and secure advanced positions.*

but took no effect. And then began a grueling race over a very rough road to Lamia, the gate to the mountain pass of Thermopylae, where the Germans hoped to cut me off. But they only wasted their time, for the wonderful power I had under me and the ability of my dependable Harley-Davidson to stand up to the terribly rough roads brought me through safely. Much of the time during that wild chase I was fairly bouncing out of the saddle."

ABOVE: *The Enthusiast naturally covered Milwaukee's succession of wins in Michigan's Jack Pine Enduro in the '30s and '40s. Jack Harding's adventurous ride from Texas to Peru was detailed in a 1950 issue.*

BELOW: *Canadian distributor Trevor Deeley was an active racer in the 1940s, coming 10th at Daytona in 1948. Earl Robinson continued his winning ways well after his cross-country runs.*

Back in Libya, Duncan was captured by Italian troops who confiscated his motorcycle. ("They abused my faithful Harley-Davidson something terrible.") Six weeks later he was liberated by British soldiers and retrieved his machine. "Although she had had a rough spin of it, I had no trouble in getting her going again."

President Franklin Roosevelt died on April 12, 1945 and was succeeded by Vice President Harry Truman. Germany surrendered on May 7, and the U.S. dropped atomic bombs on Hiroshima and Nagasaki in early August. Japan surrendered on August 15, ending World War II.

Once again Americans prepared for the shift to peaceful times, and the management of Harley-Davidson had already passed to the second-generation members of the families. With the passing of Walter Davidson and William Harley during the war years, the presidency of the company went to William H. Davidson, son of founder William

LEFT: *In the open countryside on a 1949 Hydra-Glide, what more could a fellow and his girl ask for.*

A., and the engineering title fell to Harley's son, William J. The lustre of Bill Harley's reputation shone brighter among many fans of his work when it was revealed that he had died of heart failure while sitting at the bar.

With the gentrification of America, motorcycling had developed an "image problem" long before World War II. Milwaukee had always done its part to cultivate a responsible impression among motorcycle riders and dealers, encouraging civilized, non-threatening behavior in public. At first it was simply a matter of noise, when hooligans on unmuffled machines would spook the horses in the street; as the machines grew larger and more powerful, speed created another dimension to the problem. Street racers and show-offs put pedestrians at risk, as well as other motorists.

But it was after the war that Harley-Davidson found itself confronted with a widespread public perception that hadn't existed in earlier days. The rowdies

LEFT: *Hollister, California, July 4, 1947: the famous* Life *magazine photograph that was said to have inspired director Stanley Kramer's 1953 movie "The Wild One."*

ABOVE: *A friendly gathering of bikers in 1948 at the Ozark Tavern in Secaucus, New Jersey, where riders were apparently welcome to park inside. Even Indian owners, like the couple on the right.*

of the '20s and '30s had generally been solo performers, or perhaps groups of two or three excitable boys out to raise some hell. In the mid-1940s the makers of mayhem would ride in larger groups, packs of 20 to 30 riders on modified Harleys, rolling into town with open pipes and outlaw attitudes. Motorcycle gangs.

One of these social organizations, The Boozefighters Motorcycle Club, came to national attention in Hollister, California in 1947. This relatively mild ruckus in the annals of mayhem didn't arouse a national wave of fear at the time. But in 1953, when the film loosely based on the event was released, the country recognized a new sub-culture. "The Wild One," starring Marlon Brando and Lee Marvin, didn't send the citizenry cowering into the shadows at the sight of a group of motorcyclists. But it did certify the menace of roaming bands of lawless thugs, ready to terrorize innocent hamlets at the drop of a beer bottle. And the film demonstrated the influence of actors like Brando, who made the black leather jacket fashionable.

1951-60: Post-War Prosperity Revisited

decade design evolution

"It's about time Harley got serious about high-performance bikes. The thing needs aluminum heads, which would shave a few pounds, and some lumpy cams. But it won't be long before we're kicking some Triumph butt."

FAT BURNS, MOTO PUNDIT

Although Indian was struggling to survive, Milwaukee recognized the need to broaden their appeal in the face of growing competition from England and Europe. So the move was on for more power, more color choices and accessories and increased social acceptance of the motorcycling sport. Larger intake ports on the OHV twins produced a bump in power, while quieter mufflers served to reduce the nuisance factor among the general public.

In 1952 Harley-Davidson offered its first foot shift on a production twin. The Sixty-one and Seventy-four (1000cc and 1200cc) Panheads had the option of hand or foot shift at the same price: $716.25/$727.50. The foot-shifter was fitted with a hand clutch that required a leverage booster, coined the "mousetrap." Despite its ability to retain more oil inside the engine compared to the Knucklehead, the Panhead still had a few problems with top-end lubrication. In 1953 the lifters were relocated from the top to the bottom of the pushrods, eliminating their tendency to clog up. The adoption of rotating exhaust valves helped to equalize wear and maintain compression.

The other big news in '52 was the arrival of the K model, successor to the venerable WL Forty-five and the only remaining flathead on the Milwaukee menu. With the four-speed transmission housed in the crankcases, foot-shifter on the right side and hydraulic suspension at both ends, the K bike was the picture of a major modern motorcycle. (Except for the side-valves; an OHV Forty-five [750cc] had been under development in the '40s, but was shelved as prohibitively expensive.) Stylish as it was, with 30 horsepower and 400 pounds (181kg), the K was no pinnacle of sporting performance. But the potential was there.

In 1954 an additional three-quarter inch (19mm) of stroke made the second-generation KH model a 53.9ci (883cc) engine, with considerably more urge. The KHK appeared the following year, with more muscular cams. And the racing KR version, with the assistance of tuning wizard Tom Sifton, came to dominate dirt track racing.

The Hydra-Glide big twin, now offered with only a 74ci (1200cc) engine, also got the higher performance H designation in 1955. The FLH had stronger crankcases,

LEFT: *The 1952 K model generated superlatives. "Its handling ease will astound you. You'll want to ride, ride, ride—and in competition you'll lead the pack."*

THE NEWEST ADDITION TO THE GREAT HARLEY-DAVIDSON LINE
HARLEY-DAVIDSON 45 Cu. In.

MODEL "K"

RIGHT SIDE

- All-New Engine
- Hydraulically Controlled Rear Suspension
- Hydraulic, Telescopic Front Fork
- Foot Shift—Hand Clutch
- Buckhorn, Rubber-Mounted Handlebars
- New, Streamlined, Tip-to-Tip Design

LEFT SIDE

MECHANICAL SPECIFICATIONS
1952 HARLEY-DAVIDSON 45 Cu. In.
MODEL "K"

HARLEY-DAVIDSON MOTOR CO.
MILWAUKEE 1, WISCONSIN, U.S.A.

ABOVE: As the specs indicate, the K model was much more than just those rubber-mounted buckhorn handlebars and streamlined tip-to-tip design.

ABOVE: With the adoption of the foot shift in 1952, the hand clutch needed some help, from a leverage booster fitted above the shift lever.

ABOVE: The Duo-Glide, so named for having suspension at both ends. Dual exhaust system was included in the King of the Highway option group.

larger big-end bearings and higher compression. The new tank emblem featured a bold V behind the Harley-Davidson script lettering, and the tombstone taillight was replaced by an oval unit.

In '56 the FLH was awarded new heads, high-lift cam and improved oil sealing at the valve covers. The tank badge hadn't changed but was now set off by a swath of color as background, and the new speedometer featured clock-style numbers in day-glo green and an odometer background in gold rather than silver. The 1957, and final, Hydra-Glide displayed a round plastic tank badge and a color panel atop the tank.

While the big twin remained the reigning king of the open road, the big news for 1957 was the arrival of the OHV XL 883—the Sportster. The widely rumored, long-awaited roadster didn't impress fans of the big twin, but the growing legion of street rodders accepted it with open arms and wallets. The Sportster, absent the frills and filigree of the traditional Milwaukee dresser, reflected both the accelerated development of American hot rodding and the response to the British imports.

In stock trim the first Sportster was more cruiser than dragster, but the potential was obvious; with integral transmission, four cams, overhead valves and hemispherical combustion chambers, real high performance was within reach. The short-stroke engine quickly attracted racing tuners and aftermarket parts makers.

By 1958 Milwaukee had heeded the calls from the streets and brought out the XLCH Sportster, with bigger valves, stronger gears, straight exhaust pipes and magneto ignition. With its bobbed rear fender and small 1.9-gallon (7.19lit) fuel tank pirated from the Hummer, the CH was a genuine musclebike.

The big twin hadn't been ignored in Milwaukee's advances for 1958. With a swing arm and hydraulic shock absorbers, the Duo-Glide replaced the Hydra-Glide. The new model also featured new cylinder heads, stronger clutch and transmission and hydraulic rear brake. Riders could still choose either hand or foot shift.

1951 FL Hydra-Glide; 1952 FL

"T he Fabulous Fifties debuted on a note of optimism in the country as the aftereffects of World War II were relegated to history," stated the official history ("The Big Book of Harley-Davidson"). With the "Cold War" not yet up to speed, America's consumer economy shifted into high gear and the time had come to enjoy the fruits of a hard-won peace.

Recognizing the forthcoming competition from British manufacturers, Milwaukee moved again to upgrade and civilize its products and to let people know about it. "New colors of exceeding beauty await the purchasers of all the models in our 1951 line," read the brochure. "Each is new and eye-appealing. The swellest colors ever to grace the Harley-Davidson line." The tank badge changed

from the spare speedball design to bold Harley-Davidson script, and the deluxe solo group included chrome trim throughout, crash bars and a pair of king size saddlebags for $115. The sidecar rig carried a pricetag of $240.

In 1952 Harley-Davidson took another large step for motorcycling kind and introduced foot shift to the big twin. The hand-shifter remained on the roster, and the left-foot shifter required a clutch booster nicknamed the "mousetrap." The shift from hand to foot gear selection, and

hand-operated clutch, brought Harley-Davidson into the mainstream of motorcycle configuration worldwide. And the next step, rear suspension, was on the way. Slowly. Tropical green was a new standard color in 1952; extra-charge options were metallic bronco bronze, white and metallic marine blue.

BELOW: *The clutch booster ("mousetrap") is visible between the crash bar and front cylinder. The Sixty-one sold for $955 in 1952, while the Seventy-four was up to $970. Both high-compression models were available with sidecar gearing at the same prices.*

1952 FL
Owner: John Tosta, Hanford, California
Restorer: Jones Brothers

1951 FL
Owner/restorer: Fred Lange,
Santa Maria, California

1951 FL HYDRA-GLIDE

Engine: OHV 45° V-twin
Displacement: 73.73ci (1208.19cc)
Bore & stroke: 3.44 x 4in (87 x 102mm)
Compression ratio: 7:1
Horsepower: 55 @ 4,800rpm
Carburetion: 1.31in (33.3mm) Schebler
Transmission: 4-speed
Primary drive: Chain
Final drive: Chain
Brakes: F. & R. Drum
Battery: 6-volt
Ignition: Coil/points
Frame: Steel, double downtube
Suspension: Telescopic fork
Wheelbase: 59.5in (151.1cm)
Weight: 590lb (267.6kg)
Fuel capacity: 3.75gal (14.2lit)
Oil capacity: 1gal (3.78lit)
Tires: 5 x 16in (12.7 x 40.6cm)
Top speed: 100mph (161km/h)
Colors: Brilliant black; persian red; rio blue
   (options: white; metallic green; blue)
Number built: 6,560
Price: $900

1950 WR; 1952 K

In 1952 the Harley family of flathead Forty-fives reached its fourth generation with the K model. At $865 the new machine was only $90 less than a Sixty-one Panhead, but offered the sporting rider a much lighter- and quicker-handling motorcycle.

While riders may have wished for a machine that was also faster, the benefits of an internal transmission, rear shock absorbers and uncluttered design gave the K model instant appeal. Harley had chosen a good time to introduce a sport model, since Class C competition between Milwaukee and Springfield was flourishing around the country and similar models from Britain were arriving in greater numbers. And even though the new Forty-five was rated at only 30 horsepower, astute tuners immediately saw the potential for more urge.

At Daytona in 1953, Harley avenged their succession of post-war losses when Brad Andres brought the racing KR model home first in the 200-miler (322km). The victory put Milwaukee back in the motorsports headlines, and served notice that the flathead could deal with the British overhead-valve twins. The KRTT was introduced for roadracing and TT scrambles. Thus began a new era of racing in America, with variety provided by Norton, Triumph and BSA, and the leading edge of the new movement in sportbikes for the road.

Thus the venerable W series, after 15 years of faithful service in all forms of public, commercial, police and racing duties, passed into Harley history. The WR, working man's racer, had compiled an admirable list of victories between World War II and the then current conflict in Korea. And racing versions of the new K series were poised to continue the tradition.

1950 WR
Owner/restorer: Mike Parti,
North Hollywood, California

1952 K
Owner/restorer: Fred Lange,
Santa Maria, California

FAR LEFT: *The WR flathead had been a frontrunner in dirt track racing for more than a decade. Class C racing was still growing in popularity.*

1952 K

Engine: Flathead 45° V-twin

Displacement: 45.32ci (742.66cc)

Bore & stroke: 2.75 x 3.81in (70 x 97mm)

Compression ratio: 6:1

Horsepower: 30

Carburetion: Linkert

Transmission: Unit 4-speed

Primary drive: Duplex chain

Final drive: Chain

Brakes: F. & R. Drum

Battery: 6-volt

Ignition: Coil/points

Frame: Steel, single downtube

Suspension: F. Hydraulic spring fork; R. Hydraulic spring shocks

Wheelbase: 56.5in (143.5cm)

Weight: 400lb (181kg)

Fuel capacity: 4.5gal (17.03lit)

Oil capacity: 3qts (2.84lit)

Tires: 3.25 x 19in (8.26 x 48.26cm)

Top speed: 80mph (129km/h)

Colors: Black; persian red; rio blue (option: bronco bronze metallic)

Number built: 1,970

Price: $865

ABOVE: *Though not the fastest 750 on the road, the long-awaited K model was welcomed by sport riders, racers and off-roaders. Rear suspension and foot shift were well received.*

1955 KH; 1956 KHK

By 1954, Milwaukee had applied to the K bikes the traditional divisions of responsibility for the workhorse flatheads—sportbike, Servi-Car, racer. But first Harley upped the displacement of the twin from 45 to 54ci (750 to 883cc), with a substantial increase in power and performance. The increase in stroke—to 4.56in (116mm)—brought a corresponding jump in torque, which overpowered the original transmission. Stronger gears solved the problem.

The second-generation KH was rated for 38 horsepower and had a top speed of 95mph (153km/h). The sport model engine now had a stronger bottom end, gearbox, cams and new valves and combustion chambers. The frame geometry was changed slightly and the brakes were improved, and when the hot-rod KHK arrived in 1955, it was apparent that

Harley had plans for its new sports model. The extra K denoted a factory-installed speed kit ($68) with hot cams, polished ports and a roller-bearing bottom end. And unlike the first K models, access to the transmission could be had without splitting the cases.

Since Joe Leonard had won the new Grand National Championship series on the KR in 1954, and Brad Andres repeated the feat in '55, prospects for the continued refinement of the K series looked good. But as it turned out, 1956 would be the swansong for the K model as

1955 KH

Engine: Flathead 45° V-twin
Displacement: 53.9ci (883cc)
Bore & stroke: 2.75 x 4.56in (70 x 116mm)
Compression ratio: 6:8:1
Horsepower: 38 @ 5,200prm
Carburetion: Linkert
Transmission: Unit 4-speed
Primary drive: Duplex chain
Final drive: Chain
Brakes: F. & R. Drum
Battery: 6-volt
Ignition: Coil/points
Frame: Steel, single downtube
Suspension: F. Hydraulic spring fork;
  R. Hydraulic spring shocks
Wheelbase: 56.5in (143.5cm)
Weight: 400lb (181kg)
Fuel capacity: 4.5gal (17.03lit)
Oil capacity: 3qts (2.84lit)
Tires: 3.25 x 19in (8.26 x 48.26cm)
Top speed: 95mph (153km/h)
Colors: Pepper red; atomic blue;
  anniversary yellow; aztec brown;
  black (option: hollywood green)
Number built: 1,065 (H & HK)
Price: $925

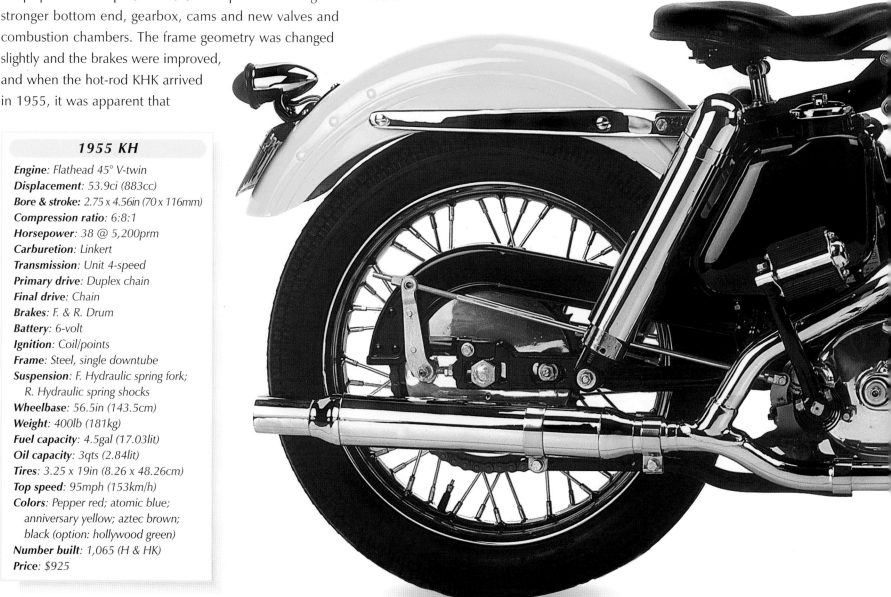

a street machine, although the racing version would be carried on for another 13 years. Milwaukee was just about ready with an overhead-valve version of the K bike, to be called the Sportster.

RIGHT: The speed kit brought the price of a KHK to $1,003. Chassis changes lowered the seat height, and kickstart gear was stronger.

1956 KHK

Owner: Otis Chandler, Ojai, California
Restorer: Glenn Bator

RIGHT: The 50-year anniversary medallion adorned the front fenders of all Harley-Davidson models in 1954. No one seems to know why it was a year late.

1955 KH

Owner: Harold Mathews,
Mathews Harley-Davidson,
Fresno, California

1955 FLH; 1955 Servi-Car

The '55 Hydra-Glide was offered in three configurations, each with the option of either foot or hand shift. Now in only 74ci (1200cc) versions, the FL Sport Solo (high-compression engine) and the FLE, with Traffic Combination motors (milder cams for police use), both listed for $1,015. The FLH Super Sport Solo, introduced at mid-year, featured stronger engine cases and bottom end bearings, and an optional compensating sprocket to reduce driveline lash. The upgraded motor, now rated at 60 horsepower, also had new aluminum rocker covers with improved oil sealing. The FLH carried a $68 price premium over the standard model.

In celebration of its 50th anniversary, Harley-Davidson adorned the 1955 FL series and the KH with chromed medallions combining the badge-and-bar logo with the V insignia. The V was also incorporated in the new script-style tank nameplate. The Hydra-Glide script disappeared from the top fork cover and reappeared as a badge on the front fender.

A new rectangular taillight was fitted in '55, and a set of auxiliary springs were available for the Buddy Seat.

The Servi-Car remained Milwaukee's all-purpose workhorse for police and commercial utility work. The three-wheeler retained the springer front end, which would be supplanted by the Hydra-Glide fork in 1959, and the trustworthy flathead

1955 FLH
Owner/restorer: Paul Wheeler,
Van Nuys, California

ABOVE: Helper springs below the seat could be pivoted up to assist in the support of the passenger.

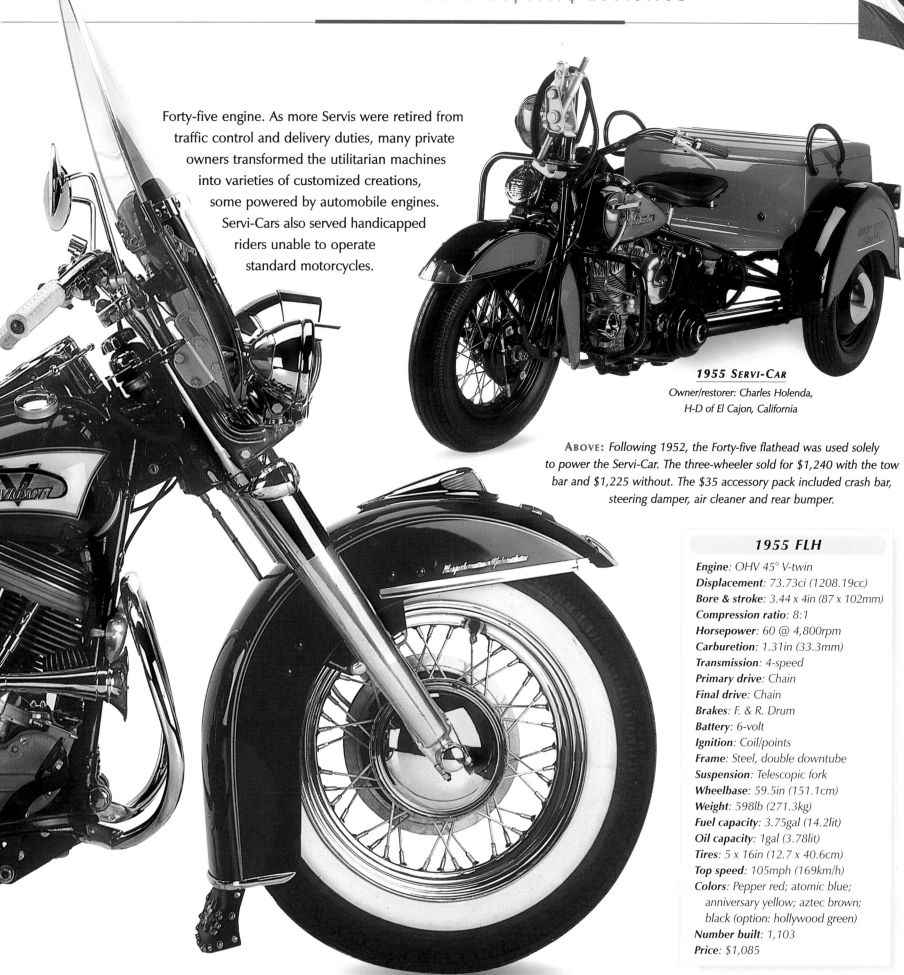

Forty-five engine. As more Servis were retired from traffic control and delivery duties, many private owners transformed the utilitarian machines into varieties of customized creations, some powered by automobile engines. Servi-Cars also served handicapped riders unable to operate standard motorcycles.

1955 SERVI-CAR
Owner/restorer: Charles Holenda,
H-D of El Cajon, California

ABOVE: *Following 1952, the Forty-five flathead was used solely to power the Servi-Car. The three-wheeler sold for $1,240 with the tow bar and $1,225 without. The $35 accessory pack included crash bar, steering damper, air cleaner and rear bumper.*

1955 FLH

Engine: OHV 45° V-twin
Displacement: 73.73ci (1208.19cc)
Bore & stroke: 3.44 x 4in (87 x 102mm)
Compression ratio: 8:1
Horsepower: 60 @ 4,800rpm
Carburetion: 1.31in (33.3mm)
Transmission: 4-speed
Primary drive: Chain
Final drive: Chain
Brakes: F. & R. Drum
Battery: 6-volt
Ignition: Coil/points
Frame: Steel, double downtube
Suspension: Telescopic fork
Wheelbase: 59.5in (151.1cm)
Weight: 598lb (271.3kg)
Fuel capacity: 3.75gal (14.2lit)
Oil capacity: 1gal (3.78lit)
Tires: 5 x 16in (12.7 x 40.6cm)
Top speed: 105mph (169km/h)
Colors: Pepper red; atomic blue; anniversary yellow; aztec brown; black (option: hollywood green)
Number built: 1,103
Price: $1,085

1957 XL Sportster

Enter the Sportster. In 1957 Milwaukee opened a new page in motorcycling history with the introduction of an overhead-valve V-twin based on the K model. The 54ci (883cc) engine with 9:1 compression was rated at 40 horsepower @ 5,500rpm, and the XL Sportster had the look and sound perfectly suited to the hot-rod era of the mid-1950s.

Harley-Davidson had proceeded cautiously in developing the Sportster, testing and refining the engine for nearly five years before its introduction. The decision over cylinder head design and material was the most troublesome. Problems with the first alloy lids on the Panhead persuaded Milwaukee engineers that cast-iron heads would do the job, and the competition from British OHV twins was an immediate challenge.

The Sportster engine was not much more powerful than its flathead ancestor the KHK, but with its shorter stroke the XL revved quicker. And the large valves and hemispheric combustion chambers, in concert with new camshaft configurations, held the promise of more power to come. And the bike's capability was established at the '57 Jack Pine Enduro in Michigan, when Harley dealer Gerald McGovern won the rugged event on a stock Sportster.

The Sportster, despite disparagement by the big twin tribe as a mere dirt bike, would go on to high achievement as a street rod, drag-, dirt- and roadracer, create another catalog of aftermarket parts and accessories, grab the attention of adventurous young ladies and make a young cat look cool just motoring down the road. In 2000 the Sportster would eclipse the Servi-Car as Milwaukee's longest continuous production model, now 45 years and counting.

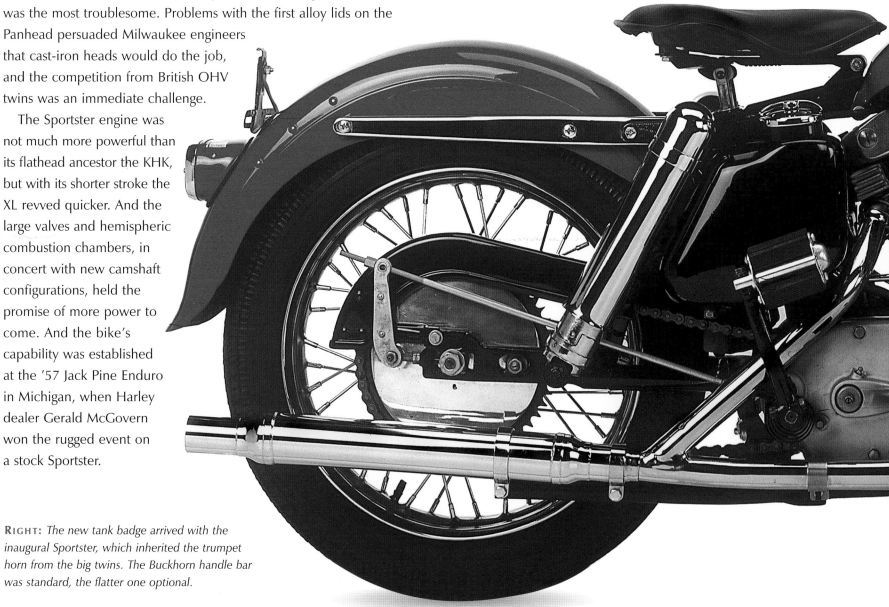

RIGHT: *The new tank badge arrived with the inaugural Sportster, which inherited the trumpet horn from the big twins. The Buckhorn handle bar was standard, the flatter one optional.*

1957 XL SPORTSTER

Engine: OHV 45° V-twin
Displacement: 53.9ci (883cc)
Bore & stroke: 3 x 3.81in
    (76 x 97mm)
Compression ratio: 9:1
Horsepower: 40 @ 5,500rpm
Carburetion: Linkert
Transmission: Unit 4-speed
Primary drive: Duplex chain
Final drive: Chain
Brakes: F. & R. Drum
Battery: 6-volt
Ignition: Coil/points
Suspension: F. Telescopic fork;
    R. Hydraulic shocks

Frame: Steel, double downtube
Wheelbase: 57in (144.8cm)
Weight: 495lb (225kg)
Fuel capacity: 4.4gal (16.7lit)
Oil capacity: 3qts (2.84lit)
Tires: 3.5 x 18in
    (8.9 x 45.72cm)
Top speed: 95mph (153km/h)
Colors: Pepper red/black;
    skyline blue/white; birch
    white/black; black/red (extra-
    charge option: metallic
    midnight blue/white)
Number built: 1,983
Price: $1,103

1957 XL

Owner: Otis Chandler, Ojai, California
Restorer: Glenn Bator

1958 XLCH; 1958 FLH; 1960 XLH

1960 XLH
*Owner: Charles Holenda,
H-D of El Cajon, California*

When the Sportster really started to add muscle, and dispense with what little fat there was, the result was the XLCH in 1958. The street scrambler marked the diversion of the model line into distinct renditions for the road and track. With a stronger gearbox, bigger valves, straight exhaust pipes and a teeny fuel tank, the CH was built to go fast.

In the tradition of its K model forebears, the XLCH could be ridden to the track, raced and, God-willing, ridden home. Both Harley and Indian had been making dual-purpose machines long before the label came along, but the CH was the closest thing to a factory racer since the first KR and the first to feature overhead valves on a roadworthy sportbike. Good for 14 seconds plus and 90mph (145km/h) in the quarter-mile (0.4km), the XLCH was an instant hot-rod hero on the boulevard.

If the advent of foot-shifting big twins had been a minor revelation in 1952, the introduction of the Duo-Glide in 1958 was a quantum leap into the present. Touring riders accustomed to having the seat perform all the rear suspension duties (which worked reasonably well) were more than a bit skeptical about the new swing-arm suspension. Advance rumors of uncontrollable wobbling and sliding out on corners were common.

1958 XLCH
*Owner: Otis Chandler, Ojai, California
Restorer: Glenn Bator*

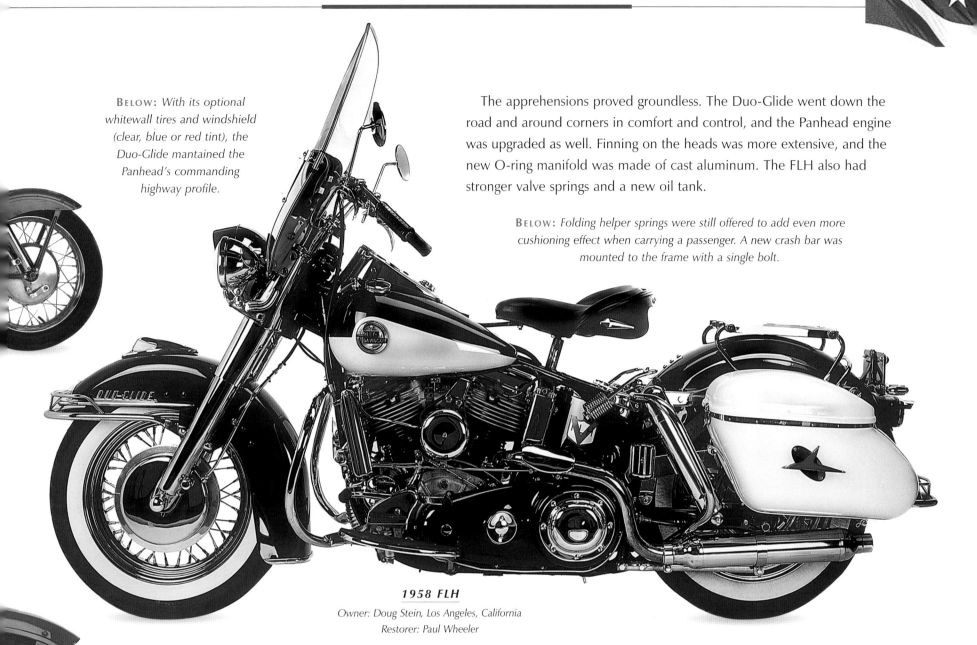

BELOW: *With its optional whitewall tires and windshield (clear, blue or red tint), the Duo-Glide mantained the Panhead's commanding highway profile.*

The apprehensions proved groundless. The Duo-Glide went down the road and around corners in comfort and control, and the Panhead engine was upgraded as well. Finning on the heads was more extensive, and the new O-ring manifold was made of cast aluminum. The FLH also had stronger valve springs and a new oil tank.

BELOW: *Folding helper springs were still offered to add even more cushioning effect when carrying a passenger. A new crash bar was mounted to the frame with a single bolt.*

1958 FLH
Owner: Doug Stein, Los Angeles, California
Restorer: Paul Wheeler

1958 XLCH

Engine: OHV 45° V-twin
Displacement: 53.9ci (883cc)
Bore & stroke: 3 x 3.81in (76 x 97mm)
Compression ratio: 9:1
Horsepower: 45
Carburetion: Linkert
Transmission: 4-speed
Primary drive: Triplex chain
Final drive: Chain
Brakes: F. & R. Drum
Ignition: Magneto
Frame: Steel, double downtube
Suspension: F. Telescopic fork; R. Hydraulic shocks
Wheelbase: 57in (144.8cm)
Weight: 480lb (217.7kg)
Fuel capacity: 1.9gal (7.19lit)
Oil capacity: 3qts (2.84lit)
Tires: F. 3.5 x 19in (8.9 x 48.26cm); R. 4 x 18in (10.16 x 45.72cm)
Top speed: 115mph (185km/h)
Colors: Skyline blue/white; calypso red/white; sabre gray metallic/white; black/white
Number built: 239
Price: $1,155

1958 FLH DUO-GLIDE

Engine: OHV 45° V-twin
Displacement: 73.73ci (1208.19cc)
Bore & stroke: 3.44 x 3.97in (87 x 101mm)
Compression ratio: 7:1
Horsepower: 52
Carburetion: Schebler
Transmission: 4-speed
Primary drive: Chain
Final drive: Chain
Brakes: F. & R. Drum
Battery: 6-volt
Ignition: Coil/points
Frame: Steel, double downtube
Suspension: F. Telescopic fork; R. Hydraulic shocks
Wheelbase: 60in (152cm)
Weight: 648lb (294kg)
Fuel capacity: 3.75gal (14.2lit)
Oil capacity: 4qts (3.79lit)
Tires: 5 x 16in (12.7 x 40.64cm)
Top speed: 100mph (161km/h)
Colors: Skyline blue/white; calypso red/white; sabre gray metallic/white; black/white (options: any standard solid color)
Number built: 3,178 (FL: 2,890)
Price: $1,320

living the dream

"Ever since World War II, California has been strangely plagued by wild men on motorcycles."

HUNTER S. THOMPSON,
"HELL'S ANGELS"

Unlike the economic aftermath of World War I, the American economy of the 1950s was one of unequalled prosperity. More people could buy more goods than at any time in the country's history, and with the advent of the "consumer" society, not even the Korean War would seriously alter the growth of a solvent middle class.

On the one hand this was good news for the motorcycle industry, since more people would be buying and riding motorcycles, and the requisite parts and accessories. On the other hand it was bad news, since the percentage of "outlaw" riders was increasing in proportion, and with the willing assistance of the news media, would have a disproportionate effect on the public's perception of motorcyclists.

This put Harley-Davidson in something of a quandary. With the demise of Indian in 1953, Milwaukee had the only motorcycle company in the country. While the great majority of their customers were law-abiding citizens, not to mention law-enforcement officers, a growing and more visible minority operated on the fringes of polite society. And while the activities of the so-called motorcycle gangs were usually more sensational in the media than in reality, their effect on the entire sport grew more difficult to ignore.

Also, while the American V-twin orthodoxy had few

RIGHT AND BELOW:
Accessory catalogs of the '50s looked much like earlier versions. Dealer imprints were included at the bottom.

ABOVE: *Motorcycle weddings gained popularity in the fun-loving '50s. A democratic attitude obviously prevailed, since most of the guests are on Harleys and the bride and groom ride a Brit bike.*

1954 Accessory Catalog

ORDER BY MAIL OR BY PHONE...OR, BEST OF ALL,
Come in and see us.

CENTRALIA MOTORCYCLE SALES   Phone 5722
1244 No. Poplar
CENTRALIA, ILLINOIS

SALES and SERVICE   ★ GENUINE PARTS AND ACCESSORIES

challengers in the 1940s, the rebuilt motorcycle industries of England, Germany, Italy and ultimately Japan, would change the market completely within a few years. The motorcycle gangsters, however, would not be persuaded to ride anything but Harleys. Milwaukee did hold one advantage in the post-war picture; thousands of surplus military Forty-fives were sold on the open market at only slightly discounted prices, forecasting a future outlet for the inventory of spare parts that Harley-Davidson had produced for the war effort.

But while Milwaukee still held the cards in the heavyweight touring division, the Forty-five was up against serious competition from overseas. When Ohioan Dick Klamfoth won the Daytona 200 in 1952 on a Norton, for the third time, it was clear that Milwaukee's venerable flathead was in need of modernization. An interesting sidelight on the '52 beach race is related in Don Emde's history, "The Daytona 200."

Heavy rains had postponed the Sunday event and Klamfoth, under the impression the date had been switched to Tuesday, decided to go fishing on Monday. Having

ABOVE: *The cover of the Saturday Evening Post, April 7, 1957, captured the youthful dreams of three lads enthralled by the majesty of Tex's dresser. Norman Rockwell influence shows in artist Stevan Dohanos' illustration.*

chartered a boat, he was waiting in a restaurant for some sandwiches to take along when a racing fan recognized him and asked how he expected to do in the race today. "You mean tomorrow," Klamfoth said. Learning that the race was but a few hours off, he rushed back to the garage to find the team had left

ABOVE: *Motorcycle stunts and group-riding tricks became staples at major events in the '50s. Daring riders entertained crowds at state fairs and during intermissions at championship racing meets.*

RIGHT: *Fifties advertising looks quaint in retrospect, but Milwaukee remained conscious of the need to maintain its level of brand identification in what was becoming a much more crowded market.*

LEFT: *Then there was the Gentle Threat style of advertising pitch. Better not miss your chance to be riding a new Hydra-Glide, or you'll regret it for the rest of your life. The Korean War cast a large shadow on the future.*

for the beach. Climbing into his riding gear, Klamfoth rode his bike to the track in time to make the start and won his third Daytona 200.

Social gatherings among the motorcycle communities of the 1950s conformed fairly closely with those of the non-riding public. Field meets were simply regional fairs or picnics for the purpose of gathering with like-minded folk to socialize, play games, eat and talk motorcycles. The more elaborately organized events might include a swap meet, hoe-down or a motorcycle race, but the focus was the ride to get there, the social get together and the ride home. Some of these gatherings became annual events, and some, like the August meet in Sturgis, South Dakota, grew into major national collectives.

BOTH ABOVE: *Field meets were popular with riders around the country. Friendly competitions included the slow race, weenie bite, inner tube toss, water balance ride and egg-and-spoon race.*

RIGHT AND FAR RIGHT: *Milwaukee's hope for the Hummer, derived from the German DKW inherited after World War II, never reached expectations.*

Local motorcycle clubs, mostly those who affiliated with the AMA, planned and organized the events with volunteer help. Most clubs included a mix of road riders and dirt riders, and a number who did both who were always willing to pitch in for the benefit of all. The local police department or fraternal organization was

and everybody's rushing to see the Harley-Davidson HUMMER!

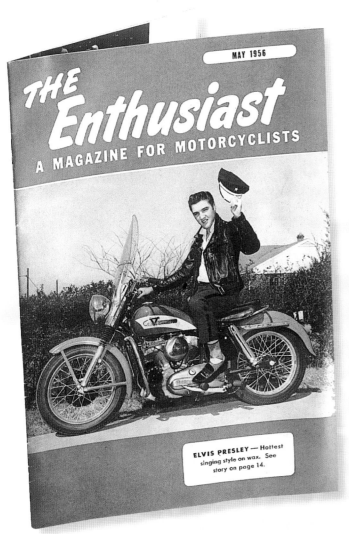

ABOVE: *Harley fan and pioneer rocker Elvis Presley made* The Enthusiast *cover in May of 1956. The KH is enshrined in the Harley-Davidson museum in Milwaukee.*

ABOVE: *The combined bar-and-shield/ V medallion was fitted to the front fenders of 1955 models.*

usually ready to handle some aspect of the food preparation or event logistics, and area motorcycle dealers were frequently willing to provide support and assistance. Often games or raffles were conducted to raise funds for local charities.

The question has often arisen, why did Harley-Davidson's foot-clutch/hand-shift system hang on so long? Fair question. After all, Velocette had introduced hand-clutch/foot-shift controls in the late '20s, and most of the world followed suit soon thereafter. Mostly it was probably just a matter of inertia; that's how it had always been done in the States, and no pressing reason to change it had ever come along.

Some of the rationale may have involved the big V-twin itself, a torque-strong motor that really didn't require a lot of gear changing to carry one down the road. And the American road itself, primarily straight and long, which also demanded little more than top gear. Plus, the size of the Harley engine itself dictated a large, strong clutch, and legs are more powerful than arms.

But with the influx of British and European bikes in the '50s, Milwaukee quickly offered the option of foot shift on the big twin and made it standard on the unit-transmission K model Forty-five in 1952. But another component in the shift from hand- to foot-shifting was the lightweight motorcycle trend that began quietly after the war, led by Harley-Davidson's own 125cc two-stroke.

While the tiddler, simply a clone of the utilitarian DKW, was beneath the dignity of big twin owners who didn't consider it a "real Harley-Davidson," the 125 introduced many youngsters to motorcycling. And it had a hand clutch and foot shift. When those young folks matured and went looking for a larger, more powerful machine, they weren't likely to be enticed by a hand-shifter and a whole new learning process.

ABOVE: *This dealer postcard showed the cute Hummer and just how keen it was to the girls.*

RIGHT: *Poster for the annual Jack Pine enduro in 1958. The Cow Bell, inscribed with the winner's name, was the trophy. Leroy Winters won in 1956 on a modified Hummer; the '57 Bell went to Gerald McGovern on a Sportster.*

BELOW: *The dominant dirt track rider of his generation, Texan Carroll Resweber won four straight national titles from 1958 through '61.*

ABOVE: *Harley-Davidson riders won the Daytona 200 each year from 1955 through 1961. Three of the victories went to Brad Andres of San Diego, California.*

BELOW: *Between them, the husband-and-wife team of Early and Dot Robinson probably won more trophies than any other twosome in motorcycling history. Dot blazed the trail for women riders.*

Plus, being hep young rock 'n' rollers, many of them would look for a fast, light middleweight motorcycle. And Harley-Davidson didn't have one.

The arrival of the Sportster in 1957 signaled Harley-Davidson's response to the imported middleweight sportbikes. Class C racing was still under the 750cc flathead/500cc OHV rule, so the new factory hot rod was intended for road use only. But, with the demise of Indian, the trusty K model had come to dominate American Grand National racing. With the talents of Joe Leonard, Brad Andres and Carroll Resweber, Harley-Davidson captured the top spot every year from 1954 through 1961.

The AMA had outlawed the DOHC Norton as a purely racing machine, outside the ostensibly production-based format of Class C. But the BSA Gold Star single would prove a worthy challenger to Milwaukee's domination; in skilled hands, the engines made close to 60 horsepower and offered a resonant counterpoint to the syncopated Harley V-twin. Carroll Resweber's domination of the sport was unprecedented in racing history. Regarded the best dirt track artist of all time, Resweber was seriously injured in a 1962 accident at Lincoln, Illinois, and retired as a racer. His record of four consecutive national titles stood for three decades, when it was matched by Harley factory rider Scott Parker.

ABOVE: *The Hydra-Glide reigned virtually uncontested as the big twin of the '50s and maintained the position through 1958, when it was renamed the Duo-Glide. The Super Sport Solo sold for $1,243 in 1957.*

ABOVE: *In 1960 the Duo-Glide Super Sport was the ultimate heavyweight road machine available, at a mere $1,375. Harleys and capri pants, stylish then and now.*

ABOVE TOP: *Actor Jimmy Stewart portrayed famed aviator Charles Lindbergh in the film "Spirit of St. Louis." Lindbergh had been a Harley rider. Other notable Hollywood motorcyclists in the 1950s were Roy Rogers, James Dean, Robert Young, Keenan Wynn and Lee Marvin.*

When the Korean War ended with an armed truce in 1953, soldiers returned to a nation ready for life without war. Many of the combatants had also served in World War II, and were fully prepared for peace, social stability and better clothes. And while many weary veterans looked forward to resuming life with their families, more than a few were eager to get a motorcycle and hit the road.

The Harley-Davidson Motor Company celebrated its 50th anniversary, noting it proudly on brass fender medallions: "50 YEARS—AMERICAN MADE." President William H. Davidson spoke of Milwaukee's rich history at the celebration dinner, acknowledging the firm's founders. "Never has a finer business heritage been handed down from one generation to the next," he said. "Let me assure you that my generation holds the same unwavering faith in America's future as did our fathers before us."

But dramatic change was sweeping the country. With prosperity at hand, the market was full of choices. The fully recovered British industry was offering powerful, agile twins derived from European roadracing heritage. Young Americans were ready to cut loose, with hot rods, sports cars, cafe racers, rock 'n' roll and a broad, unfocused restlessness that would reshape the nation's consciousness. It was time to shake, rattle and roll.

1961–70: Motorcycling Redefined

decade design evolution

"Drags! Scrambles! Trials! Enduros! Climbing! Anything! You name it … you ride it … the CH loves it! Here is the sporting Sportster … ready to take a challenge … willing to meet any odds … and always able to win."

1960s ADVERTISEMENT

The big twin was slower to evolve than the Sportster, since Milwaukee's position in the touring market still remained strong. The foremost issues were the sportbike division, which the Sportster addressed, and the growing lightweight segment. Since the Hummer was deemed inadequate to the challenge, Harley-Davidson bought a half-interest in the Italian Aermacchi factory.

The first Aermacchi/Harley-Davidson was the 1961 Sprint, powered by a 250cc overhead valve four-stroke engine in a single-strut backbone frame. While the Italian styling didn't win wide approval among most U.S. riders, or Harley-Davidson dealers for that matter, the lightweight did attract budget-conscious sport and commuter riders and racers. In 1962 the standard C model road version was accompanied by the H version—a street-scrambler with high pipe, small fuel tank and seat.

The Sprint was imported in limited numbers for the first few years, fewer than 2,000 a year until 1965 when the total was up to 3,000. The dual-purpose H model outsold the street version about five to one, and would later be called the Scrambler and ultimately the Sprint SS. With higher compression, larger carburetor and exhaust system, horsepower grew from 18 to 25. The Sprint fared well in short track and scrambles competition, but was soon outpaced by faster two-strokes from Europe and Japan. The Sprint's numbers peaked in 1967, when Milwaukee brought in more than 9,000 machines, including a few roadracing versions. In 1969 the SS model arrived as a 350cc.

The pure competition version of the Sportster was the XLR, which had its magneto mounted at the front of the cases in place of the standard model's generator. With its ball-bearing lower end, purpose-built heads, cams, valves and pistons, the race motor was good for about 75 horsepower.

The civilian Sportster inherited a full-width front brake hub from the Sprint in 1964, and was upgraded to a 12-volt electrical system the following year. The XLH was fitted with

HARLEY-DA
topper motor scoot
modern wheels for modern

Catching the commuter special…getting to school on time … or just out for real, downright fun … you can't beat the Topper H. These are fun 'wheels' the whole family can enjoy with super gas mileage economy to boot! The Topper H is easy to ride, too, with "Scootaway"

AVAILABLE AS OPTIONAL EXTRA EQUIPMENT FOR TOPPERS

NEW SEAT Styled from new, jet black waterproof Hy-palon plastic. Material is easy to keep clean with soap and water. A passenger Seat Strap is optional.

ENGINE – DRIVE Topper's **Scootaway** automatic drive eliminates shifting—gives you fast smooth acceleration. Engine delivers 9½ horsepower for your pleasure.

WHEELS – RIDE Large diame wheels take you o holes and bum safely. Smooth su pension, front an rear, gives you a ver. gliding ride.

topper h GREATEST FUN VALUE ON

automatic throttle ani lighting sys any road su modern Harley-Davi

LEFT: *Harley-Davidson Rider Handbooks are especially sought after by both those who restore older models and riders buying one for their own use.*

automatic spark advance, while the CH still used a manual advance on the left handgrip. In 1966 new cams and carburetor brought increased horsepower, and in '67 the XLH was fitted with an electric starter. The basic Sportster look—peanut tank, solo saddle, eyebrow headlight and staggered dual exhausts—was typified by the XLCH.

The big twin had undergone largely cosmetic changes in the early 1960s. The Panhead was awarded an electric starter in 1965, and its title changed from Duo-Glide to Electra-Glide. A new frame and oil tank accompanied the switch to 12-volt electrics, with the large battery fitted below the seat on the right side. Automatic spark advance was included in the upgrades, along with a stronger crankcase and clutch. After 18 years' service, this would be the final year for the Panhead, assuring its collector status.

New aluminum cylinder heads, derived from the Sportster design, graced the FLH in 1966 and created the nickname Shovelhead. With improved combustion chambers came an increase of five horsepower, but an accompanying rise in vibration. Despite the incremental advances in design, engineering and performance, Harley-Davidson's market share had slipped badly in the '60s. Faced with the growing popularity of Honda and other Japanese marques, Milwaukee needed financial help to both meet production demands and develop new products. The subsequent merger with American Machine and Foundry, which proved both blessing and curse, at least kept the only American motorcycle company alive.

ABOVE LEFT: *The Topper set no sales records for Harley, but it was a cute motor scooter and enjoyed some popularity as a runabout in the city and for parade duties of fraternal organizations.*

ABOVE: *Nicknamed the "tombstone" speedometer for the center panel, the model was used from 1962–67. Clock-style numerals were fashionable and easy to read.*

RIGHT: *For many tastes, the Shovelhead had the most pleasing engine architecture since the Knucklehead. The balance of chrome and polished and unpolished aluminum somehow unified form and function. American industrial folk art.*

1961 Sprint; 1962 Topper; 1963 Scat

In its first half-century, Harley-Davidson had far more experience in exporting than importing motorcycles. But in the early '60s it became increasingly apparent that the lightweight market in the U.S. was growing, and that developing new models would be both expensive and tardy. So Harley bought half of the Italian Aermacchi firm, which built small two- and four-stroke singles.

The 250cc Sprint, designed for both road and trail applications with a bit of racing thrown in, was powered by a horizontal overhead-valve single. The four-speed, wet-sump 18-horsepower engine was hung in a single-strut backbone frame, suspended telescopically at both ends, and with six-volt coil/points ignition. At under 300 pounds (136kg), the Italian lightweight was presented as an easy handling machine for entry-level riders and low-budget buyers. Although the Sprint would stay on the Milwaukee roster for 13 years, and include a 350cc version, its development fell behind the Japanese imports.

In 1960 Milwaukee had taken another market-broadening step with the Topper motor scooter. Driven by a 165cc two-stroke engine, the scooter arrived too late to capitalize on the market previously owned by the Italian Vespa and Lambretta models, which were being displaced by the 50cc Honda minibike. By 1962 the Hummer family of two-stroke lightweights had evolved into the Pacer, Scat and Ranger models for road, on/off road and track/trail use respectively. The Ranger was gone in '63, and the Scat was awarded a swing arm with shocks mounted below the engine. The 175cc model was offered with a Hunting and Fishing Gear Kit with larger rear and smaller front sprockets.

BELOW: *Harley's only motor scooter, the Topper was built to compete with the Cushman and the Italian imports. It was also offered with a sidecar or utility box. A five-horsepower engine was standard with a nine-horsepower motor optional.*

RIGHT: *The 250cc Aermacchi Sprint was offered in standard or cafe racer trim. In 1963 a dual-purpose model joined the roster; the 350cc version came in 1969.*

1962 TOPPER
Owner: Tom Perkins, San Francisco, California

1963 Scat

Owner: Trev Deeley Museum,
Vancouver, British Columbia

1961 Sprint

Owner: Otis Chandler,
Ojai, California

1961 Sprint

Engine: OHV horizontal single
Displacement: 15ci (246.2cc)
Bore & stroke: 2.59 x 2.83in
  (66 x 72mm)
Compression ratio: 8.5:1
Horsepower: 18 @ 6,750rpm
Carburetion: Dell'Orto
Transmission: 4-speed
Primary drive: Helical gear
Final drive: Chain
Brakes: F. & R. Drum
Battery: 6-volt
Ignition: Coil/points
Frame: Steel tube, single strut
Suspension: F. Telescopic fork;
  R. Hydraulic shocks
Wheelbase: 52in (132cm)
Weight: 275lb (124.7kg)
Fuel capacity: 4gal (15.14lit)
Oil capacity: 2qts (1.89lit)
Tires: 3 x 17in (7.62 x 43.18cm)
Top speed: 75mph (121km/h)
Colors: Red/white; red/silver; gray/black
Number built: n/a
Price: $690

1962 XLR; 1964 XLCH; 1964 XLH

The Sportster had ascended quickly in the musclebike division, and the next logical move in Milwaukee was to answer the growing need for a raceworthy scrambler. The XLR was distinguished by its magneto ignition in place of the generator on the street models, and the option of a close-ratio gearbox and broad selection of gearing choices.

But the important differences were inside the engine. The crankshaft was supported by ball bearings; the flywheels, rods, pistons, valves and heads were all purpose-built for racing, and the engine made 60 plus horsepower. In the hands of a talented rider,

the R model was a potent weapon on TT tracks, and was also adapted by many riders for roadracing and drag strip competition. An enlarged XLR engine was later used in the Manning/Riley/Rivera streamliner in which pilot Cal Rayborn set a new Bonneville speed record at 265mph (426.5km/h).

1962 XLR

Owner/restorer: Sam Mathews,
Mathews Harley-Davidson, Fresno, California

ABOVE: *The XLR was the meanest of the mighty Sportsters. The racing version of the XLCH is identified by the magneto mounted in front of the engine in place of the generator. The brace below the steering head has been added to strengthen the frame.*

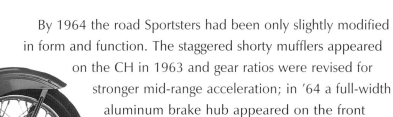

By 1964 the road Sportsters had been only slightly modified in form and function. The staggered shorty mufflers appeared on the CH in 1963 and gear ratios were revised for stronger mid-range acceleration; in '64 a full-width aluminum brake hub appeared on the front wheel, and the tank insignia lost the checkered flag design.

1965 XLH
Owner/restorer: Randy Janson,
El Cajon, California

RIGHT: *Standad colors for both Sportsters were black/white or blue/white, with options of Hi-Fi blue/white or red/white. In 1964 the XLCH was $1,360 while the XLH sold for $1,295.*

1964 XLCH
Owner/restorer: Randy Janson, El Cajon, Caifornia

With its six-volt system and manual spark advance, the Sportster could be a challenge to kickstart. In 1965 Harley switched to a 12-volt system and provided the XLH with an automatic spark advance. The stacked dual mufflers remained standard equipment on the H model, and options included the Buddy Seat, windshield, saddlebags and crash bars. The XLH sold for $1.295 and the XLCH for $1,360.

1962 XLR

Engine: OHV 45° V-twin	**Suspension**: F. Telescopic fork;
Displacement: 53.9ci (883cc)	R. Hydraulic shocks
Bore & stroke: 3 x 3.81in	**Wheelbase**: 57in (144.8cm)
(76 x 97mm)	**Weight**: 340lb (154.2kg)
Compression ratio: 10:1	**Fuel capacity**: 1.9gal (7.19lit)
Horsepower: 60	**Oil capacity**: 3qts (2.84lit)
Carburetion: Linkert	**Tires**: F. 3.5 x 19in
Transmission: 4-speed	(8.9 x 48.26cm);
Primary drive: Triplex chain	R. 4 x 18in (10.16 x 45.72cm)
Final drive: Chain	**Top speed**: 120mph (193km/h)
Brakes: F. & R. Drum	**Colors**: Red/white; blue/white
Ignition: Magneto	**Number built**: n/a
Frame: Steel, double downtube	**Price**: $1,500

1965 FLH Electra-Glide

M ilwaukee entered the modern age of motorcycling in 1965 with the Electra-Glide, the electric-start successor to the Duo-Glide. And the first thumb-start big twin would gain added cachet in terms of exclusivity, since it would also be the final version of the Panhead.

Bringing the FLH to contemporary specs required more than just grafting on a starter motor. Given the displacement and generally heavy-duty nature of the big Harley, other components had to be correspondingly robust. A new frame with a cast-aluminum primary cover helped support the added weight of starter and 12-volt battery, which eliminated the tool box. Stronger engine cases and clutch were also on the upgrade list, and primary chain adjustment was enhanced by an access hole in the cover. And the foot-shift model (now outpacing the hand-shifter by almost 4:1) was fitted with a 5-gallon (18.9lit) fuel tank, while the hand-shifter retained the 3.75-gallon (14.2lit) container. All of which meant a heavier motorcycle.

BELOW: *With the advent of non-kickstarting, Electra-Glide sales reached their highest point in 15 years. Riders could still choose hand or foot shift. Milwaukee offered a long menu of accessories, including the Super Deluxe Buddy Seat in red or blue and white.*

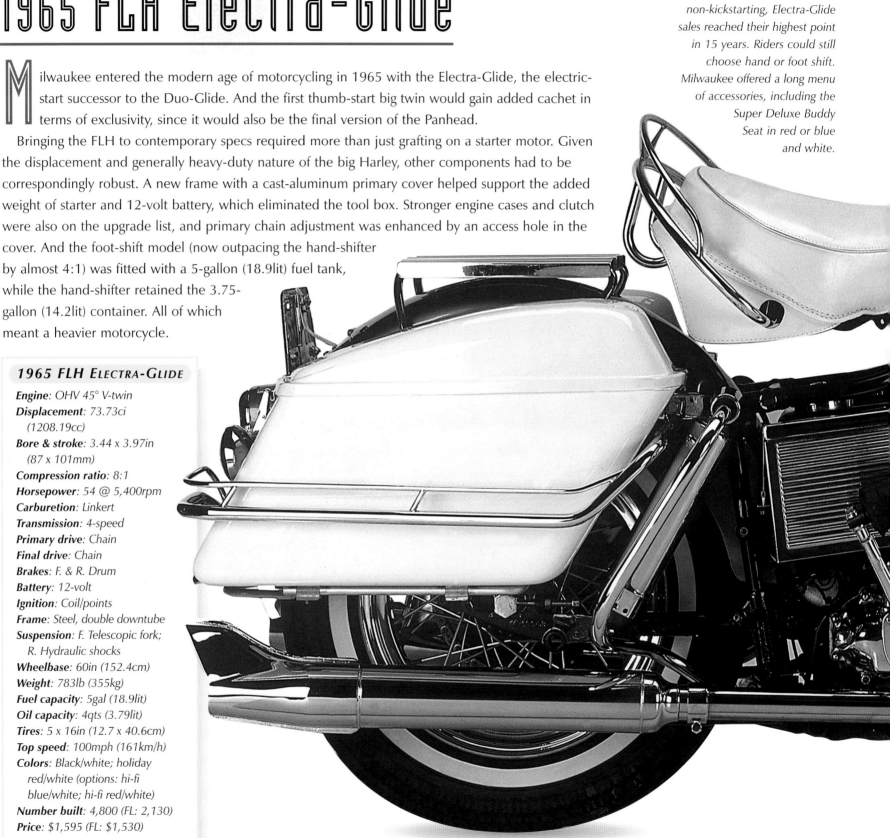

1965 FLH ELECTRA-GLIDE

Engine: OHV 45° V-twin
Displacement: 73.73ci
  (1208.19cc)
Bore & stroke: 3.44 x 3.97in
  (87 x 101mm)
Compression ratio: 8:1
Horsepower: 54 @ 5,400rpm
Carburetion: Linkert
Transmission: 4-speed
Primary drive: Chain
Final drive: Chain
Brakes: F. & R. Drum
Battery: 12-volt
Ignition: Coil/points
Frame: Steel, double downtube
Suspension: F. Telescopic fork;
  R. Hydraulic shocks
Wheelbase: 60in (152.4cm)
Weight: 783lb (355kg)
Fuel capacity: 5gal (18.9lit)
Oil capacity: 4qts (3.79lit)
Tires: 5 x 16in (12.7 x 40.6cm)
Top speed: 100mph (161km/h)
Colors: Black/white; holiday
  red/white (options: hi-fi
  blue/white; hi-fi red/white)
Number built: 4,800 (FL: 2,130)
Price: $1,595 (FL: $1,530)

BELOW: *The foot-shift model included a neutral light on the instrument panel. Handlebar options were the Buckhorn or Speedster. The tool kit was no longer standard; the oil cooler is not original equipment.*

The additional weight and complexity of the Electra-Glide was met with disapproval among many of the traditional Harley faithful. Kickstarting a big twin was widely regarded as a rite of manhood, and to add an "electric leg" just meant having a bunch of sissies riding Harleys. But the kickstart lever remained in place on the right side, and the macho segment was mollified by optional plates to cover the holes when they removed the starter and solenoid. The kickstarter was retained for another two years. For 1965 the trumpet horn was replaced by a disc below the headlight, and ball-end clutch and brake levers were fitted for the first time. Now more than 800 pounds (363kg) fully dressed, in its 18th and last year of production the Panhead was the undisputed king of the road among touring bikes.

1965 FLH
Owner/restorer: Fred Lange,
Santa Maria, California

1965 Sprint H; 1966 Sprint CRS; 1968 KRTT

By 1965 the light- and middleweight markets, especially in the on/off-road category, had exploded in the U.S. Motorcycle sales were on a steep climb, Honda was well in the lead and all the other manufacturers were scrambling for market share. More than 30 manufacturers sought pieces of the pie.

Milwaukee had introduced the H model Sprint in 1962, but the four-stroke single was slipping against the invasion of Japanese and European two-strokes. Although the road model Aermacchi 250s would easily top 80mph (129km/h) in stock trim, they were eclipsed by the lighter, faster-accelerating two strokes. The on/off-road H version, with 25 horsepower, had a better reception in the States. Although the

Sprint was at a disadvantage in roadracing, Bart Markel and other Harley riders continued doing well in the short dirt track races. And at Bonneville, George Roeder took a streamlined Sprint 250 to a new record of 177mph (285km/h). Late in 1966 the Sprint racing engine was reconfigured with larger bore and shorter stroke. With 12:1 compression, the short-stroke motor was good for 32 horsepower.

Milwaukee continued to campaign the venerable KR model in U.S. roadracing, but was up against the fast Doug Hele-tuned Triumphs at Daytona. Buddy Elmore and

1965 SPRINT H

Owner: Trev Deeley Museum,
Vancouver, British Columbia

1968 KRTT

Owner: Hayashi collection

1965 SPRINT H

Engine: OHV horizontal single
Displacement: 15ci (246.2cc)
Bore & stroke: 2.83 x 2.4in
   (72 x 61mm)
Compression ratio: 12:1
Horsepower: 35 @ 10,000rpm
Carburetion: Dell'Orto
Transmission: 4-speed
Primary drive: Helical gear
Final drive: Chain
Brakes: F. & R. Drum
Ignition: Magneto
Frame: Steel tube, single strut
Suspension: F. Telescopic fork;
   R. Hydraulic shocks
Wheelbase: 52in (132cm)
Weight: 245lb (111.1kg)
Fuel capacity: 4gal (15.14lit)
Oil capacity: 2qts (1.89lit)
Tires: 3 x 17in
   (7.62 x 43.18cm)
Top speed: 110mph
   (177km/h)
Colors: Red/white; red/silver;
   gray/black
Number built: 350
Price: $1,050

LEFT: The Sprint H (H-D's traditional letter designation for the high-performance edition) accounted for most of the imports' sales over a five-year period. The SS model would take the lead in 1967.

ABOVE: In 1967 the KR roadracers got new low-boy frames, dual carburetors and improved fairings. In 1968 Cal Rayborn became the first rider to average over 100mph (161km/h) in the Daytona 200.

Gary Nixon had put the British marque first in 1966 and 1967, but a concerted effort by Harley racing chief Dick O'Brien and rider Cal Rayborn won the Daytona 200 for Harley in 1968 and '69. The two stirring performances would mark Milwaukee's final Grand National roadracing victories.

1966 SPRINT CRS

Owner: Trev Deeley Museum,
Vancouver, British Columbia

ABOVE: The roadracing Sprints did well in the 250cc class in the early 1960s, and Dick Hammer won the 100-mile (161km) Daytona races in '63 and '64. But by 1965 the Yamaha two-strokes ruled the class.

1966 FLH; 1966 XLH

The FLH 1200 entered a new era in 1966 with the introduction of new aluminum "Power Pac" heads patterned on the Sportster design. While the official model name remained Electra Glide (de-hyphenated), the new nickname reflected the shape of the engine's aircraft-style rocker boxes, so the successor to the Panhead was called the Shovelhead.

With more efficient combustion chambers and a new diaphragm carburetor, the latest Seventy-four gained five horsepower in the high-compression FLH; the standard FL was rated at 54 horsepower. The new cast-aluminum rocker boxes made the big twin more oil-tight than the Panhead, and somewhat easier in terms of routine maintenance. On the debit side, the additional power added a moderately higher level of vibration.

In its continuing efforts to keep the big twin current in the increasingly crowded motorcycle market, Milwaukee expanded its list of options. The King of the Highway group included front and rear bumpers, Extra Quiet dual mufflers, Buddy Seat, crash bars, saddlebags and windshield. Dozens of chrome covers were available to hide nearly every non-shiny piece on the machine.

In 1966 the Sportster was also granted a power increase, afforded by high-performance cams and a new carburetor, for a claimed 60 horsepower. A new air cleaner, which came to be called the "ham can," was fitted to meet new federal emissions standards. Like the big twin, the Sportster was growing marginally more modern in incremental fashion, but remained a spartan roadburner in most respects. And 1966 signaled the final edition of the kickstart-only Sportster, last of the true tough guys. Naturally, the electric starter added weight to the Sportster, but even at 475 pounds (215.5kg) the XLCH could still run low 14s in the quarter-mile (0.4km)

1966 FLH	
Engine: OHV 45° V-twin	**Wheelbase:** 60in (152.4cm)
Displacement: 73.73ci (1208.19cc)	**Weight:** 783lb (355.2kg)
Bore & stroke: 3.44 x 3.97in (87 x 101mm)	**Fuel capacity:** 5gal (18.93lit)
Compression ratio: 8:1	**Oil capacity:** 4qts (3.79lit)
Horsepower: 60 @ 5,400rpm	**Tires:** 5 x 16in (12.7 x 40.64cm)
Carburetion: Linkert	**Top speed:** 100mph (161km/h)
Transmission: 4-speed	**Colors:** Black/white; indigo metallic/ white (options: hi-fi blue/white; sparkling burgundy/ white)
Primary drive: Chain	
Final drive: Chain	
Brakes: F. & R. Drum	**Number built:**
Battery: 12-volt	5,625
Ignition: Coil/points	(FL: 2,175)
Frame: Steel, double downtube	**Price:**
Suspension: F. Telescopic fork; R. Hydraulic shocks	$1,610

BELOW: *With tighter federal controls on engine emissions, 1966 would be the final year for the round air-cleaner cover, soon to be replaced by the less appealing "ham can" enclosure. The saddlebags, bumpers, windshield, Buddy Seat chromed luggage carrier, crash bars and front hub cap were included in the King of the Highway Group. Whitewall tires were a separate option.*

1966 XLH
Owner: Trev Deeley
Museum, Vancouver,
British Columbia

ABOVE: *The staggered shorty dual mufflers were standard on the XLCH and optional on the XLH, which came standard with stacked mufflers and crossover pipe. These and the large fenders and assorted cosmetics made the XLH heavier and slower than the CH.*

1966 FLH
Owner: Paul Wheeler, Van Nuys, California

1969 Sprint SS 350; 1969 CRTT; 1970 Rapido 125

The Sprint grew to 350cc in 1969, which provided a significant boost in power but no real advance against the growing number of Japanese lightweights flooding the U.S. market. The SS 350 was the road model, followed three years later by the SX scrambler rendition. A limited number of competition editions, designated ERS, were offered in '69, one of which took a victory in the 500-mile (805km) Greenhorn National Enduro.

Despite the rising sea of opposition in the road model ranks, Sprint-based racers continued doing well in short track events. And in Europe the CRTT roadracing versions were humbling more sophisticated machines; the Aermacchis were second and third in the Junior TT at the Isle of Man in 1969 and second again in 1970. The same year American star Bart Markel came from behind to pass the field and win the Chicago short track national. Italian ace Renzo Pasolini secured his reputation in the mid-1960s by coming third in the World Championship on the Aermacchi 350 single, competing against multi-cylinder bikes.

Harley-Davidson would phase out the Italian four-strokes in 1974 in favor of the more economical two-stroke models. The Rapido grew to 125cc in 1968 and was offered in both street and on/off-road models the following year. The last road version appeared in 1970, while the dual-purpose 125 SS continued through 1972. Later models featured a full-loop frame with 175 and 250cc engines, including a motocross version. Milwaukee discontinued the Aermacchi models in 1978.

BELOW: *The 350 CRTT roadracer was no match for the increasingly faster two-strokes by 1969, and no longer a force in big races.*

1969 SPRINT SS 350	
Engine: OHV horizontal single	*Weight*: 325lb (147.4kg)
Displacement: 21ci (344cc)	*Suspension*: F. Telescopic fork;
Bore & stroke: 2.91 x 3.15in	R. Hydraulic shocks
(74 x 80mm)	*Wheelbase*: 53.3in (135.4cm)
Compression ratio: 9:1	*Fuel capacity*: 2.5gal (9.5lit)
Horsepower: 35 @	*Oil capacity*: 2qts (1.89lit)
10,000rpm	*Tires*: F. 3.25 x 19in
Carburetion: Dell'Orto	(8.26 x 48.26cm);
Transmission: 4-speed	R. 3.5 x 18in
Primary drive: Helical gear	(8.9 x 45.72cm)
Final drive: Chain	*Top speed*: 95mph
Brakes: F. & R. Drum	(153km/h)
Ignition: Magneto	*Colors*: Blue; black
Frame: Steel tube,	*Number built*: 4,575
single strut	*Price*: $840

1969 350 CRTT
Owner: Otis Chandler, Ojai, California

RIGHT: The two-stroke Rapido 125 was available in both street and dual-purpose models from 1968–70. The on/off roader lasted through '72, and was replaced in '73 by a full-loop frame version.

BELOW: The SS 350 Sprint was still upholding Milwaukee's lightweight hopes in the late 1960s, but was steadily losing the battle to two-stroke imports. Nonetheless, the Sprint continued to supply the transportation and/or recreational needs of budget-conscious commuters, students and those who simply wanted to ride something a little different. Rebels with an American/Italian cause.

1970 RAPIDO ML 125 S
Owner: Trev Deeley Museum,
Vancouver, British Columbia

1969 SPRINT SS 350
Owner: Trev Deeley Museum, Vancouver, British Columbia

ABOVE: While some riders had difficulty with the appearance of a single cylinder hanging out in the breeze, the Aermacchi overhead-valve engine was well built and a surprisingly strong performer.

1970 XR 750

The one competition venue in which Harley-Davidson still held a strong hand was the traditional American sport of dirt track. Harley roadracing star Cal Rayborn won at Daytona in 1968 and '69 on the aging KR flathead, but that would be the model's swansong. The XR 750, fundamentally a de-stroked XLR engine in a chrome-moly steel frame based on the KR, became Milwaukee's purpose-built racer in 1970.

After overcoming initial overheating problems, racing chief Dick O'Brien and his crew were getting about 65 horsepower from the hybrid engine, and a broad spread of torque. But reliability remained a serious problem and Milwaukee experienced one of its worst records in national championship history. The engine was improved for 1971, but the Harleys were still down on speed against the British machines. Returning to competitive status would mean a new engine.

1970 XR 750

Owner: Otis Chandler, Ojai, Calfornia

ABOVE: *The second-generation XR 750 immediately became the once and future king of American dirt track racing. With improved combustion chambers, each with a 36mm carburetor, 10:1 compression and 90 horsepower, it went good.*

RIGHT: *The iron-head XR 750 was the racing cousin of the Sportster. Although it was fast, the engine could overheat severely in long racing events.*

1970 XR 750

ABOVE: *Decreasing compression from 9.5:1 to 8.5 helped to minimize the overheating problems, but also reduced power output.*

With the decision to build a short-stroke engine with alloy cylinders and heads, including smaller valves at narrowed angles to each other, the science of intake and exhaust flow in the management of power gained influence. Compression and power both went up, the bottom end got more beef and the new Harley XR 750 was ready to race. The machine wasn't ready for Daytona in 1972; it was prepared for the remaining season and took factory rider Mark Brelsford to the championship by year's end. And Cal Rayborn won two roadrace nationals with the XR.

Without significant modifications, the XR 750 would carry on for the next three decades as the bike to beat on the mile and half-mile (1.6 and 0.8km) dirt tracks. No production racing machine in any category has amassed a similar record of victories or national championship titles.

1980 XR 750

Engine: OHV 45° V-twin
Displacement: 45ci (750cc)
Bore & stroke: 3.125 x 2.983in (79 x 76mm)
Compression ratio: 10.5:1
Horsepower: 90
Carburetion: Two 36mm Mikuni
Transmission: 4-speed
Primary drive: Triplex chain
Final drive: Chain
Brakes: Rear disc
Ignition: Magneto
Frame: Steel, double downtube

Suspension: F. Telescopic fork; R. Hydraulic shocks
Wheelbase: 57in (144.8cm)
Weight: 320lb (145.2kg)
Fuel capacity: 2.5gal (9.5lit)
Oil capacity: 3qts (2.84lit)
Tires: 4 x 19in (10.16 x 48.26cm)
Top speed: 130mph (209km/h)
Color: Jet fire orange/black
Number built: 160 (1980); total production approx. 530
Price: $4,000

living the dream

Motorcycling would see more changes, and growth, in the 1960s than it had in the previous 50 years. The elements for a two-wheeled revolution seemed to fall into place as if by design. Simply put, the demand had been greater than the supply for several years. Youngsters weaned on Cushman or Allstate scooters or Harley Hummers were yearning to step up to real motorcycles. Those with a dad, uncle or neighbor who rode a Harley or Indian had a good idea of what their first mount would (or wouldn't) be.

Then, as the first wave of post-war baby boomers came of age, the selection of motorcycles confronting them expanded enormously. The British and German machines that had begun coming to the States as a trickle in the 1950s constituted a major river by the '60s. Then the flow expanded with lightweight motorcycles from Spain, Sweden, Czechoslovakia, Italy and Japan. The marketplace had gone, seemingly overnight, from famine to feast.

Harley-Davidson dealers had petitioned the company to build sporting middleweights for nearly a decade to no avail. Milwaukee had witnessed the failure of all its domestic competitors, and was convinced that its traditional models, methods and policies would see it through what was merely a temporary influx of foreign machines. Nonetheless, to hedge their bets Harley-Davidson acquired Aermacchi of Italy to cover the lightweight sport/budget market, and set about upgrading the size and performance of the Hummer. But in most respects, it was already too late.

No one could fault Harley-Davidson for not predicting the groundswell of affluence in America, or the sudden and widespread enthusiasm for new forms of recreation and entertainment. But Milwaukee soon had to pay the piper for the traditional tune of piecemeal progress and insular self-protection. While "you meet the nicest people on a Honda" may have just been an advertising slogan, it was also a siren call that the rules of the game had changed. Motorcycling may have still had a

ABOVE LEFT: Rider Handbooks for the 1965 Electra Glide have become collectible items, since the year marked the end of the Panhead engine and the first electric starter.

LEFT: Chicago's 1962 International Championship Rod and Custom Show included a few bikes for added flavor. Carine Barome demonstrates kickstart style on a 1962 Panhead.

LEFT: *The Duo-Glide remained Harley's top seller in the mid-1960s, when fun galore was still a possibility for substantial numbers of American riders. The Vietnam conflict would soon affect the market.*

LIGHTWEIGHT... PACER 175 c.c.

ABOVE: *As the two-stroke engines went up in size, commuting to work was more reasonable. But one still had to carry his own lunch box.*

BELOW: *The Topper scooter, even with Scootaway Drive and a price of $460, was a hard sell in a marketplace grown crowded with smaller, cheaper imported minibikes.*

lingering image problem, but it was barely an issue for machines built anywhere other than Milwaukee.

Harley's sales did swing upward in the 1960s, due mostly to the 175cc two-strokes and Aermacchi Sprint. But these were low-profit machines compared to the Duo-Glide and Sportster, whose numbers remained static. While both motorcycles maintained their attraction for the committed corps of "buy-American" riders, their numbers in proportion to the total buying public were growing steadily smaller. Harley seemed to be watching helplessly as its market share fell away.

In what many observers considered a curious move, in 1962 Harley-Davidson bought a fiberglass company for the purpose of building golf carts. This expansion into unrelated recreational markets was no doubt part of a broad plan to diversify, but the timing seemed odd when Milwaukee was taking a beating in the field it knew best.

Meanwhile, the motorcycle sport was itself expanding exponentially in all directions. Spidery-looking imported roadsters called cafe racers were

ABOVE: *The handbooks in the '60s looked quite similar to those of the '50s, much like the bikes.*

1963 HARLEY-DAVIDSON Topper H

NEW HORIZONS in fun

with a '63 HARLEY-DAVIDSON Topper H

AUTOMATIC "SCOOTAWAY" DRIVE
LARGE WHEELS & BIG BRAKES FOR A SMOOTH SAFE RIDE
new JET-BLACK HYPALON SEAT

Rider Hand Book

HARLEY—DAVIDSON

Topper

Motor Scooter

ABOVE AND LEFT: *The appeal of the Topper to students and business commuters was the obvious slant of Harley-Davidson's advertising, but scooter sales overall had begun to decline.*

LEFT AND BELOW: *Even Harley-Davidson advertising adopted the psychedelic style in the 1960s. Ohio's George Roeder won two Nationals, but the title went to Gary Nixon on Triumph.*

ABOVE: *Ralph White put his Harley KR in the winner's circle at Daytona in 1963, the first year for full fairings in AMA competition. Other Harley-Davidson riders won Nationals, but the title went to Dick Mann who rode BSA and Matchless.*

showing up on the streets; an imported off-road form of racing called motocross was attracting enthusiasts all over the country, European-style roadracing was gaining interest and the more traditional categories of dirt track and scrambles were drawing full rosters of competitors. And the imported street machines, especially those from Japan, were growing larger, faster and more user-friendly.

Motorcycle racing entered upon another golden age of close, exciting competition in the mid-1960s. The success of imported machines led to direct or indirect factory support for distributor or dealer-sponsored teams, and the speeds and level of racing rose accordingly.

AMA Grand National racing, formerly the stronghold of Harley-Davidson, was now equally divided between Milwaukee iron and Triumph and BSA machines from England. Even though the flathead/overhead displacement rule was still in effect, performance parity was evident on the track. In 1965 Roger Reiman made it two in a row for Harley at Daytona, but it was his teammate Bart Markel who went on to win the championship, followed by Dick Mann on BSA/Matchless. Both riders won three Nationals on the year.

RIGHT: *By 1964 the Duo-Glide was only $1,450, and still available with either food or hand shift. But the motorcycle market was now changing quickly, and Harley-Davidson was soon struggling to keep pace.*

BELOW: *While the Electra Glide may not have been the sportiest model on the road in 1968, it still looked mighty fetching among a field of racing cars. And the addition of a pretty girl didn't hurt.*

1968 ELECTRA GLIDE

Unique in all the cycling worl

HARLEY-DAVIDSO

New 125 cc!
Over 70 mph!
Under 175 lbs!
Over 70 mpg!
Under $400!

Harley-Davidson
priced to meet competition
+ engineered to beat it.

RIGHT: *Even though the Harley two-strokes were falling farther behind the imported competition, the marketing department never gave up on them. And the pretty girl…*

In 1966 Cal Rayborn's Harley KR was the fastest qualifier at Daytona, running at 134mph (216km/h). But an oil leak put him out of the race, which was won by Texan Buddy Elmore on a Triumph. Markel repeated his title win in 1966, trailed by the Triumph of Gary Nixon in second place. In 1967 and '68 the championship went to Maryland's Gary Nixon on the increasingly rapid and reliable Triumph twins. The Grand National calendar grew from 17 races in 1967 to 23 in 1968 and 25 in '69.

They weren't called the Gypsy Tours for nothing. Most motorcyclists were simply part-time gypsies, from the tidy uniformed corps of AMA road riders of the 1940s and '50s, the itinerant racers always on the road during the racing season, to the casual groups of weekend riders. The so-called "one-percenters," who had never approached such a high ratio of active motorcyclists, were closer to the nomadic tribes of the middle ages. But their clank and swagger evoked the posture of costume drama, the trappings of the professionally disenchanted; lifestyle masquerading as life.

But motorcycling's image problem was a minor blip on the social radar of the late 1960s. America's growing disunity over the Vietnam War was the foremost galvanizing issue of the day, and would be focused even more sharply by the election of Richard Nixon in 1968. The United States' position as leader of the free world had become a tenuous proposition, and despite a thriving motorcycle market, Harley-Davidson's future was in serious doubt.

In ten years the number of Harley dealerships had dropped by 40 percent. Facing the possibility of bankruptcy, Milwaukee management began the search for either a buyer or a corporate merger. The ensuing

LEFT: *Alfred E. Neuman was joined by Peter Fonda, Dennis Hopper and Michael Parks on the cover of* Mad *magazine, June, 1970.*

ABOVE: *With the release of several movies, and a book by Hunter Thompson, the Hell's Angels were back in the news in the mid-1960s. The group's rides never failed to attract public attention.*

"The Angels' collective viewpoint has always been fascistic. They insist and seem to believe that their swastika fetish is no more than an antisocial joke, a guaranteed gimmick to bug the squares ..."

HUNTER S. THOMPSON, "HELL'S ANGELS"

struggle for control between Bangor-Punta and American Machine and Foundry (AMF) drove the price of Harley stock up by a factor of seven, to the great profit of many shareholders. AMF won the tussle and retained Harley-Davidson's management team.

In his book, Hunter Thompson suggested that the Angels could bug the squares more effectively if they dropped the swastika and decorated their bikes with the hammer and sickle. "That would really raise hell on the freeways ... hundreds of Communist thugs roaming the countryside on big motorcycles, looking for trouble."

Thompson would go on to write more widely read examples of gonzo journalism on other subjects, but his experience with the Hell's Angels was punctuated with a severe beating administered by "four or five Angels who seemed to feel I was taking advantage of them." Years later he was asked by the author of this book just what prompted the punishment. After a long pause he said, "They wanted half the money from the book." Following the death of man at a 1972 Rolling Stones concert in California, where the Hell's Angels had been hired to provide security, the club chose to adopt a lower profile in the media.

Nearly 20 years later Sonny Barger, president of the Oakland, California chapter, published his own story "Hell's Angel, The Life and Times of Sonny Barger and the Hell's Angels Motorcycle Club."

"A group of Hell's Angels cruising down the road, riding next to each other and traveling at a speed of over 80mph is a real sight. It's something else, a whole other thing, when you're in the pack riding. It's fast and dangerous and by God, you better be paying attention. Whatever happens to the guy in front of you is going to happen to you. It's different from other vehicles. You gotta be alert. Like Fuzzy, an Oakland Angel, once said, 'God damn, we do 85 or 90 in the rain sometimes. I don't even go that fast in my car!'"

LEFT AND BELOW: *The film most responsible for expanding the market for chopper accessories, and country-rock music, was "Easy Rider." The movie also jump-started the career of Jack Nicholson.*

1971—80: Surviving the Sixties

decade design evolution

"Harley was improving their machines, but they couldn't keep up with the demand. So they went in with AMF and started to turn out more motorcycles, but they lost control of the quality in the process. That made lots of folks unhappy, and for a while it looked like Harley-Davidson just might go belly-up."

EUGENE WEAVER,
FORMER CUSTOMER

RIGHT: *The Low Rider's traditional fat bob fuel tanks were conjoined by a flat black instrument panel housing the speedometer and tachometer in that order. The headlight nacelle held the neutral and oil pressure lights.*

William G. Davidson, company design director, artist and motorcyclist, viewed the partnership with AMF with more than passing concern. Fortunately, for the company's prospects and Harley-Davidson fans, his creative freedom as a designer went unthreatened.

The first Willie G. factory custom, the FX Super Glide of 1971, was a hybrid combination of the big twin and the Sportster. The idea had been percolating in Willie's brain for a few years, and the AMF connection provided the opportunity to give it a try. The sport-cruiser met with mixed response in terms of styling, but the platform itself was received with widespread approval.

Since all manner of cruisers, choppers and miscellaneous customs had been created from the big twin foundation, Davidson made the obvious choice to follow the same route. The Super Glide, tagged the "All-American Freedom Machine" and resplendent in red, white and blue livery, was the first installment in a succession of factory customs that would continue for the next two decades.

The Sportster was offered with a modified boattail seat in 1970-71, but was also dismissed as a "non-Harley" styling feature. A wet clutch came into use in '71, and the ignition points moved into the timing case, which incorporated an automatic advance mechanism.

In 1972 the Sportster was enlarged to 61ci (1000cc) with a bore increase, and in '73 a disc brake appeared on the front wheel. The XL 1000, rated at 61 horsepower for a convenient match with the cubic inches, would run the quarter mile (0.4km) in the low 13-second bracket, and top speed in the *Cycle World* road test was 116mph (186.7km/h). The new Showa front fork improved handling on cobbled roads.

Although the British motorcycle industry was dissolving, the Japanese builders were producing larger and better machines each year. So the former security of Milwaukee's big twins was no longer taken for granted; and increasingly stringent safety and environmental regulations by the federal government had to be met. In 1972 the Electra Glide received a front disc brake, as did the Super Glide the following year. But Harley-Davidson's primary concern was making the big twins run clean enough to meet national emissions standards. Then the Honda Gold Wing arrived to take the touring bike bar up several notches.

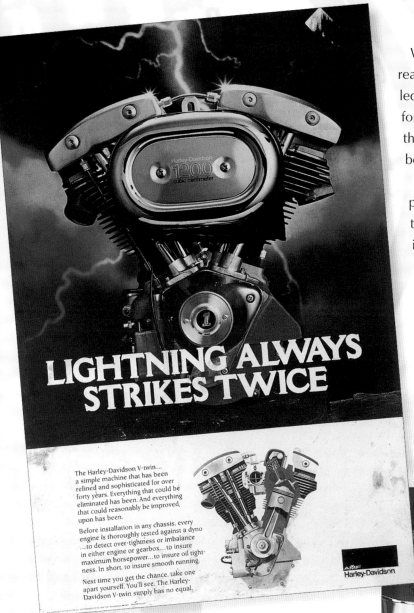

LIGHTNING ALWAYS STRIKES TWICE

The Harley-Davidson V-twin...
a simple machine that has been
refined and sophisticated for over
forty years. Everything that could be
eliminated has been. And everything
that could reasonably be improved,
upon has been.

Before installation in any chassis, every
engine is thoroughly tested against a dyno
...to detect over-tightness or imbalance
in either engine or gearbox...to insure
maximum horsepower...to insure oil tight-
ness. In short, to insure smooth running.

Next time you get the chance, take one
apart yourself. You'll see. The Harley-
Davidson V-twin simply has no equal.

AMF
Harley-Davidson

Willie G. now had two new designs in the pipeline, both of which appeared in real steel in 1977. Given the lukewarm reception to the original Super Glide, which led to its less sporting configuration, the designer chose the Sportster as the basis for a cafe racer and the Super Glide for a new low rider cruiser. Thus the XLCR and the FXS, also known as the Cafe Racer and the Low Rider. (Milwaukee has never been shy about adopting names from the public lexicon.)

While the XLCR was a handsome piece, it was outclassed in terms of performance and lasted only two years. The FXS on the other hand was a hit from the start, since it conformed more closely to the custom cruiser market for which it was intended. With the moderate chopper image invoked by the raked front end, deeply stepped seat, cast-alloy wheels, bazooka muffler and fat bob tank, the Low Rider had The Look down pat.

Its success led directly to the FXEF in 1978, sure enough called the Fat Bob, with a 5-gallon (18.9lit) fuel tank and either the Seventy-four (1200cc) engine or the new 80ci (1340cc) motor. The FX series was hugely successful and Willie G. was on a roll. His next variation was the FXB Sturgis in 1980, with a black-on-black paint scheme and the reintroduction of belt drive. And the FLT Tour Glide, also powered by the new Eighty, with a five-speed transmission and rubber-mount engine, showed that Harley wasn't going to relinquish the touring market without a fight.

ABOVE: The V-twin may have been refined and sophisticated for over 40 years, but the big Shovelhead was a real shaker until it was broken in, a process that could involve several thousand miles and blurred vision, loose dentures, etc. Thus the assurance that engines were pre-tested for "over-tightness."

RIGHT: More than a few riders were suspicious about the longevity of drive belts, but the concerns proved unwarranted. Developed by the Gates Rubber Company using nylon fiber reinforcement, the belts were good for 30–40,000 miles. And they were quiet, and not messy.

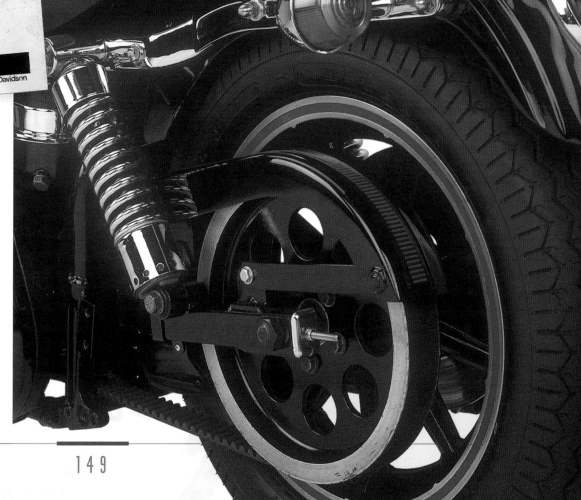

1971 FX Super Glide

William G. Davidson, son of Harley president William H. and grandson of founder William A., joined Harley-Davidson as director of styling in 1963. He retains the position today (2002) and seems to enjoy the job security.

As an artist/designer, Willie G. decided that with so many Harley owners modifying their machines there was no reason for the factory not to have its own custom models. The 1971 FX Super Glide was the inaugural effort, a 74ci (1200cc) FLH from the steering head back, a Sportster front end and streamlined Anglo-American bodywork. While the boattail seat didn't win many admirers, the muscular stance and patriotic paint scheme grabbed plenty of attention.

RIGHT: *The red, white and blue "Sparkling America" paint scheme was optional on the inaugural Super Glide. Patriotism cruised in style.*

BELOW: *For years the custom creators had been subtracting bits from the touring models. The FX offered a simpler platform.*

1971 FX
Owner: Trev Deeley Museum,
Vancouver, British Columbia

1971 FX
Owner: Otis Chandler, Ojai, California
Restorer: Jerry Sewell

The Super Glide had the look of a serious roadburner, and the relatively light weight and big twin combination moved the sport-cruiser smartly down the road. With the XL front end, and no electric starter, the FX was 150 pounds (68kg) lighter than the Electra Glide and only about 60 pounds (27kg) heavier than a Sportster. The Super Glide had the power and poise of a muscle bike, although the style would change quickly.

In 1972 the boattail seat was replaced by a standard seat/fender, and in '73 the large fuel tank gave way to a smaller one from the Sprint. Super Glide sales climbed immediately, ensuring that the evolution of the FX series was set in place. Willie G. would go on to design more factory specials, but the Super Glide would have the most lasting effect on ensuing model development.

1971 FX SUPER GLIDE

Engine: OHV 45° V-twin
Displacement: 73.73ci (1208.19cc)
Bore & stroke: 3.44 x 3.97in
  (87 x 101mm)
Compression ratio: 8:1
Horsepower: 65
Carburetion: Bendix
Transmission: 4-speed
Primary drive: Chain
Final drive: Chain
Brakes: F. & R. Drum
Battery: 12-volt
Ignition: Coil/points
Frame: Steel, double downtube
Suspension: F. Telescopic fork;
  R. Hydraulic shocks
Wheelbase: 62in (157.5cm)
Weight: 560lb (254kg)
Fuel capacity: 3.5gal (13.25lit)
Oil capacity: 4qts (3.79lit)
Tires: F. 3.5 x 19in (8.9 x 48.26cm);
  R. 5 x 16in (12.7 x 40.64cm)
Top speed: 110mph (177km/h)
Colors: Black; birch white (options: sparkling green; burgundy; blue; turquoise; red; copper; "sparkling America" [red, white and blue])
Number built: 4,700
Price: $2,500

1971 & 1972 XLH; 1972 RR 250

By 1971 the Sportster was breathing hard against the imported competition. New heads, valves and exhaust system had brought a power increase in 1969, but the contest between the British and Japanese builders had elevated the performance bar.

An abbreviated version of the Super Glide tail section was offered as an option on the '71 Sportster, but few buyers opted. Sporty riders preferred the traditional distinctions between the XLH and XLCH, so the configuration remained relatively unchanged. In 1972 Milwaukee responded to the power challenge in traditional fashion—more displacement. The Shovelhead Sportster consequently grew to 1000cc, a Sixty-one incher like the original Knucklehead.

Even though the Sportster was still underpowered compared to the multi-cylinder imports, sales continued upward. Milwaukee produced more than 18,000 of the lean machines in '72 and nearly 20,000 the following year. A front disc brake arrived on the Sportster in 1973.

The Harley/Aermacchi two-stroke lightweights remained on the Milwaukee roster, though few of the specialized 250cc racing twins came to the U.S. Built to compete with the new Yamaha roadracers, the RR 250 was a 230-pound (104kg) machine

1972 XLH

Owner: James Kirchner,
San Diego, California

RIGHT: *The two-stroke Aermacchi roadracers were successful in Europe but not in the U.S.*

1972 RR 250

Owner: Trev Deeley Museum, Vancouver, British Columbia

1971 XLH

Owner: Eva Mathews, Mathews Harley-Davidson, Fresno, California

ABOVE: *The XLH had grown more like the XLCH, but retained the larger fuel tank. A front disc brake would arrive in 1973.*

with 50 horsepower. Italy's Walter Villa dominated the class in the mid-1970s and added the 350 title in 1976. Canadian Harley distributor Trev Deeley campaigned the racers in the U.S., and factory rider Gary Scott rode the little twin to victory in the 250 class at the Loudon, New Hampshire round in 1974.

1972 XLH

Engine: *OHV 45° V-twin*
Displacement: *61ci (1000cc)*
Bore & stroke: *3.19 x 3.81in (81 x 97mm)*
Compression ratio: *9:1*
Horsepower: *61*
Carburetion: *Bendix/Zenith*
Transmission: *4-speed*
Primary drive: *Triplex chain*
Final drive: *Chain*
Brakes: *F. & R. Drum*
Battery: *12-volt*
Ignition: *Coil/points*
Frame: *Steel, double downtube*
Suspension: *F. Telescopic fork; R. Hydraulic shocks*
Wheelbase: *58.5in (148.6cm)*
Weight: *530lb (240kg)*
Fuel capacity: *3.7gal (14lit)*
Oil capacity: *3qts (2.84lit)*
Tires: *F. 3 x 19in (7.62 x 48.26cm); R. 4 x 18in (10.16 x 45.72cm)*
Top speed: *116mph (187km/h)*
Colors: *Black; white; sparkling burgundy; green; red; blue*
Number built: *7,500 (XLCH: 10,650)*
Price: *$2,120*

1972 FLH; 1973 Sprint SX 350; 1974 XLH

The Electra Glide marked the 50th anniversary of the Harley Seventy-four in 1972, and was awarded a front disc brake. While the big twin may have suffered a perceived disadvantage to the imports in terms of technology, those faithful to the marque continued to find plenty to like in the only remaining American machine. Demand was up and Harley-Davidson, now under the corporate management of American Machine and Foundry, struggled to meet it.

By 1972 the reorganized AMF Harley-Davidson produced almost 60,000 motorcycles, and close to 70,000 the following year. But the rush to meet the demand created problems with quality control, and many machines that had been improperly assembled were shipped to dealers. This created problems between the dealers and customers, and ultimately with the factory. In 1974 AMF moved

chassis construction and final assembly to their plant in York, Pennsylvania, leaving Milwaukee responsible for engines and transmissions. The move created more difficulties, including a three-month labor strike that crippled production.

The Sportster for 1973 arrived with a Japanese Showa fork and both models had a front disc brake. By 1974 push/pull throttle controls had been mandated by the federal government, so the set-it and forget-it throttle was consigned to history.

The Sprint models were also awarded electric

1972 FLH

Owner: Bob Rocchio, San Francisco, California

starters in 1973, but the SX 350 would mark the final model in the line of Aermacchi four-strokes under the Harley banner. The Italian connection would last another five years for two-stroke lightweights.

1974 XLH
Owner: Sam Williams,
Los Angeles, California
Restorer:
Richard Brazas

RIGHT: *With the new front disc brake came a Showa fork, which improved handling and comfort. Carb was also new.*

RIGHT: *The SX 350 added a full-cradle double-loop frame to the Sprint, which also had electric start.*

1973 SPRINT SX 350
Owner: Trev Deeley Museum
Vancouver, British Columbia

1972 FLH

Engine: OHV 45° V-twin
Displacement: 73.73ci (1208.19cc)
Bore & stroke: 3.44 x 3.97in (87 x 101mm)
Compression ratio: 8:1
Horsepower: 66
Carburetion: Bendix
Transmission: 4-speed
Primary drive: Chain
Final drive: Chain
Brakes: Drum
Battery: 12-volt
Ignition: Coil/points
Frame: Steel, double downtube

Suspension: F. Telescopic fork; R. Hydraulic shocks
Wheelbase: 61.5in (156.2cm)
Weight: 738lb (355.2kg)
Fuel capacity: 5gal (18.93lit)
Oil capacity: 4qts (3.79lit)
Tires: 5 x 16in (12.7 x 40.64cm)
Top speed: 100mph (161km/h)
Colors: Black; sparkling purple; sparkling burgundy; sparkling blue; sparkling red; sparkling turquoise; "sparkling America"
Number built: 8,100 (FL: 1,600)
Price: $2,500

1975 FLH; 1975 MX/SX 250; 1975 Z-90

The pressing need to increase production continued through 1975, and few modifications were made to any Milwaukee models. As a touring machine, the Electra Glide was now up against the smooth four-cylinder Honda Gold Wing, which immediately set new standards for comfort and reliability. Harley-Davidson now faced the need to make better, as well as more, motorcycles.

While the big twin engineers looked into the needs for more power, less vibration and lower maintenance, the marketing department was working to capitalize on the strong market for light-weight dirt bikes. The AMF/Harley-Davidson/Aermacchi 175 had been bumped to 250cc in 1974, in the hope of contending with Yamaha's popular DT1. Milwaukee also offered a motocross version, and sponsored a factory team, but development of the Japanese

entries was progressing so quickly that the MX 250 was left in the dust.

The SX 250 dual-purpose model, and the 125 and 90cc two-strokes, would be Milwaukee's final attempt to sell lightweight imports. In 1978 Harley-Davidson would sell the Aermacchi division to the Cagiva Group of Italy.

The good news in 1975 was provided by factory rider Gary Scott, who wrestled the Grand National title from Yamaha's Kenny Roberts and returned it to Milwaukee. In third place was young Jay Springsteen, who in 1976 would win the first of three successive championships on the Harley XR 750. Even though Harley-Davidson was up against hard times in the touring and sport bike segments of the market, their continued support of dirt track racing went a long way to encourage the faithful to remain believers.

1975 Z-90
Owner: Trev Deeley Museum,
Vancouver, British Columbia

ABOVE: *The 90cc Aermacchi was a diminution of the TX-125, which had replaced the Rapido. The same engine was used in the X-90 minibike. This would be the last years for the tiddlers in the Milwaukee lineup, and the large two-stroker models would also soon fade out.*

RIGHT: *Most Shovelheads were modified to meet the personal riding and appearance needs of their owners. This example has been given a light retro treatment teens-style tank lettering, beehive taillight and staggered dual exhausts. The oil cooler is a modern touch.*

RIGHT: *According to the company history, 11,000 of the SX 250s were produced in 1975. The dual-purpose model shared few parts with the MX version below.*

BELOW: *Milwaukee had a brief fling with motocross in 1976, building 86 examples of the MX 250, which was gone in '77.*

1976 MX 250

Owner: Oliver Shokouh, H-D of Glendale, Glendale, California

1975 SX 250

Owner: Trev Deeley Museum, Vancouver, British Columbia

1975 FLH

Engine: *OHV 45° V-twin*
Displacement: *73.73ci (1208.19cc)*
Bore & stroke: *3.44 x 3.97in (87 x 101mm)*
Compression ratio: *8:1*
Horsepower: *66*
Carburetion: *Bendix*
Transmission: *4-speed*
Primary drive: *Chain*
Final drive: *Chain*
Brakes: *Disc*
Battery: *12-volt*
Ignition: *Coil/points*
Frame: *Steel, double downtube*
Suspension: *F. Telescopic fork; R. Hydraulic shocks*
Wheelbase: *61.5in (156.2cm)*
Weight: *738lb (355.2kg)*
Fuel capacity: *5gal (18.93lit)*
Oil capacity: *4qts (3.79lit)*
Tires: *5 x 16in (12.7 x 40.64cm)*
Top speed: *100mph (161km/h)*
Colors: *Black; red; blue*
Number built: *7,400*
Price: *c. $3,100*

1975 FLH

Owner: Bartels' Harley-Davidson, Marina Del Rey, California

1977 FXS Low Rider; 1977 FLH

1977 FLH

Owner: Jim Furlong, Northridge, California

The next factory custom from Willie G. and the designers was the 1977 FXS Low Rider, devolved from the Super Glide. The chopper look had become a permanent feature among custom-builders, so another hybrid of the Seventy-four and Sportster took its place on the showroom floors, to immediate acclaim. Most everyone agreed that this time Willie had got the look right.

The Low Rider sold out quickly, established the cruiser style once and for all and improved Harley's prospects in a tough market. Production of the FXS went to almost 10,000 machines in 1978 and outsold the Super Glide and Electra Glide. The scooped seat was both stylish and friendly to the short of leg, and the burly exhaust system and disc brakes all around gave the cruiser a touch of attitude.

1977 FXS LOW RIDER

Engine: OHV 45° V-twin
Displacement: 73.3ci (1208.19cc)
Bore & stroke: 3.44 x 3.97in
(87 x 101mm)
Compression ratio: 8:1
Horsepower: 65
Carburetion: Bendix
Transmission: 4-speed
Primary drive: Chain
Final drive: Chain
Brakes: Triple disc
Battery: 12-volt
Ignition: Coil/points
Frame: Steel, double downtube
Suspension: F. Telescopic fork;
R. Hydraulic shocks
Wheelbase: 63.5in (161.3cm)
Fuel capacity: 3.5gal (13.25lit)
Oil capacity: 4qts (3.79lit)
Weight: 623lb (282.6kg)
Tires: F. 3.5 x 19in
(8.9 x 48.26cm);
R. 5 x 16in (12.7 x 40.64cm)
Top speed: 100mph (161km/h)
Color: Gunmetal gray
Number built: 3,742
Price: $3,475

RIGHT: *The Electra Glide had changed little, at least in terms of appearance, over the years. But improvements among engine components and running gear were made continuously. The repair index improved accordingly.*

BELOW LEFT: *The Low Rider was the hit of the season in 1977. By consensus, Willie G.'s best yet.*

1977 FXS

Owner: Oliver Shokouh, H-D of Glendale, Glendale, California

1977 XLCR Cafe Racer

1977 XLCR CAFE RACER

Engine: OHV 45° V-twin
Displacement: 61ci (1000cc)
Bore & stroke: 3.19 x 3.81in (81 x 97mm)
Compression ratio: 9:1
Horsepower: 68
Carburetion: Keihin
Transmission: 4-speed
Primary drive: Chain
Final drive: Chain
Brakes: Triple disc
Battery: 12-volt
Ignition: Coil/points
Frame: Steel, double downtube
Weight: 515lb (234kg)

Suspension: F. Telescopic fork; R. Hydraulic shocks
Wheelbase: 58.5in (148.6cm)
Fuel capacity: 4gal (15.14lit)
Oil capacity: 3qts (2.84lit)
Tires: F. 3 x 19in (7.62 x 48.26cm); R. 4 x 18in (10.16 x 45.72cm)
Top speed: 110mph (177km/h)
Color: Black
Number built: 1,923
Price: $3,623

William G. Davidson counted himself fortunate that the AMF corporate suits paid little attention to the design department. And although he was under cost constraints in terms of developing entirely new models, the director was free to mix and match parts from the existing inventory. He also recognized that a contender in the sportbike market would have to be based on the Sportster. So he built the XLCR, as in Cafe Racer.

With its bikini fairing, racy seat/tail section, low bars and black-on-black motif, the XLCR struck a dramatic pose. And it wasn't style without substance—with its rear-set footpegs, cast-alloy wheels and triple disc brakes, the Cafe Racer could be hustled through the twisties with some agility. But it enticed few riders weaned on either British twins or Japanese multis, and Sportster fans considered it a curiosity. As a consequence, the XLCR lasted only two years in production and forever as a collector's item.

LEFT: Many sport riders thought the Cafe Racer was the best thing since espresso. But their numbers were too small for its survival.

Milwaukee would steer clear of the sportbike market for years to come, but not forever.

1977 XLCR CAFE RACER
Owner: Otis Chandler, Ojai, California

1979 FXEF

1979 FXEF

Engine: OHV 45° V-twin
Displacement: 81.65ci (1338cc)
Bore & stroke: 3.5 x 4.25in
(89 x 108mm)
Compression ratio: 8:1
Horsepower: 66
Carburetion: Bendix
Transmission: 4-speed
Primary drive: Chain
Final drive: Chain
Brakes: Triple disc
Battery: 12-volt
Ignition: Coil/points
Frame: Steel, double downtube
Suspension: F. Telescopic fork;
R. Hydraulic shocks
Wheelbase: 63.5in (161.3cm)
Weight: 642lb (291kg)
Fuel capacity: 5gal (18.9lit)
Oil capacity: 4qts (3.79lit)
Tires: F. 3.5 x 19in (8.9 x 48.26cm);
R. 5 x 16in (12.7 x 40.64cm)
Top speed: 105mph (169km/h)
Colors: Vivid black; brilliant red;
concord blue; chestnut brown
Number built: 5,264 (1200: 4,678)
Price: $4,260

In 1978 Harley served up another dose of displacement for the Super Glide, bringing the big twin to 80ci (1340cc). Milwaukee was committed to the V-twin, and the short route to more power had always been cubic inches/centimeters. The big motor showed up the following year in the Low Rider, and in the next variation on the Super Glide, the FXEF Fat Bob.

The Eighty was intended to regain some of the market lost to Honda's touring bike, while the same engine in the Low Rider and Fat Bob targeted the riders who prized prodigious torque in a leaner street machine. The FXE was offered as either a Seventy-four or Eighty, with options of spoked or cast wheels and dual exhausts. Easier to chop or customize than an FL, the big bob covered a market not addressed by the Japanese. And it marked the fifth model in the FX series, which now accounted for more than half of Harley's total production.

ABOVE RIGHT: *The Fat Bob came in large (74ci/1200cc) and extra large (80ci/1340cc) with twin instruments on the tank console. Neither engine ever had the need to touch the 5,500rpm redline, especially the Eighty with its bags o' torque. Nor would either hit 150mph (241.4km/h).*

1979 FXEF

*Owner: Brad Richardson,
Hemet, California*

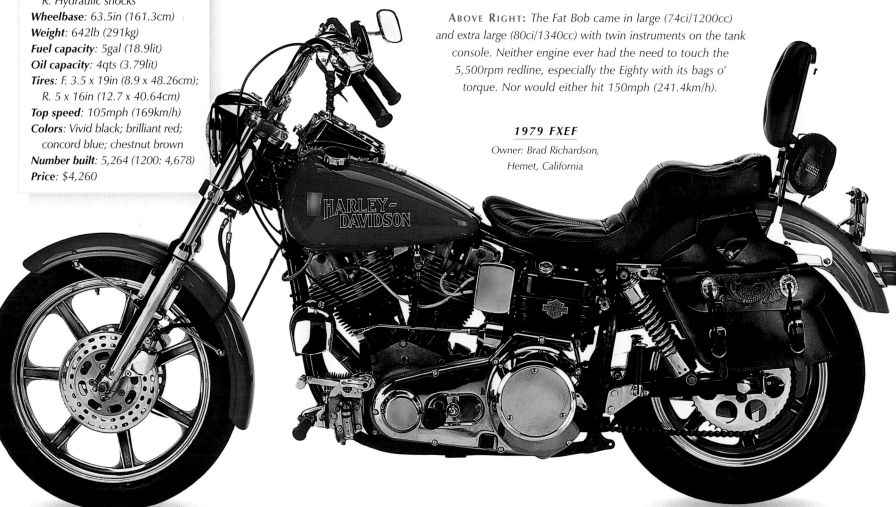

1980 FXB Sturgis; 1980 FLT Tour Guide

The FXB Sturgis, the next Super Glide progeny, was distinguished by the first use of belt drive in 70 years. Reinforced with nylon fiber, the belts proved quieter, required less adjustment than chains (and no lubrication) and were more durable. A limited production model, just over 5,000 Sturgises were made in two years. The FLT Tour Glide, Harley's next generation touring bike, also debuted in 1980. The new Eighty featured a five-speed transmission and transistorized ignition, fitted in a new frame with three-point rubber mounts, revised steering geometry and a fully enclosed drive chain. The Tour Glide marked a major step toward reclaiming some of the touring riders who had been defecting.

LEFT: *The Tour Glide engine's rubber-mount system eliminated most of the big twin's characteristic vibration, and the enclosed drive chain meant higher reliability and lower maintenance.*

1980 FLT
Owner: Doug Holden,
Gustine, California

1980 FXB
Owner: Otis Chandler, Ojai, California

1980 FXB STURGIS

Engine: OHV 45° V-twin
Displacement: 81.65ci (1338cc)
Bore & stroke: 3.5 x 4.25in
  (89 x 108mm)
Compression ratio: 8:1
Horsepower: 65
Carburetion: Bendix
Transmission: 4-speed
Primary drive: Belt
Final drive: Belt
Brakes: Triple disc
Battery: 12-volt
Ignition: Electronic
Frame: Steel, double downtube
Suspension: F. Telescopic fork;
  R. Hydraulic shocks
Wheelbase: 64.7in (164.3cm)
Weight: 610lb (277kg)
Fuel capacity: 3.5gal (13.25lit)
Oil capacity: 4qts (3.8lit)
Tires: F. 3.5 x 19in
  (8.9 x 48.26cm);
  R. 5 x 16in (12.7 x 40.64cm)
Top speed: 106mph (171km/h)
Color: Black
Number built: 1,470
Price: $5,687

living the dream

BELOW: *Mert Lawwill, Grand National Champion in 1969, set a new qualifying record at the Indianapolis Mile (96mph/154.5km/h) in 1973.*

ABOVE: *Cal Rayborn, Harley-Davidson's undisputed roadracing master, on the pit wall at California's Ontario Speedway in 1971.*

RIGHT: *Rayborn's machine lacked the speed of the BSA triples and the agility of the new two-strokes from Japan. But Calvin went on to demonstrate his skill, and the old KR's, at the Trans-Atlantic match races in England.*

The explosion of motorcycle sales in the United States had peaked by the 1970s, although the market was still strong. But even though Harley-Davidson had managed to resolve some of its financial and production problems, the merger with AMF didn't prove to be a marriage made in motorcycle heaven. Milwaukee was in for a tough decade.

Somehow, largely due to the efforts of manager Dick O'Brien, the racing department would go on to new heights. The new Sportster-based XR 750 arrived just as the AMA dropped the old equation and declared that 750cc machines would compete on an equal basis with any sort of valve configuration. Now there would be no more grumbling about the inequities imposed by what many felt was Milwaukee's undue influence on the AMA.

But the rule change didn't work to Harley's benefit in roadracing. Cal Rayborn's Daytona bike was slower than the earlier KR, while the BSA and Triumph teams had found more speed. Dick Mann had won the 1970 event on the Honda four and rode the BSA triple to victory in 1971, also taking the national championship. In 1972 Rayborn won the Indianapolis and Laguna Seca Nationals on the new alloy-head XR 750, but thereafter the roadracing category would be locked up by the new two-stroke entries from Japan. Henceforward, the XR 750 would find its best application on the dirt tracks, recording a long list of victories. The XR would also be the last racing-only engine from Harley-Davidson for more than two decades.

In spite of the glamor and publicity conferred by Hollywood in recent years, Harley Davidson had its hands full in the real world. In the rush to increase

ABOVE: *For flamboyance and showmanship, no one could match the exploits of Evel Knievel, who jumped (and crashed) Harleys in the '60s and '70s.*

LEFT: *There was no shortage of magazines covering the chopper and custom markets in the 1970s, when modified bikes were widely popular.*

ABOVE: *Harley-Davidson enjoyed almost complete domination of the police bike market for decades. But the 1970s brought new contenders from Japan and Germany.*

production, quality control plummeted at the same time prices shot up. Nonetheless, sales were staying at reasonable levels, but the factory's relationship with dealers, who often got stuck with repair costs, was suffering.

Many dealers, and more than a few formerly faithful Harley customers, put the blame squarely on AMF. "Some of those damn Shovelheads were a real pain in the ass," one dealer recalled. "We got to the point where we had to take a new machine, strip it all down and take the engine to a machine shop, balance the crank and everything, and man, what a difference. I mean you had to spend $1,500, but it was terrific." Some dealers just couldn't hang in until Harley-Davidson finally managed to turn it around, which would be ten years down the road. Those who could secure the franchise for imported motorcycles usually switched to a combination of Japanese and European brands. Ironically, more custom and chopper shops were appearing at the same time, serving Harley owners.

ABOVE: *Harley-Davidson celebrated the American bicentennial with a colorful poster featuring the four founders. The eagle/logo art also adorned the tank of the Liberty Edition Superglide.*

"The fact is, most of Harley-Davidson's second-generation managers didn't give a damn about motorcycles and wanted out before Hondas even arrived." FAT BURNS, MOTO PUNDIT

American motorcycling matured in the 1970s, shifting from what had been largely a hobbyist pastime to both a mainstream recreation and successful business enterprise. Aftermarket parts and accessory firms flourished, modern showrooms filled with better motorcycles in all categories and more sophisticated, well-informed customers came to look them over.

The effect was worldwide by the mid-1970s, but it was due in largest measure to the combination of American economic muscle and the remarkable success of Honda motorcycles in the '60s. Soichiro Honda had raised the bar, and every other manufacturer in the business enjoyed some of the residual effect. Honda had effectively made motorcycles socially acceptable in the States, the only part of the world in which they had previously been widely disdained. Harley-Davidson, like everyone else, had been unprepared for this revolution, and had to hook up with AMF to have any hope of keeping up with the phenomenon.

But the drive to accelerate production and introduce new models had some unintended consequences, in addition to the quality-control issue. With the growth of the custom bike and chopper themes, a substantial market for parts and accessories was going unserved by the factory. As a result, independent entrepreneurs simply copied Harley-Davidson parts, designed their own bits and pieces and had them manufactured in Taiwan. Many parts were represented as original factory spares, and the Harley-Davidson logo was widely affixed to all manner of clothing and accessories that had no connection to Milwaukee. By the end of the decade, Harley would take broad legal actions to reclaim their trademark.

Touring riders whose patriotism wore thin in the 1970s acquiesced and switched to the Honda Gold Wing. Customizers and cruisers who simply couldn't bear not to buy American were largely satisfied with the Super Glide, while street and drag racers kept faith with the Sportster. Harley-Davidson could still count on a fairly substantial core group of riders, but most of them removed the AMF logo as soon as possible.

American dirt track racing in the 1970s was thrilling stuff. Dick Mann (BSA) took

FAR RIGHT: *In the mid-1970s, Milwaukee tried sex appeal in the marketing campaign for the two-stroke lightweights.*

the title away from Gene Romero (Triumph) in 1971, which set the stage for the battle of the young guns. Mark Brelsford grabbed the #1 plate back for Harley-Davidson in 1972, but a horrendous accident at Daytona in 1973 effectively ended his racing career.

In 1973 the focus shifted to the running battle between Kenny Roberts' Yamaha and Ohio's Gary Scott for Harley-Davidson. The two young riders had come up through the ranks together, both exhibiting exceptional talent and determination. Roberts won the championship in 1973 and '74, with Scott edging him out for the title in 1975. With the added flavor of Harley's "Michigan Mafia"—Corky Keener, Rex Beauchamp and Jay Springsteen—dirt track fans were treated to some of the finest racing ever staged.

BELOW: *The term "dresser" took on a new meaning in the 1970s when some riders built rolling light shows. Cleveland, Ohio's Sam Green built a display that included chrome balls, horns and a television canopy.*

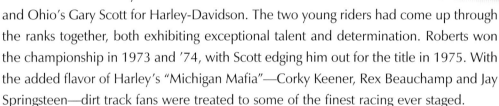

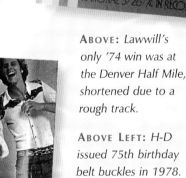

ABOVE: *Lawwill's only '74 win was at the Denver Half Mile, shortened due to a rough track.*

ABOVE LEFT: *H-D issued 75th birthday belt buckles in 1978.*

LEFT: *The discerning Harley rider, even on the two-stroke tiddler, remained unaffected by the glitz and glitter of the 1970s disco era.*

RIGHT: *The traditional rigid frame chopper with a Shovelhead engine was the ride of choice in the mid-1970s. The occasion was the bicentennial Fourth of July parade, Corte Madera, California, 1976. The great American freedom machine on parade.*

AMF
Harley-Davidson
Fat Bob FXE/F-1200

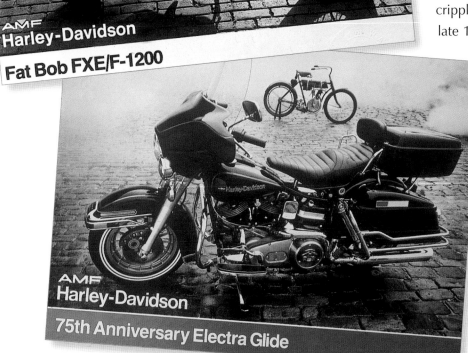

AMF
Harley-Davidson
75th Anniversary Electra Glide

BOTH ABOVE: *The Fat Boy, chubby cousin of the Low Rider, arrived in time for the 75th anniversary. The special edition Electra Glide II was contrasted with the original 1903 single in the background.*

Harley-Davidson had managed to slide into the slipstream of the motorcycle sales boom, and the AMF connection allowed them to nearly triple production in three years. Despite the aforementioned quality control problems having crippled Milwaukee's relationship with many dealers and customers, by the late 1970s there were signs of a turnaround.

While dyed-in-the-wool Harley riders weren't dissuaded by the deficiencies in the first few AMF years—most of them could fix the problems themselves—new riders were another matter. And they would soon account for higher numbers of potential buyers. So the Low Rider and the Cafe Racer were significant symbols of Harley's return from the brink of disaster.

Former dealer John Klocko recalled, "They came out with that special Cafe Racer, whenever it was—'76; now that was a super machine. Rode, handled, run like a champ. Why couldn't they build the rest of 'em like that? The quality was there, and the one right along side of it, a dresser or a Low Rider, and it wasn't."

But, quality control or not, the Low Rider had something the Cafe Racer didn't: The Look. So the Euro-style roadster was soon gone, and riders queued up for the chopper-style cruiser.

AMF
Harley-Davidson
MX-250

BELOW: *Factory customs were now appearing annually. The Wide Glide, a Super Glide with the front end from the Electra Glide, had the 80ci (1340cc) engine and the look of bobbers from the 1950s.*

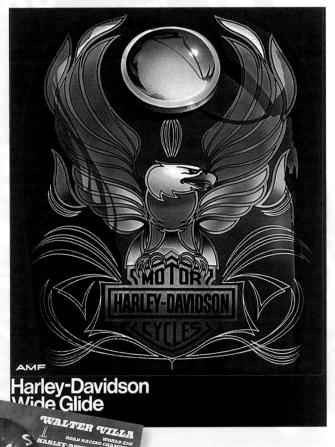

AMF

Harley-Davidson Wide Glide

FAR RIGHT: *Milwaukee's concerted attempt to recapture some of the touring market lost to the Japanese imports resulted in the Tour Glide. The machine had a five-speed transmission and more nimble steering geometry.*

LEFT: *Italy's Walter Villa won consecutive 250cc world roadracing titles in 1974–75 on the Aermacchi twin.*

FAR LEFT: *The two-stroke MX-250 showed promise in the hands of Rex Staten, but was soon discontinued.*

Most of the mainstream motorcycle publications were harsh on Harley-Davidson in the 1970s. The world's motorcycles, forcibly upgraded by the Honda effect, had improved so much in a relatively short time that editors felt justified in scolding Milwaukee for their foot-dragging.

The criticism wasn't entirely unjustified. Harley could have introduced new, improved models shortly after World War II, but chose not to. The company was in sound economic shape, the technology was available and the market was eager for new products. But history conspired against Harley-Davidson in that respect. They had survived a half-century of peaks and valleys, enduring to stand alone as the only American motorcycle manufacturer. Indian had finally buckled, and Milwaukee was triumphant. Nobody was going to tell them what to do.

These were emotional choices, not practical business decisions. Harley-Davidson had rarely been an innovative company. In terms of design, engineering or technical experimentation, they were followers rather than leaders; the silent gray fellows. Also, unlike automobiles, motorcycles in the United States were a hobby, not a necessity. The demand for improvement, a function of strong competition, was absent until the mid-1960s. And second-generation family ownership rarely exhibits the sort of drive and commitment of its forebears.

But general-interest motomag editors largely ignored the fact that Harley retained what none of its current competitors could match, regardless of their technological efficiency: tradition. Milwaukee survived the '70s because of the lineage established in the '20s and '30s, handed down to succeeding generations. The quality of the product may have slipped, but the tradition was still in place. In this case, patriotism trumped technology.

This was personal. The Harley was still a horse; the Honda was an appliance.

The Tour Glide showed that Harley-Davidson hadn't reached the end of the line after all. That despite the turmoil of the '60s and the uncertainty of the '70s, Milwaukee was still involved in the design and

Announcing the Harley -Davidson Tour Glide.

The first touring bike built to handle like a sport bike.

Harley-Davidson. More than a machine.

construction of touring motorcycles which, while making no quantum leaps into the technological mainstream, were better than the ones that had gone before. And that was enough to persuade enough riders that their faith in American iron may not be lost.

Although the Shovelhead was coming to the end of its run, most of its annoyances had been refined. The Tour Glide addressed the fundamentals of handling, comfort, ease of operation and maintenance, and proved that the engineers hadn't been napping.

1981-90: New Tricks for an Old Hog

decade design evolution

"AMF's substantial capital investment … permitted Harley-Davidson revenues to grow from $49 million to approx. $300 million … the most tangible evidence of their success is the company's ability to now stand on its own once again."

VAUGHN BEALS, H-D COO

ABOVE: *The Evo engine looked perfectly at home in the Fat Boy, Willie G.'s homage to industrial design as a mid-American craftwork. Some observers ranked the chubby one the best-styled machine since the Knucklehead.*

While Harley-Davidson's model design and development process had been conducted largely in piecemeal fashion for years, with the '80s came the opportunity to redesign the company itself. Some of the old hands in Milwaukee, including Willie G. himself, could see that home control was essential to their survival, and American Machine and Foundry was ready to sell. None of the prospective buyers looked too appealing to the factory veterans, a group of whom pooled their resources and bought the company themselves.

Faced with an economic recession that had put motorcycle sales, especially expensive heavyweight touring bikes, in the basement, the new management team confronted an imposing roster of challenges. Not only were new design and engineering requirements high on the list; production techniques and procedures were due to be overhauled, the relationship between management and labor tuned up and marketing efforts devised and implemented to persuade potential customers that Harley was building a worthwhile product. All of which had to be accomplished without delay.

The enormity of this task can scarcely be overstated. Naysayers on the outside were all but unanimous in their conviction that Harley-Davidson was on its way down the tube, or that at best would be swallowed by another conglomerate with no understanding of Milwaukee's unique market. Or even by another powerful motorcycle company, meaning Honda. That none of these scenarios would prevail was by no means clear in the early 1980s.

Although the FX series was still selling moderately well, the Electra Glide was sorely strained against the success of the Honda Gold Wing. Many veteran touring riders, those who buy a new motorcycle every few years, had defected to the virtually trouble-free Honda. So Milwaukee not only had to build a better heavyweight machine, but also convince satisfied owners to give Harley another look.

The Evolution engine, in development since 1977, was still a few years from completion. The first machine to be upgraded was the FXR Super Glide II, with a five-speed transmission and rubber-mount engine. Its new frame, improved shift mechanism and electronic ignition combined to elevate both handling and reliability. In 1983 the surprise was the XR-1000, a skunk works hot rod hatched by Willie G., racing director Dick O'Brien and marketing director Clyde Fessler. The 70-horsepower street racer was too potent, and costly, for most riders, but the basic and significantly cheaper XLX-61 Sportster attracted plenty of attention.

By late 1983 the V2 Evolution engine was ready. The Shovelhead, after 18 years of yeoman duty, was approaching consignment to history and an all new 45-degree twin

RIGHT: *Given the apprehension about belts, Milwaukee felt compelled to explain at some length the advantages they held over other final-drive systems. This was reassuring, but in the end it was word of mouth that convinced buyers.*

BELOW: *The Tour Glide Ultra Classic has a cockpit that invites long hours in the saddle. Touring riders appreciated the many built-in amenities.*

To destroy a few myths about shaft drive, here's an exploded view of our belt.

In recent years, there has been a transformation in motorcycle drive systems. A steady movement away from chain drive, primarily in the touring and custom categories.

Some manufacturers have switched their motorcycles to shaft drive, proclaiming its indestructible nature as state-of-the-art motorcycle technology.

But take a closer look. We did, over 40 years ago. We built a shaft drive motorcycle in 1942. That experience convinced us that shaft drive does not belong on a motorcycle. It's not worth the sacrifice in performance and handling.

At Harley-Davidson, we still believe that form follows function. And in our experience, a more functional drive system for the modern American motorcycle is one built into the very first motorcycles—belt drive.

Not the leather belts used earlier this century. Rather, tough-as-steel aramid fiber composition belts.

The Harley-Davidson belt drive system is a product of American ingenuity. Built by motorcyclists, for motorcyclists. Here are its advantages:

Belt drive is more efficient than a shaft.

Engineering data show that belt drive transmits an unbeatable 99% of the engine's power. Shaft drive, on the other hand, saps 7-10% of the engine power.

It's been reported that, to compensate for this power loss, some manufacturers have had to boost engine displacement in their shaft drive models just to make performance equal to a chain.

Belt drive handles better than a shaft.

The ring-and-pinion in the rear wheel of a shaft drive machine transmits a torque reaction that jacks the back end up and down with every twist of the throttle.

Even on straight, perfectly paved roads, shaft drive is unacceptable. As you close the throttle, a shaft-driven bike sinks on its suspension. That reduces ground clearance, for an uncomfortable if not scary ride, especially around corners and over bumps.

Belt drive is just as clean as a shaft.

A belt requires absolutely no lubrication. In addition, after initial break-in, it can go up to 8,000 miles before it needs adjustment.

Belt drive is lighter weight than a shaft.

Shaft drive makes a motorcycle noticeably heavier, especially in back. The extra weight reduces payload and acceleration.

Belt drive is less complicated than a shaft.

No extra gears means smoother, quieter riding.

Belt drive is featured on all 1985 Harley-Davidson touring motorcycles—the Sport Glide,™ the Electra Glide,® and the Tour Glide.® In the custom category, belt drive is on the Low Rider,™ the Wide Glide,® and is a new feature on the 1985 Low Glide.™

In the showroom or out on the road, a close look reveals major differences between belt drive and shaft drive. When it comes to choosing between the two, go with the one that belongs on a motorcycle. Belt drive.

was set to carry Harley-Davidson into a still uncertain future. The Evo motor was designed from the outset to retain as much of the traditional Harley look and sound as possible, while also being more powerful, oil tight, cooler running, lighter, cleaner, more reliable and achieving better fuel economy. And requiring less maintenance.

To offset what might seem to some a too "modern" engine, Milwaukee housed the Evo in a retro-styled cruiser called the Softail, with a bobbed rear fender and a swing arm disguised as a rigid frame section from the '40s. By 1985 every model in the Harley-Davidson stable except the Sportster was powered by the Evolution engine, and in '86 the XL series also had the new motor. The Softail was an almost instant success, while the FL touring machines took a bit longer to catch on. All machines but the Sportster were now belt drive, which would have to wait until '91 before losing its chain and gaining a five-speed transmission.

With the new powerplant and running gear in order, Milwaukee turned its attention to styling and marketing considerations. The nostalgic theme was further advanced in 1986 by the FLST Heritage Softail with its Hydra-Glide fork, and the FX series evolved into a wide selection of Low Riders and Super Glides. The Sportster got up to speed in '88 with a 1200cc/74ci version, while the FX Springer combined an 80ci (1340cc) Evo engine with a '40s-style girder/spring fork.

The arrival in 1990 of the Fat Boy, another Willie G. styling coup, signaled Harley-Davidson's phenomenal return to prominence in less than a decade. The company now had its feet firmly planted—one in the past and the other in the present.

1981 FLH; 1981 XLH

The showdown between AMF corporate directors and Harley-Davidson management arrived in 1981. AMF didn't forecast a profitable future for Milwaukee iron, and had actively searched for a buyer. Finding no takers, they accepted the offer of a leveraged buyout by 13 Harley managers headed by chief executive Vaughn Beals. The deal was completed in June and the new owners declared, "The Eagle Soars Alone."

The 1981 Electra Glide, last of the big twins with AMF on the tank, was offered in a limited run (784) appropriately called the Heritage Edition. The orange and green special featured fringed seat and saddlebags, whitewall tires and plenty of chrome bits. While the FLH was a largely cosmetic gesture to big twins of

the past, most of the production and quality problems had been sorted out as well. While the mighty Shovelhead was still straining against the increasingly sophisticated imports, at least it had regained some reliability. And a new engine was in the works.

Concurrent with the design work on the new powerplant, Milwaukee engineers worked overtime to meet new federal emission standards on the current models. The move to lower octane and no-lead gasoline created a rush to find solutions that would meet national regulations. So the ham can air-cleaners got bigger and compression ratios came down.

1981 FLH
Owner: Trev Deeley Museum,
Vancouver, British Columbia

RIGHT: *The last of the AMF Sportsters were among the fastest, since lower octane fuels would force lower compression ratios.*

1981 XLH
Owner: Clay Osincup, Los Osos, California

LEFT: *Electra Glides were holding at about 8–10,000 bikes a year, about one-third of FX-series production. The figure would drop to 6,000 in 1982 in a sagging economy, but plans for a new engine were proceeding regardless.*

ABOVE: *The Sportster would lose its dual front discs in 1983, and some of its lean, mean demeanor. But production stayed above 10,000 until 1984 when it dropped below 6,500.*

The Sportster got a new frame in 1981 but was largely unchanged otherwise. The XL remained second only to the FX series in overall sales, and would be the last model up for modification as Milwaukee put its highest priority on the design and engineering of the forthcoming Evolution engine.

1981 FLH

Engine: OHV 45° V-twin
Displacement: 81.65ci (1338cc)
Bore & stroke: 3.5 x 4.25in (89 x 108mm)
Compression ratio: 7.4:1
Horsepower: 65
Carburetion: Bendix
Transmission: 4-speed
Primary drive: Chain
Final drive: Chain
Brakes: Triple disc
Battery: 12-volt
Ignition: Electronic
Frame: Steel, double downtube
Suspension: F. Telescopic fork; R. Hydraulic shocks
Wheelbase: 61.5in (156.21cm)
Weight: 740lb (335.7kg)
Fuel capacity: 3.5gal (13.25lit)
Oil capacity: 4qts (3.8lit)
Tires: 5 x 16in (12.7 x 40.64cm)
Top speed: 105mph (169km/h)
Color: Green/orange
Number built: 784
Price: $6,200

1982 FXR; 1982 XLH

The Super Glide took another techno-step in 1982 with the introduction of the FXR. The new chassis featured a box-section backbone frame and rubber-mount system in the R model with its five-speed transmission. The standard FX retained the solid-mount attachment and four-speed gearbox.

1982 XLH
Dudley Perkins Co.,
San Francisco, California

1982 FXRS SUPER GLIDE II

Engine: OHV 45° V-twin
Displacement: 81.65ci (1338cc)
Bore & stroke: 3.5 x 4.25in
  (89 x 108mm)
Compression ratio: 8:1
Horsepower: 65
Carburetion: Bendix
Transmission: 5-speed
Primary drive: Duplex chain
Final drive: Chain
Brakes: F. Dual discs; R. Disc
Ignition: Electronic
Frame: Steel, double downtube
Battery: 12-volt

Suspension: F. Telescopic fork;
  R. Hydraulic shocks
Wheelbase: 64.7in (164.3cm)
Weight: 610lb (277kg)
Fuel capacity: 3.5gal (13.25lit)
Oil capacity: 4qts (3.8lit)
Tires: F. 3.5 x 19in (8.9 x 48.26cm);
  R. 5 x 16in (12.7 x 40.64cm)
Top speed: 115mph (185km/h)
Colors: Vivid black; candy red;
  metallic blue; metallic green;
  brown and black
Number built: 3,190 (FXR: 3,065)
Price: $6,690

The new transmission shifted more easily and was more willing to find neutral. The 80ci (1340cc) Shovelhead also had a better lubrication system, improved valve guides, electronic ignition and dual front disc brakes. While the FXR was still a heavyweight (over 600 pounds/272kg), it handled reasonably well and became the sportiest of Milwaukee's muscle cruisers.

The Sportster turned 25 years old in 1982, the occasion celebrated in Milwaukee with anniversary editions for the XLH and XLS models. Compression was dropped to compensate for the newly mandated low-octane fuels, which meant a slight decline in horsepower.

1982 FXR
Owner: Ginger Gammon, Cranleigh, England

1983 XR-1000; 1983 XLX-61

In 1983, responding to increasing requests for a real street racer, Harley presented the XR-1000. With new alloy heads on shortened cast-iron cylinders, lumpy cams, big carbs and pipes, the XR made 70 horsepower and went like hell. But it was too expensive ($7,000) and hard-edged for a streetbike and lasted only two years. The XR helped draw attention to the bare-bones XLX-61 at $4,000, making the Sportster affordable to more buyers.

1983 XLX-61

Owner: Trev Deeley Museum, Vancouver, British Columbia

LEFT: *With the ranks of buyers for bikes in the $6–8,000 range thinning, the XLX built showroom traffic.*

BELOW: *By contrast, the factory hot rod XR-1000 was expensive to build, being a hybrid of the Sportster and the XR 750 racer. So it was fast, uncomfortable and costly.*

1983 XR-1000	
Engine:	OHV 45° V-twin
Displacement:	61ci (1000cc)
Bore & stroke:	3.19 x 3.81in (81 x 97mm)
Compression ratio:	9:1
Horsepower:	71 @ 5,600rpm
Carburetion:	Two 36mm Dell'Orto
Transmission:	4-speed
Primary drive:	Chain
Final drive:	Chain
Brakes:	Triple disc
Battery:	12-volt
Ignition:	V-Fire CDI
Frame:	Steel, double downtube
Suspension:	F. Telescopic fork; R. Hydraulic shocks
Wheelbase:	60in (152.4cm)
Weight:	490lb (222kg)
Fuel capacity:	2.5gal (9.5lit)
Oil capacity:	2.5qts (2.36lit)
Tires:	F. 110/90-19; R. 130/90-16 (18in/45.72cm rear wheel optional)
Top speed:	125mph (201km/h)
Color:	Slate gray (option: orange/black in 1984)
Number built:	1,108
Price:	$6,995

LEFT: *Some of the XRs became production roadracers, with considerable success. Others became museum pieces.*

1983 XR-1000

Owner: Oliver Shokouh, H-D of Glendale, Glendale, California

1984 FXST; 1984 FLH; 1984 FXEF

1984 FXEF
Mathews Harley-Davidson, Fresno, California

Evolution of the Milwaukee species was marked by the 1984 arrival of the Softail, designated FXST. The next-generation Super Glide housed the first new Harley-Davidson engine in decades, and held the promise of reliable performance, riding comfort combined with classic styling and lasting value.

The Evolution engine was the keystone in Harley's revival process, while the design crew continued looking to the past for styling hints. Their collaboration produced the Softail with its rigid-look rear frame section and shock absorbers fitted below the engine. The retro look, anchored by a traditional but upgraded 45-degree V-twin, was calculated to move Harley into the future without ignoring the past. Success didn't follow immediately, but when it came, it was huge.

While the Evolution engine was in the spotlight, the Shovelhead inventory was exhausted in the early '84 FL and FX series. The Wide Glide showed signs of the future with a new final belt drive system. Early attempts to employ belt-drive primaries in the FX had poor results, so Milwaukee stuck with primary chains.

The FX series had grown to five models, which combined accounted for nearly half the factory's production. And as they all received the Evolution engine, sales increased even further.

BELOW LEFT: *Everything old is new again. The Softail, combining traditional design, custom styling and a new engine in orthodox configuration, put Harley back on the road.*

1984 FLH

*Owner: Steve Alamango,
Hot Bikes, Venice, California
Restorer: Richard Brazas*

LEFT: *Although the V2 Evolution engine was new only above the cases, it was sufficiently improved to give Harley-Davidson another chance in an increasingly competitive market. While Japanese engineering and build quality had also improved, their attempts at American styling were dubious.*

ABOVE: *The last of the Shovelheads remained popular platforms for custom treatments, such as this retro piece of '50s-style nostalgia.*

1984 FXST

Engine: OHV 45° V-twin
Displacement: 81.65ci (1338cc)
Bore & stroke: 3.5 x 4.25in
   (89 x 108mm)
Compression ratio: 8.5:1
Horsepower: 55
Carburetion: 38mm Keihin
Transmission: 4-speed
Primary drive: Duplex chain
Final drive: Chain
   Brakes: Disc F. & R. Disc
   Battery: 12-volt
   Ignition: CDI
   Frame: Steel, double downtube
   Suspension: F. Telescopic fork;
   R. Shocks
   Wheelbase: 66.3in (168.4cm)
   Weight: 628lb (285kg)
   Fuel capacity: 5gal (18.9lit)
   Oil capacity: 3.5qts (3.3lit)
   Tires: F. 3 x 19in
      (7.62 x 48.26cm);
      R. 5 x 16 in (12.7 x 40.64cm)
Top speed: 110mph (177km/h)
Colors: Vivid black with pinstripes;
   candy red with pinstripes
Number built: 5,413
Price: $7,999

1984 FXST

*Dudley Perkins Company,
San Francisco, California*

1985 FLHTC; 1986 FLST; 1986 FXSTC

By 1985 the new generation of Harleys was in place, all but the Sportster now fitted with the Evo engine. The FLHTC Electra Glide Classic wore the traditional bar-and-shield logo on the fuel tank and the old-style handlebar fairing, and now had a smoother engine with a five-speed transmission.

While the FL series was slow to draw touring riders back to the Harley showrooms, the Softail success story was well on its way into the record books. More cross-pollination was in order, so in 1986 Milwaukee offered the FLST, a Softail with the venerable Hydra Glide front end, and created an instant classic. In fact the following year, in even more retro trim, it would be called the Heritage Softail Classic.

The Sportsters and the FX series remained the top-selling machines in 1986, with the Super Glide derivations spanning a lineup of 11 models. The FXSTC led in production numbers, followed by the standard Softail and the FXR Super Glide. As a final evolutionary step in 1986, the V2 engine was conferred on the Sportster as well.

The Evo engine, in concert with the Softail models, effectively re-established Harley-Davidson's credibility in the mid-1980s. What many industry observers had written off as a defunct enterprise was now a thriving business and national success story. When Harley stock was listed on the New York Stock Exchange in 1987 at $20 a share, the turnaround was complete.

1985 FLHTC

Engine: OHV 45° V-twin
Displacement: 81.65ci (1338cc)
Bore & stroke: 3.5 x 4.25in
  (89 x 108mm)
Compression ratio: 8.5:1
Horsepower: 55
Carburetion: 38mm Keihin
Transmission: 5-speed
Primary drive: Duplex chain
Final drive: Belt
Brakes: F. Dual discs; R. Disc
Battery: 12-volt
Ignition: CDI
Frame: Steel, double downtube
Suspension: F. Telescopic fork;
  R. Shocks
Wheelbase: 62.9in (159.8cm)
Weight: 760lb (345kg)
Fuel capacity: 5gal (18.9lit)
Oil capacity: 4qts (3.8lit)
Tires: F. 3 x 19in (7.62 x 48.26cm);
  R. 5 x 16in (12.7 x 40.64cm)
Top speed: 110mph (177km/h)
Colors: Vivid black; candy red; candy
  blue; tan/cream; candy burgundy/
  slate gray (all with pinstripes); candy
  burgundy/candy pearl
Number built: 3,409
Price: $9,199

BELOW: *Had there been any doubts about Milwaukee's commitment to regaining its share of the touring market, they were diminished by the appearance of the Electra Glide Classic. The five-speed gearbox and belt drive were encouraging signs.*

1985 FLHTC
Bartels' Harley-Davidson,
Marina Del Rey, California

RIGHT: Willie G.'s the name, cross-pollination is the game. The Softail was a hit from the git-go, so variations on the theme were quick to follow. The Heritage Softail covered design cues from the '40s through the '60s, stylishly.

1986 FLST

Owner: Harley-Davidson Motor Co., Milwaukee, Wisconsin

© Harley-Davidson Archive photo

ABOVE: Shock absorbers for the rigid-look frame were neatly hidden below the transmission. Staggered shorty dual exhausts added a muscular touch to the stately Hydra-Glide profile, and the traditional paint scheme was elegant.

LEFT: The bar-mounted fairing remained the popular choice over the large, frame-mount enclosure. Electra Glide sales were still in decline, but more touring riders had taken renewed interest in the big Harleys.

1986 FLST

Engine: OHV 45° V-twin
Displacement: 81.65ci (1338cc)
Bore & stroke: 3.5 x 4.25in (89 x 108mm)
Compression ratio: 8.5:1
Horsepower: 55
Carburetion: 38mm Keihin
Transmission: 5-speed
Primary drive: Duplex chain
Final drive: Belt
Brakes: F. & R. Disc
Battery: 12-volt
Ignition: CDI

Frame: Steel, double downtube
Suspension: F. Telescopic fork; R. Shocks
Wheelbase: 62.5in (158.75cm)
Weight: 650lb (295kg)
Fuel capacity: 5gal (18.9lit)
Oil capacity: 3qts (2.84lit)
Tires: MT-90S-16
Top speed: 112mph (180km/h)
Colors: Signal red/creme; bronze/creme
Number built: 2,510
Price: $9,099

1986 FXSTC

Owner: John Kingston, Atascadero, California

1988 FXSTS; 1989 FLHTC; 1988 XLH 1200

The Softail's success afforded Harley the opportunity to conduct some test marketing on even more nostalgic themes. With the 1988 FXSTS Springer, Willie G. and the design elves reached back to the Knucklehead era for the fork layout. And while the front suspension looked like a '40s piece, its engineering and performance were contemporary.

The new Springer was timed for Harley-Davidson's 85th anniversary, and was appropriately designated with commemorative insignias on the front fender and tank. Produced in limited numbers for '88 (1,356), the FXSTS was another instant hit and production nearly tripled the following year. The Softail Custom remained the sales leader of the FX lineup, followed by the Springer, Low Rider and Super Glide.

The FL roster now included the Electra Glide Sport, fitted with fiberglass bags and a windshield, the FLHTC Classic, with handlebar fairing and tail trunk, and Ultra Classic versions of both the Electra and Tour Glides. All the touring models featured a new alternator and self-canceling turn signals; the Ultras were fitted with cruise control.

The XLH 1200 Sportster, a few of which were built in 1986, went into full production in '88. The larger diameter FX fork tubes were fitted to all Sportsters, of which 16,500 rolled off the line.

BELOW: By 1989 the Electra Glide division accounted for more than 9,000 motorcycles. Part of the renewed volume could be attributed to riders returning to motorcycling after years of not owning a touring bike, and part to long-term riders coming back to Harley-Davidson after owning imported machines.

1989 FLHTC

Engine: OHV 45° V-twin
Displacement: 81.65ci (1338cc)
Bore & stroke: 3.5 x 4.25in
   (89 x 108mm)
Compression ratio: 8.5:1
Horsepower: 55
Carburetion: 38mm Keihin
Transmission: 5-speed
Primary drive: Duplex chain
Final drive: Belt
Brakes: F. Dual discs; R. Disc
Battery: 12-volt
Ignition: CDI
Frame: Steel, double
   downtube
Suspension: F. Telescopic fork;
   R. Shocks
Wheelbase: 62.9in (159.8cm)
Weight: 760lb (345kg)
Fuel capacity: 5gal (18.9lit)
Oil capacity: 4qts (3.8lit)
Tires: F. 3 x 19in (7.62 x 48.26cm);
   R. 5 x 16in (12.7 x 40.64cm)
Top speed: 110mph (177km/h)
Colors: n/a
Number built: 3,969
Price: $12,265

1989 FLHTC
*Harley-Davidson of Atascadero,
Atascadero, California*

1988 FXSTS

Owner: Harley-Davidson Motor Co., Milwaukee, Wisconsin

© Harley-Davidson Archive photo

1988 FXSTS

Engine: OHV 45° V-twin	**Frame**: Steel, double downtube
Displacement: 81.65ci (1338cc)	**Suspension**: F. Springer fork; R. Shocks
Bore & stroke: 3.5 x 4.25in (89 x 108mm)	**Wheelbase**: 64.5in (163.8cm)
Compression ratio: 8.5:1	**Fuel capacity**: 6.4gal (24.2lit)
Horsepower: 55	**Oil capacity**: 3qts (2.8lit)
Carburetion: 38mm Keihin	**Tires**: F. MT90-21; R. MH90-16
Transmission: 5-speed	
Primary drive: Duplex chain	**Top speed**: 114mph (183km/h)
Final drive: Belt	**Color**: Black with red pinstripes
Brakes: F. & R. Disc	
Battery: 12-volt	**Number built**: 1,356
Ignition: CDI	**Price**: $10,279
Weight: 635lb (288kg)	

ABOVE: The new version of the Springer front end was a nearly exact replica of the original version, but it worked much better. And while the disc brake may have been at stylistic odds with the retro fork and skinny wheel, it also performed in contemporary fashion. It was another design triumph, showing that form and function aren't mutually exclusive.

1988 XLH 1200

Bartels' Harley-Davidson, Marina Del Rey, California

LEFT: Here again Milwaukee was determined to prove that traditional motorcycles, based on decades-old designs, could still be built to modern standards of performance, comfort and reliability. And since those qualities hold high priority among touring riders, the success or failure of the Electra Glide held an equal measure of importance for Harley-Davidson. Thus the adoption of items like cruise control.

ABOVE: While the Sportster may have been slower to evolve than other models, in 1988 it did get bumped to 1200cc/74ci with a 12 percent increase in power. Tighter gear ratios enhanced the acceleration curve, and better carburetion improved the low-speed manners. Larger fork tubes from the FX made the front end stronger, but the look remained vintage Sportster.

1990 FLSTF; 1990 FLTC Ultra

As Harley-Davidson returned to economic health, and Willie G. remained relatively undisturbed in the design department, the special editions kept coming. But the FLSTF Fat Boy wasn't turned out in limited numbers to test market reaction; this time the production run was 4,440 machines, so the confidence level in Milwaukee had obviously risen.

The Fat Boy was another Softail retro rider, but not one based on any specific design element of the past. This was the designer's tribute to the techno-futuristic stylings of the '50s, when industrial and commercial art began to overlap. With its monochromatic treatment, subtle graphics, disc wheels and shotgun pipes, the Fat Boy presented an image of fashion, style and humor. And it worked perfectly well as a motorcycle.

With the FX roster covered, attention turned to the touring models. The Tour Glide had fallen well behind the less distance-oriented Electra Glide in popularity, which led to the FLTC Ultra Classic in 1990. Within its protective frame-mount fairing, the Tour Glide featured an 80-watt stereo, citizen's band radio, rider/passenger voice-activated intercom system and cruise control. The same amenities were also available on the Electra Glide.

Few more than 1,000 Tour Glides were built for 1990, compared to about 7,000 of the Classic and Ultra Classic Electra Glides. But it signaled Milwaukee's conviction that they weren't about to call it quits in the touring category.

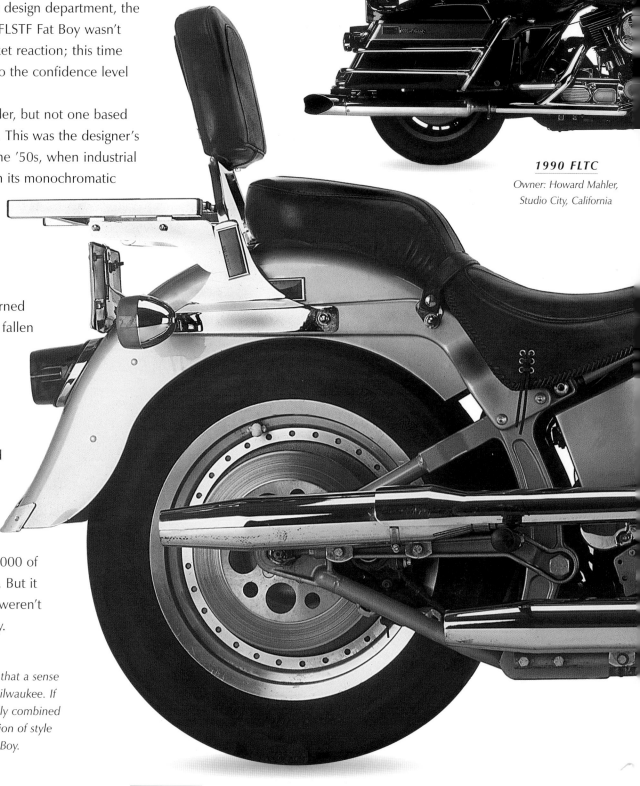

1990 FLTC
*Owner: Howard Mahler,
Studio City, California*

RIGHT: *The Fat Boy was another good indication that a sense of fun and adventure was still alive and well in Milwaukee. If any motorcycle of the late 20th century successfully combined past and present in a coherent and attractive union of style and grace, it was the perfectly named Fat Boy.*

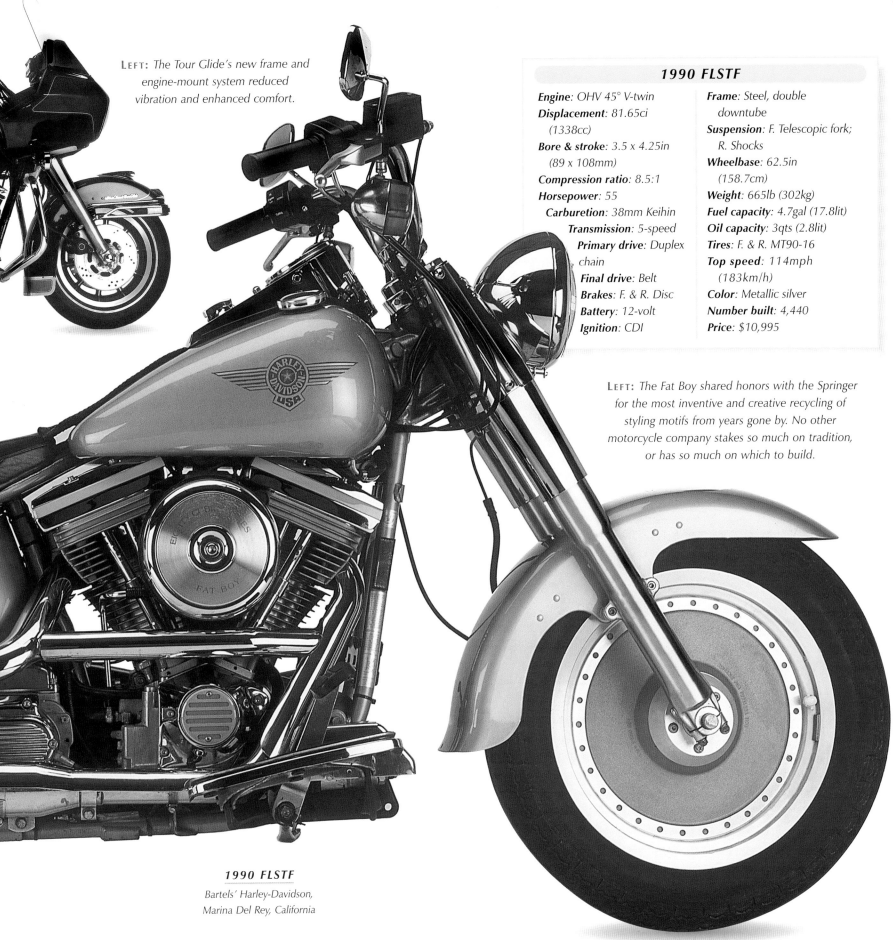

LEFT: *The Tour Glide's new frame and engine-mount system reduced vibration and enhanced comfort.*

1990 FLSTF

Engine: OHV 45° V-twin
Displacement: 81.65ci (1338cc)
Bore & stroke: 3.5 x 4.25in (89 x 108mm)
Compression ratio: 8.5:1
Horsepower: 55
Carburetion: 38mm Keihin
Transmission: 5-speed
Primary drive: Duplex chain
Final drive: Belt
Brakes: F. & R. Disc
Battery: 12-volt
Ignition: CDI

Frame: Steel, double downtube
Suspension: F. Telescopic fork; R. Shocks
Wheelbase: 62.5in (158.7cm)
Weight: 665lb (302kg)
Fuel capacity: 4.7gal (17.8lit)
Oil capacity: 3qts (2.8lit)
Tires: F. & R. MT90-16
Top speed: 114mph (183km/h)
Color: Metallic silver
Number built: 4,440
Price: $10,995

LEFT: *The Fat Boy shared honors with the Springer for the most inventive and creative recycling of styling motifs from years gone by. No other motorcycle company stakes so much on tradition, or has so much on which to build.*

1990 FLSTF

Bartels' Harley-Davidson, Marina Del Rey, California

living the dream

"...some people ... had been using the Harley-Davidson name and logos on various products without company permission. In some instances ... on items of questionable taste or in conjunction with profanity or vulgarity."

THOMAS C. BOLFERT,
"THE BIG BOOK OF HARLEY-DAVIDSON"

ABOVE: *The Electra Glide, now with belt drive and electronic ignition, was commemorated with a limited edition of 920 FLHX models with special paint, decals and hand-painted striping.*

ABOVE RIGHT: *Harley-Davidson had produced badges, pins, buckles and assorted decorative bits and pieces for decades. Outside companies had also used the Harley-Davidson symbols on their merchandise for years, but unlicensed use was coming to an end.*

Although the motorcycle sales boom had leveled off in the 1970s, the machines themselves kept improving. The market may not have had the breadth or legs that some manufacturers foresaw, but the competition among them, especially the Japanese, sustained the stream of engineering and performance innovation. Honda's achievement in elevating the user-friendliness of motorcycles simply provoked others to go them one better. Horsepower, handling, braking and comfort all moved up the scale.

Harley-Davidson's management was well aware of the need for product improvement, but their internal problems with AMF retarded the supply of solutions. In the meantime, a new, more demanding generation of riders had come of age. They had come to expect better motorcycles, and in many cases would influence the decisions of their fathers and older brothers.

"We rode Harleys in the '50s and '60s," recalled Kentuckian Don Sullivan. "They were fine. Of course you had to tinker with 'em now and then, but that was part of the fun. And they weren't real fast or anything, but that probably helped keep us out of trouble. But then we got a Shovelhead, '73 I think it was, and that thing was just a pain in the ass. Had to take a full set of tools with you on a trip, everything would come loose ... real aggravating."

One day Sullivan's son showed up on a Kawasaki Z1. "Gene let me ride that thing, and Lord Almighty. I mean it was sorta top heavy, but brother was it smooth. And fast? ... took it out on the highway, looked down and I was doin' almost ninety! And it had great brakes, too," he said. "Wasn't long before I sold that Harley."

As more people discovered the joys of trouble-free motorcycling, and more Harley dealers pressured the factory for better machines, the quicker the pace of improvement in Milwaukee. The elements were in place by the time the AMF era ended; more qualified engineers, better quality control and a new engine coming along. Then, just as the picture looked rosy, the motorcycle market went flat and Harley-Davidson was in money trouble again.

"We knew they were working hard to get it together," said longtime Harley fan Hank Wilson. "Some of us decided to just hold off buying anything until they had a good chance to turn it around. And as it turned out, that's what happened in the long run. It just took them a couple years longer than they figured."

LEFT AND BELOW: *Scott Parker went on to become the most dominant dirt tracker since Carroll Resweber. The Enthusiast for spring 1982 included coverage of Daytona in March.*

ABOVE: *Various chapters of the Hells Angels (no apostrophe in their spelling) made the scene in Sturgis, South Dakota, such as this event in August, 1982.*

HARLEY-DAVIDSON Wins Indy Mile, Sets New Record

Harley-Davidson factory rider Scott Parker won his first ever Indianapolis, Indiana Mile Race on August 25, 1985 in a big way. Not only did he take the checkered flag, but he broke the race time record by 7.288 seconds.

Credit for this tremendous victory goes to Scotty's hard charging riding ability, a perfect track and an all night session putting the bike together by tuner Bill Werner.

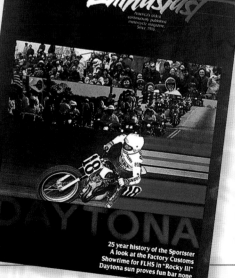

One member of the "Harley 13" buy-back group was Timothy Hoelter, a former member of Harley's law firm. As Vice President and general counsel, Hoelter's job was to provide the new company with protection from trademark infringement.

"Are you going to control your promotional effort, or do you intend to leave it in the hands of third parties?" he said in David Wright's book, "The Harley-Davidson Motor Company." Hoelter's campaign to eliminate the use of Harley's logo on items of questionable taste alienated many independent shop owners who employed it on T-shirts. "The law doesn't distinguish between 'good infringement' and 'bad infringement,'" he said. "They tell you to protect your trademark against those who use it or give it up and let everyone use it. That doesn't give us much choice in prosecuting."

RIGHT: *The FX series came to include a half dozen variations on the model theme. Outfitted in different selections of gear, the Junior Glides were profitable accessory platforms.*

FAR RIGHT: *One of the last AMF-era limited-edition specials was the Electra Glide Classic with Sidecar.*

BELOW: *Tenacious, built by Denis Manning of BUB pipes, sponsored by the Harley Owners Group and S&S Engineering and driven to 278mph (447.4km/h) by Dan Kinsey in 1984. Manning called Kinsey "the bravest man I've ever seen."*

YOUR BASIC, UNADORNED BEAUTY: EVERYTHING A PURIST COULD ASK FOR.

Stock 1988 FXR

BUT THEN AGAIN, EVERYONE'S GOT A MIND OF HIS OWN.

For a look that's purely personal, look at the difference genuine make in this FXR. Like seats and sissy bars. Windshields chrome trim, and more. Even custom paint and Screamin' our new catalog at your Harley dealer. And build your bike.

Harley-Davidson® accessories can and leather bags. Exhaust systems, Eagle® Performance Parts. Pick up any way you have a mind to.

Custom Built with Harley Accessories

HARLEY ACCESSORIES

THE SIDECAR by HARLEY-DAVIDSON®

Harley-Davidson is the grandest name in the history of American touring. Now your King of the Highway can be equipped with the ultimate accessory, the luxurious and functional Harley-Davidson Sidecar.

Our FLHT and FLT models boast the new V² Evolution™ engines with smooth five speed transmissions and provide ample power for sidecar use. A state-of-the-art front end and hydraulic steering damper on these vehicles improve handling and stability. Move up to the ultimate touring experience, the sidecar by Harley-Davidson.

HARLEY-DAVIDSON MOTOR CO., INC.

Land Speed Record holder Dan Kinsey and Tenacious, the H.O.G./Harley-Davidson sponsored Streamliner.

LEFT: *The first and last Harley Rider comic book, published by Carl Hungness Publishing in 1988.*

Once clear of the AMF malevolence and the Citicorp incongruity as financiers, the Harley-Davidson Motor Company opened its latest chapter. No longer either a family company or a conglomerate cog, Harley was now under professional management, albeit a group mortgaged up to its necktie. What was the consensus within the industry?

"We thought they were nuts," said one multi-brand dealer. "Harley was so far behind the rest of the crowd, there didn't seem any way they could pull it off. I mean how much can you do with that big lump of an engine?" More, as it turned out, than most might have imagined.

A curious sidelight of this period was Harley's purchase of the Trihawk, a 1,300-pound (590kg) three-wheeler powered by a 1300cc Citroen four-cylinder engine. Chairman Vaughn Beals saw "a definite market niche between current motorcycle and sportscar offerings." The acquisition raised eyebrows in the light of Milwaukee's recent plea for tariff relief on Japanese imports from the federal government. The trike was quietly shelved about a year later.

AMF had discovered that there was no way Harley-Davidson could compete with the Japanese. The buy-out team was aware of that, but also convinced that they didn't

BELOW: *The "Charlie's Angels" TV show perpetuated the Farah Fawcett hairstyle well into the 1980s. And when it came to accessories, what could be more fetching than a lovely blonde? Harley-Davidson continued to expand the fashion and accessory catalog.*

AMF Harley-Davidson 1981 Motorcycle Fashions and Accessories

have to; that there existed among the motorcycling public a reservoir of goodwill and, yes, patriotism, that would not only restore Milwaukee to its former glory, but carry the big V-twin thundering into the 21st century. Profitably.

All of this made the old guard nervous. The Evo engine looked like "a Jap motor;" the dealerships were filling up with "motorcycle fashions" and silly little knick-knacks; the new breed of "rubs" (rich urban bikers) were buying into the Harley lifestyle, a bunch of phonies who talked the talk but "couldn't walk the walk." And so forth. In fact, by the mid-1980s there were so few of the outlaw types, real or imagined, left that it made little difference to Milwaukee. Those few who could afford the new Evo models would eventually buy one and be converted; those who stuck with their Panheads and Shovelheads supported the aftermarket parts industry and maintained their brotherhood of honorable suffering.

Harley fans past and present, and most of the fence-sitters, recognized by the mid-1980s that the boys in Milwaukee were accomplishing what they set out to do: change just about everything but the look, sound and feel of the motorcycle. Even the skeptical magazine testers admitted that the 1985 FXRT set new marks for comfort, handling and braking. *Cycle Guide* magazine staffers praised the refinements, and the belt drive, noting that the new model achieved a pleasant balance between the sport and touring modes.

Regaining the California Highway Patrol motorcycle contract with the FXRT was another public relations plus for Milwaukee at the time, and it was renewed again in 1987, '88 and '89. Obviously the corner had been turned.

Milwaukee had struck the right combination of engineering and manufacturing improvement, national pride and "biker lifestyle" to overcome 20 years of losing ground to other manufacturers. The Harley Owners Group gave new riders a free pass into the motorcycling scene; instant acceptance by the fraternity formerly perceived as a closed society of unsavory folks. While it may all have been anathema to the growling geezers of the Panhead and Shovelhead generations, the new order of Harley owners were having a swell time on their motorcycles.

ABOVE: *Willie G. introduced the new Low Rider Custom on the cover of* The Enthusiast *for Fall, 1986. The design chief was the company's most familiar face.*

RIGHT: *Harley-Davidson got the California Highway Patrol contract in 1984, the first time in ten years Harley could meet the tough CHP standards.*

HARLEY-DAVIDSON DEALER NEWS

©HARLEY-DAVIDSON MOTOR CO. INC., FEBRUARY, 1984

Police Sales Grow...
C.H.P. contract is iceberg's tip

The recent contract to provide the California Highway Patrol with a minimum of 135 police motorcycles represents an important milestone. And it is important, perhaps for no better reason than it gives Harley-Davidson and its nationwide dealer network an unparalleled opportunity to open the doors at other police and law enforcement agencies around the country.

In today's market, police sales can be an important plus in the dealer's success and profit picture. And Harley-Davidson has the programs to help dealers capitalize on the opportunity.

In recent months, these programs have put 15 police motorcycles on the roads in Ft. Lauderdale. El Paso, Texas, police climbed off their Kawasakis and onto 22 FXRP Harleys. Atlantic City, New Jersey got 10 FLHTPs; Mobile, Alabama, 12; and Nassau, County, New York, 10.

Let's start the overview of police-sales programs with a look at the motorcycles. Harley-Davidson offers three police motorcycles, suited to a variety of purposes. The all-new FXRP, the model sold to the CHP, is a light and agile, pursuit-oriented motorcycle, designed to compete with Kawasaki. The FLHP and FLHTP which round out the lineup, are larger, "image-oriented" motorcycles, ...

fleet. An order for 135 motorcycles, with its economies of production, provides areas for cost and price reductions. 2. The CHP contract, because of its ramifications, was handled on a direct ...

Meet "Vector Bender."

BELOW: *There's that face again. One of Willie G.'s personal favorites, the Fat Boy of 1990, complements the massive Harley-Davidson Freightliner transporter.*

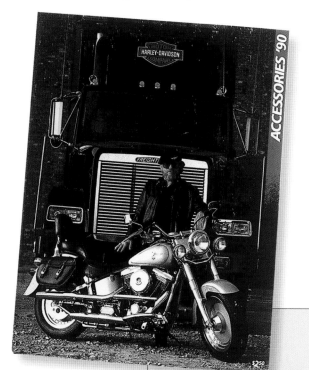

In 1987 Harley-Davidson went public with an initial offering on the New York Stock Exchange. The brokerage agency, Dean Witter Reynolds, produced a television commercial featuring Harley executives riding down Wall Street, lined with American flags, and into the stock exchange. The patriotic theme projected Harley's return to financial health, and signaled the company's celebration of its almost rags-to-riches success story.

There were other signs of a healthy bank balance. The advertising spreads had the characteristically stylish look of an upscale agency, with large, professional photographs, snappy headlines and crisp, trendy copywriting. At the end of the year Harley-Davidson bought the Holiday Rambler Corporation, a manufacturer of motor homes, commercial vans, truck bodies and related stuff, including an injection-molding plastics subsidiary.

Some of the more cynical observers suggested that Milwaukee wanted a motor home company to serve the needs of their aging biker clientele who could no longer manage the operation of a two-wheeler. The next logical acquisition for Harley after motor homes, some suggested, would be a casket manufacturer.

By 1988 it was fairly conclusive that Harley-Davidson was, as President Reagan had said, "serious about getting back in fighting shape." Major magazines, newspapers,

ABOVE: *Harley-Davidson turned out this handsome buckle for the 1980 "Artistry is Iron" show in Los Angeles.*

RIGHT: *The Ultra Classic line was introduced in 1989, with the Tour Glide and Electra Glide. Cruise control and C.B. radio were standard.*

THE NEW ULTRA CLASSIC ELECTRA GLIDE.
TOURING ON A HIGHER PLANE.

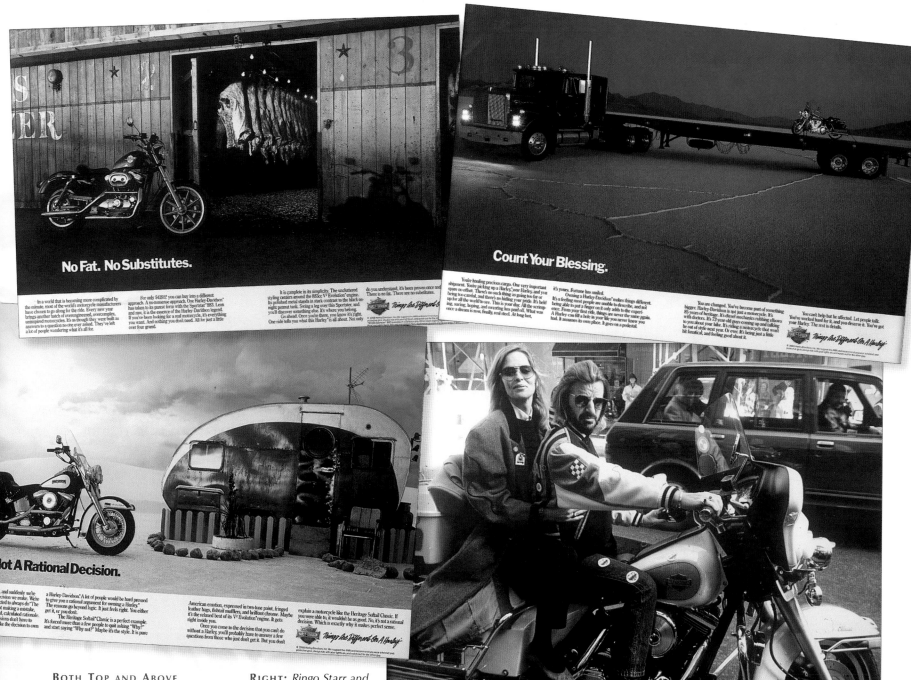

No Fat. No Substitutes.

Count Your Blessing.

Not A Rational Decision.

BOTH TOP AND ABOVE LEFT: *The handsome photography of Harley-Davidson ads in the late 1980s reflected the successful rebound the company had established in five years. The trend was to continue into the 1990s and beyond.*

RIGHT: *Ringo Starr and his lovely passenger, Barbara Bach, on their way to Abbey Road. As the former drummer in a band called The Beatles, Ringo appreciated the syncopation of the Harley engine, its resonant bass and prominent paradiddle.*

television shows and assorted Hollywood celebrities were glad to publicize the enormous reversal achieved by The Motor Company. Congratulations were in order all around.

The Milwaukee gathering celebrating Harley's 85th anniversary attracted about 35,000 enthusiasts. The company management, led by Willie G. and his wife Nancy, were on hand to meet and greet the customers, and to show off the special-edition Anniversary models. The highlight was the Springer Softail, a stylish retro nod to Milwaukee's long history.

1991-2000: Profits Up Down the Road

decade design evolution

"Harley managed to regain their purpose in the '80s, and engineered their own salvation. If they can maintain that focus, they might well be around for another century."

VIRGIL GRANT, RIDER

ABOVE: *Among the six Anniversary Editions in 1993 was the Dyna Wide Glide. Each had silver/charcoal paint, jeweled cloisonné tank emblems and serialized nameplates.*

With the century's last decade came substantial reason for renewed optimism in Milwaukee. Harley-Davidson stock was doing well, plans were underway for the 90th anniversary celebration and the new engine and chassis technology had proved out. Many riders who had given up on Harley had returned to the fold.

The first version of the Sturgis in 1981 was more successful in terms of style than engineering. The combination and design of primary and final belt drive systems made service difficult, but many fans were favorably impressed with the unified look of the motorcycle, enhanced by the black-on-black motif.

None of which was lost on Willie G., who happened to admire the bike himself. So in 1991 the new, improved Sturgis appeared with chain primary drive, a single front disc brake and absent the oversized air-cleaner cover. The Dyna Glide frame situated the Evo engine farther forward and inclined four degrees aft. Built to showcase the new chassis, the Sturgis was a considerable improvement on the original in terms of engineering but remained a limited edition model, with only 1,546 examples built.

Harley's sales at home and abroad had been growing steadily for five years, and Milwaukee was once again positioned to produce limited-run specials based on current production models. Their stock price had quintupled in the same period, then split two-for-one. The management team of 13 men who had bought the company ten years earlier were now wealthy, as were those with the foresight or luck to have bought lots of Harley stock early on.

Fortunately no widespread profit-taking among the principals diluted Harley-Davidson's capacity to reinvest in the company, and to maintain the pace of product development it had established in the early '80s. Which they did. As plans for the revolutionary phase of engine design were in the preliminary stages, the company finalized preparations for its 90th anniversary celebration in 1993. The FX series (Low Rider/Super Glide) now covered a range of six models, and the topmost Electra Glide was fitted with an American-made C.B. radio, automotive-style cruise control and air suspension.

Had there been any doubts about Milwaukee's sense of restored fortunes and sense of security, they were put to rest in 1994 with the unveiling of Harley-Davidson's first purpose-built racing machine in its history. The VR 1000 roadracer, developed to compete in AMA Superbike racing, was recently retired after eight years of what could only charitably be called limited success. But it served as a demanding test bed for Harley's secrecy shrouded power cruiser to be unveiled in 2001.

Harley-Davidson was now in the enviable position of struggling to keep up with the demand for its products. With most of the design and engineering resources now

RIGHT: *The 1992 Dyna Daytona commemorated 50 years of racing in Florida. The gold pearlglo/indigo blue metallic color combination was Harley's first true pearl paint. Only 1,700 limited-edition models were built.*

ABOVE: *The Twin Cam 88 made its debut in 1999. The number indicated cubic inches, which brought a healthy increase in torque, horsepower and acceleration.*

devoted to the forthcoming V-Rod, existing models received minor modifications in style and function. The FLHR Road King replaced the Electra Glide Sport, and featured a new 5-gallon (18.9lit) tank fitted with an electronic speedometer and digital odometer. The Dyna Low Rider got similar instrument upgrades in 1995, plus a half-inch (1.27cm) reduction in seat height.

The FXDS Convertible Low Rider displaced the Sport model in 1996, and the Sportster line added Custom and Sport models. The Softails, in both FX and FL configurations, went largely unchanged but for color options and graphics. Fuel injection was now standard on the Ultra Classic Tour Glide, and optional on the Classic and Ultra Classic Electra Glides. The Weber-Marelli system not only improved the tourers' fuel mileage, but met the strict California emissions requirements without using a catalytic converter.

The second-generation Evolution engine, the Twin Cam 88, was unveiled at Harley-Davidson's 95th anniversary celebration in 1998. The bigger-inch twin featured single-fire ignition in place of the wasted spark system, made more horsepower and torque and was offered with either a carburetor or fuel injection. Introduced in the Road Glide, the Twin Cam was fitted to the Softails in 1999. Improvements continued to be made in Milwaukee, and the Twin Cam 88B appeared in 2000 with vibration-reducing counterbalancers.

Evolution at Harley-Davidson was moving on apace, and the stage was set for something a bit more revolutionary.

1991 FXDB Sturgis; 1992 FXDB

Willie G. and the designers had had such fun with the Fat Boy, they figured it was time the Sturgis made its encore. With the enhancement of the Evolution engine, a new chassis and belt-drive system, the new FXDB was all but a completely different machine.

The Dyna Glide frame, with square-section backbone, forged junctions and two rubber-mount engine attachments, moved the oil tank below the transmission. Slightly longer than the original Sturgis, the '91 had a higher handlebar and seat and a single disc front brake. The black-on-black color scheme with orange highlights remained distinctive.

The belt drive system had been improved considerably in the interim, in terms of both performance and ease of maintenance. Since many riders had been asking for a new version of the Sturgis for nearly a decade, the time was right for a new example that would also serve to introduce yet another sort of Super Glide with the new bits of technology.

The next platform for the computer-aided Dyna chassis design was the FXDB Daytona,

BELOW: *Seat height on the Sturgis was a manageable 29 inches (74cm). Traditional racing colors maintained continuity.*

1991 FXDB

Bartels' Harley-Davidson,
Marina Del Rey, California

BELOW LEFT: *As Milwaukee's first computer-aided chassis design, the Sturgis marked another significant step in the modernization of Harley-Davidson. With more young, qualified engineers on the staff, the pace of progress had quickened.*

LEFT: *The Daytona marked the introduction of Harley-Davidson's first "true pearl paint." Double front disc brakes were standard on the Dyna Glides and some of the Super Glide models, while the Softails still had a single disc.*

1992 FXDB
Owner: Trev Deeley Museum, Vancouver, British Columbia

LEFT: *The Sturgis gained 2 inches (5cm) in wheelbase over the '81 model, and the price doubled.*

1992 FXDB DYNA DAYTONA

Engine: OHV 45° V-twin
Displacement: 81.65ci (1338cc)
Bore & Stroke: 3.5 x 4.25in (89 x 108mm)
Compression ratio: 8.5:1
Horsepower: 72 @ 4,000rpm
Carburetion: 40mm Keihin
Transmission: 5-speed
Primary drive: Duplex chain
Final drive: Belt
Battery: 12-volt
Ignition: CDI
Frame: Steel, double downtube

Brakes: F. Dual discs; R. Disc
Suspension: F. Telescopic fork; R. Shocks
Wheelbase: 65.5in (166.4cm)
Weight: 630lb (286kg)
Fuel capacity: 4.9gal (18.5lit)
Oil capacity: 3qts (2.8lit)
Tires: F. 100/90-19; R. 130/90-16
Top speed: 103mph (166km/h)
Color: Gold pearlgo/indigo blue metallic
Number built: 1,700
Price: $12,120

built as a limited edition for the 50th anniversary of the Florida race in 1991. Released as a '92 model, the Daytona featured commemorative graphics on gold pearl/indigo blue metallic paint and an inscribed air-cleaner cover. Production of the Daytona was limited to 1,700 examples.

1993 FXDWG; 1991 FXRS; 1992 FXSTS

H arley-Davidson had pumped its motorcycle production from under 30,000 in 1982 to over 65,000 in 1991. Having successfully upgraded the engine, running gear and accessory components, Milwaukee continued the proven process of spinning off more variations of established models.

Since 1993 marked Harley's 90th anniversary, no fewer than six special Anniversary Edition models were readied for the large party held in Milwaukee. The FXDWG Wide Glide took the theme back to the big twin choppers of the '60s, with kicked-out fork, spoked wheels and a bobbed rear fender. With 21- and 16-inch (53.3 and 40.6cm) wheels fore and aft, forward-mount foot controls and custom seat, the Wide Glide was a burly boy for the boulevard. The jeweled cloisonné emblems and silver/charcoal satin-brite paint set it apart from the crowd. Production was limited to 1,993 machines.

In 1991 the FXR Low Rider, in Standard and Custom trim, accounted for about a third of the FX output of some 9,000 motorcycles. The FXR Super Glide and the Convertible both gained popularity, while the Sport Glide and Low Rider Sport filled out the six-model roster.

The FXSTS Springer was in its third model year in 1992, now with a more form-fitting front fender, studded seat and saddlebags.

1992 FXSTS
Dudley Perkins Company, San Francisco, California

1993 FXDWG

Engine: OHV 45° V-twin	**Suspension**: F. Telescopic fork; R. shocks
Displacement: 81.65ci (1338cc)	
Bore & stroke: 3.5 x 4.25in (89 x 108mm)	**Wheelbase**: 66.1in (167.9cm)
Compression ratio: 8.5:1	**Weight**: 615lb (279kg)
Horsepower: 72 @ 4,000rpm	**Fuel capacity**: 5.2gal (19.7lit)
Carburetion: 38mm Keihin	**Oil capacity**: 3qts (2.8lit)
Transmission: 5-speed	**Tires**: F. MH90-21; R. 130/90-16
Primary drive: Duplex chain	
Final drive: Belt	**Top speed**: 110mph (177km/h)
Brakes: F. & R. Disc	**Colors**: Vivid black; victory red/sun-glo; aqua sun-glo/silver
Battery: 12-volt	
Ignition: CDI	**Number built**: 5,602 (including 1,993 Anniversary)
Frame: Steel, double downtube	**Price**: $12,550

OPPOSITE TOP LEFT: *The Softail Springer adopted the cowboy motif in 1992. Optional accessories included a windshield, two-into-one exhaust system with fishtail muffler and stylishly curved luggage rack. Traditionalists could even choose a chromed '40s-style ribbed tool box to complete the retro look in style and fashion.*

1991 FXRS
Harley-Davidson of Sacramento, Sacramento, California

ABOVE: *The FXRS upheld the sporting segment of the lineup. With four Low Rider models, the Super Glide, Sport Glide and Convertible, Harley had their gliders in order.*

RIGHT: *In celebration of their 90th anniversary, Harley-Davidson adorned the 1993 limited-edition commemorative models with special paint and graphics.*

1993 FXDWG
Los Angeles Harley-Davidson, South Gate, California

ABOVE: *The Wide Glide, the more politically correct form for Fat Bob, also had the benefit of the Dyna chassis. The Low Rider version had cast-alloy wheels, with spoked rims an option.*

1993 FLHTC; 1995 FLHR; 1994 VR 1000

Naturally the Electra Glide didn't go unrecognized in the spread of 90th Anniversary Editions. The run of 1,340 of the mighty Eighties was distinguished by the silver/gray black paint scheme and cloisonné emblems, and a new auto-type cruise control package.

The oil pan now resided below the engine, and the level checked by a dipstick. The battery had moved from the saddlebag to below the seat, and the stronger new bags had permanently attached lids. The suspension at both ends was adjustable by air pressure, a feature shared by all FL models.

The Electra Glide Sport, the economy model of the line, had been the hindmost hog for several years. It was succeeded in 1994 by the FLHR Road King which, while still sporty by FL standards, offered more versatility as a cruiser/tourer. Quick-detach passenger seat, windshield and saddlebags meant the Road King could change outfits, and purposes, in a matter of minutes.

1993 FLHTC ULTRA CLASSIC

Engine: OHV 45° V-twin
Displacement: 81.65ci (1338cc)
Bore & stroke: 3.5 x 4.25in (89 x 108mm)
Compression ratio: 8.5:1
Horsepower: 72 @ 4,000rpm
Carburetion: 38mm Keihin
Transmission: 5-speed
Primary drive: Duplex chain
Final drive: Belt
Brakes: F. Dual discs; R. Disc
Battery: 12-volt
Ignition: CDI
Weight: 774lb (351kg)

Frame: Steel, double downtube
Suspension: F. Telescopic fork; R. Shocks
Wheelbase: 62.9in (159.9cm)
Fuel capacity: 5gal (18.9lit)
Oil capacity: 4qts (3.8lit)
Tires: F. & R. MT90-16
Top speed: 110mph (177km/h)
Colors: Vivid black; victory red sun-glo; two-tone aqua sun-glo/silver; two-tone victory red sun-glo/silver (option: 90th anniversary livery)
Number built: 3,702
Price: $15,349

BELOW: *The travel trunk lid was now hinged on the side for easier access, and saddlebag capacity went up by 15 percent. The rider's back rest was detachable.*

LEFT: *Rider and passenger got separate sound system controls, the pilot's situated on the left of the handlebar.*

1993 FLHTC ULTRA

Bartels' Harley-Davidson, Marina Del Rey, California

Harley's solvency was best illustrated by the appearance of the VR 1000 in 1994. After two decades' absence from roadracing, during which time the Japanese and Italians had gained considerable experience, Milwaukee issued forth a Superbike racing machine. With a 60-degree liquid-cooled V-twin, co-engineered by Porsche, and a twin-spar aluminum frame, the VR weighed 375 pounds (170kg) and made 135 horsepower. The racer faced a hard future in AMA National Superbike competition, and would be shelved after eight years.

BELOW: *The Road King was another example of Milwaukee's successful blending of traditional styling and contemporary technology. The '60s look and modern conveniences ensured the model's success.*

BELOW: *The solo seat and wide whitewall tires evoked the Road King's ancestry. The tank panel included a digital odometer and electronic speedometer. Optional fuel injection arrived in '96.*

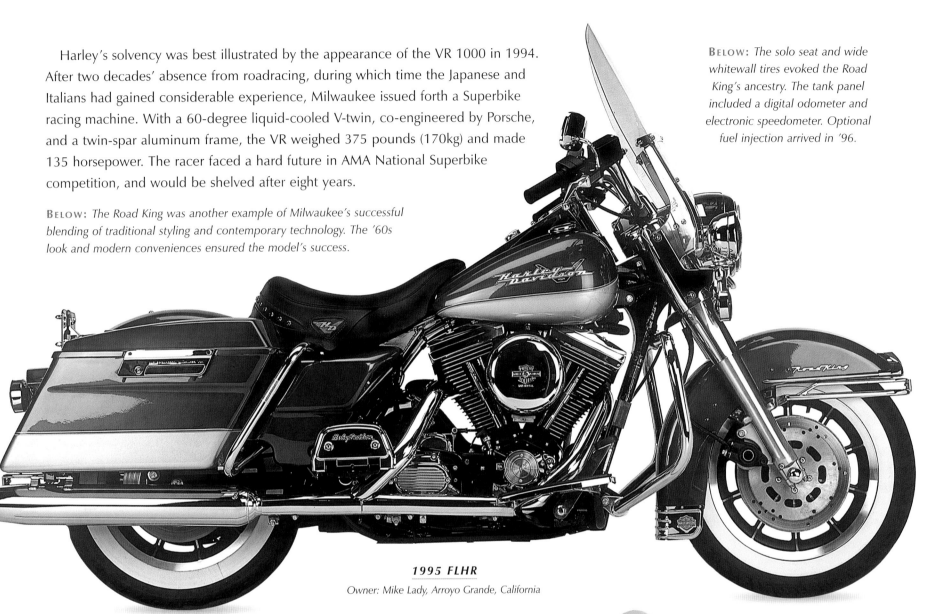

1995 FLHR
Owner: Mike Lady, Arroyo Grande, California

1995 FLHR ROAD KING

Engine: OHV 45° V-twin
Displacement: 80ci (1340cc)
Bore & stroke: 3.5 x 4.25in (89 x 108mm)
Compression ratio: 8.5:1
Torque: 77lb-ft @ 4,000rpm
Carburetion: 40mm Keihin
Transmission: 5-speed
Primary drive: Duplex chain
Final drive: Belt
Brakes: F. Dual disc; R. Disc
Battery: 12-volt
Ignition: Electronic
Frame: Steel, double downtube

Suspension: F. Air-adjustable fork; R. Dual air-adjustable shocks
Wheelbase: 62.9in (159.8cm)
Weight: 719lb (326kg)
Fuel capacity: 5gal (18.9lit)
Oil capacity: 4qts (3.8lit)
Tires: F. & R. MT90B-16
Top speed: 112mph (180km/h)
Colors: Vivid black; two-tone aqua pearl/silver; two-tone vivid black/silver; two-tone burgundy pearl/silver
Number built: 7,910
Price: $13,475

1994 VR 1000
Owner: Petersen Automotive Museum, Los Angeles, California

LEFT: *The VR 1000 showed promise in its first two years of Superbike competition, but never developed into a frontrunner. While the machine exhibited excellent handling characterstics, its power output, delivery and top speed remained at a slight deficit compared to the more well-established teams. Despite the talents of top riders, and engine assistance from Porsche, Harley withdrew the bike in 2001.*

1996 FXDS; 1996 XL 1200S

By 1996 the Low Rider outstripped the Sport by a wide margin in the FX stable, so the Convertible remained as the single sporting model of the lineup. With the Dyna chassis, the steering head angle tightened up a few degrees and the wheelbase was a bit shorter, which quickened the Convert's handling in the twisties.

Like its royal brother the Road King, the Convertible offered quick-detach accessories to facilitate the switch from sport to touring. The staggered shorty dual mufflers enhanced the sporty look, and buyers could choose between cast-alloy or standard spoked rims. At the sport-touring end of the Super Glide geneaology, the Convertible came to be well regarded by multi-purpose riders.

The next model to get the sport treatment was the Sportster itself, unveiled in both Sport and Custom models for 1996. All five XL models now featured five-speed transmissions and belt drive.

The Sport was fitted with adjustable suspension front and rear, double disc brakes in front and Dunlop Sport Elite tires. And the complaints about the limited range imposed by tiny fuel tanks were answered by the return of the 3.3-gallon (12.5lit) container. The Sportster Sport handled and stopped better, and went farther. The Custom featured shorter suspension, a disc rear wheel and 21-inch (53.3cm) spoked front wheel.

1996 XL 1200C
Owner: Harley-Davidson Motor
Co., Milwaukee, Wisconsin
© Harley-Davidson Archive photo

ABOVE: *Some Sportster enthusiasts had been calling for a sportier version for years, and it arrived in the 1200S. A more backroad-worthy Sporty was overdue.*

1996 XL 1200S
Los Angeles Harley-Davidson,
South Gate, California

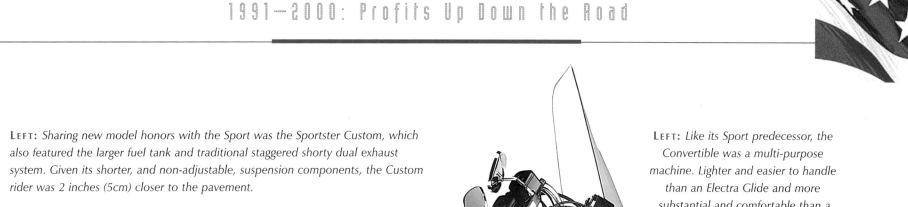

LEFT: *Sharing new model honors with the Sport was the Sportster Custom, which also featured the larger fuel tank and traditional staggered shorty dual exhaust system. Given its shorter, and non-adjustable, suspension components, the Custom rider was 2 inches (5cm) closer to the pavement.*

BELOW: *Some prospective buyers bemoaned the loss of the Low Rider Sport, but the Convertible proved even more agile and added the versatility of easy on/off saddlebags and windshield. The FXDXS was heavier by some 35 pounds (16kg), but had a bit more ground clearance.*

LEFT: *Like its Sport predecessor, the Convertible was a multi-purpose machine. Lighter and easier to handle than an Electra Glide and more substantial and comfortable than a Sportster, the Convert appealed to riders whose mileage divided fairly equally between day rides on the backroads, commuting to and from work and making the occasional long haul with or without a passenger.*

1996 FXDS

*Bartels' Harley-Davidson,
Marina Del Rey, California*

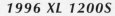

1996 XL 1200S	
Engine: OHV 45° V-twin	**Suspension:** F. 1.53in (3.9cm) cartridge fork; R. Dual gas-reservoir shocks
Displacement: 73.2ci (1200cc)	
Bore & stroke: 3.5 x 3.81in (89 x 97mm)	**Wheelbase:** 60.2in (152.9cm)
Compression ratio: 9:1	**Weight:** 512lb (232kg)
Horsepower: 63	**Fuel capacity:** 3.3gal (12.5lit)
Carburetion: 40mm Keihin CV	**Oil capacity:** 3qts (2.8lit)
Transmission: 5-speed	**Top speed:** 120mph (193km/h)
Primary drive: Triple-row chain	**Colors:** Vivid black; patriot red pearl; states blue pearl; violet pearl; two-tone victory sun-glo/platinum; two-tone violet/red pearl; two-tone platinum silver/black
Final drive: Chain	
Brakes: F. Dual disc; R. Disc	
Battery: 12-volt	
Ignition: CDI	
Frame: Steel, double downtube	
Tires: F. 100/90-19; R. 130/90-16	**Number built:** n/a
	Price: $7,910

1996 FXDS	
Engine: OHV 45° V-twin	**Suspension:** F. Telescopic fork; R. shocks
Displacement: 81.65ci (1338cc)	
Bore & stroke: 3.5 x 4.25in (89 x 108mm)	**Wheelbase:** 63.9in (162.3cm)
Compression ratio: 8.5:1	**Fuel capacity:** 4.9gal (18.5lit)
Horsepower: 72 @ 4,000rpm	**Oil capacity:** 3qts (2.8lit)
Carburetion: 38mm Keihin	**Tires:** F. 100/90-19; R. 130/90HB-16
Transmission: 5-speed	
Primary drive: Duplex chain	**Top speed:** 112mph (180km/h)
Final drive: Belt	**Colors:** Vivid black; patriot red pearl; states blue pearl; violet pearl; two-tone victory sun-glo platinum; two-tone violet/red pearl; two-tone platinum silver/black
Brakes: F. Dual discs; R. Disc	
Battery: 12-volt	
Ignition: CDI	
Frame: Steel, double downtube	
Weight: 638lb (289kg)	**Number built:** n/a
	Price: $13,330

1999 FLTRI Road Glide

Another large party in Milwaukee celebrated Harley's 95th anniversary in 1998. And the centerpiece was the second generation of the Evolution engine, the Twin Cam 88, as in cubic inches (1450cc), with an increase of 8 horsepower and 10 percent jump in torque. The new engine breathed through a 40mm CV carburetor (or optional sequential-port fuel injection) and sparked on a single-fire ignition system.

The bigger Evo powered the Road Glide tourer, with a frame-mount fairing and dual headlights, and a premium sound system. The objective was to offer more of everything—power, comfort and reliability—in the big tourer. The Twin Cam 88 would power the Softails a year later.

BELOW: *The Road figured more strongly in Harley model names in the late '90s. Joining the Road King (FLHR) and the Road King Classic (FLHRCI) was the Road Glide (FLTR/FLTRI) successor to the Tour Glide. Introduced in 1998, the mighty "custom touring" machine was the true monarch of the open road.*

The architecture of Milwaukee's massive frame-mount fairing served as the housing for the new heavy-duty wiring harness, full complement of instruments (including ambient air temperature gauge, clock and cigarette lighter), oval headlamps and stereo system. Cruise control was optional on the Road King.

1999 FLTRI ROAD GLIDE

Engine: OHV 45° V-twin
Displacement: 88ci (1450cc)
Bore & stroke: 3.75 x 4in (95 x 102mm)
Compression ratio: 8.9:1
Torque: 86lb-ft @ 3,500rpm
Carburetion: 40mm Keihin/ESPFI
Transmission: 5-speed
Primary drive: Duplex chain
Final drive: Belt
Brakes: F. Dual disc; R. Disc
Battery: 12-volt
Ignition: Electronic
Frame: Steel, double downtube
Suspension: F. Air-adjustable fork; R. Dual air-adjustable shocks
Wheelbase: 63.5in (161.3cm)
Weight: 750lb (340.2kg)
Fuel capacity: 5gal (18.9lit)
Oil capacity: 4qts (3.8lit)
Tires: F. & R. MT90B-16
Top speed: 112mph (180km/h)
Colors: Vivid black; lazer red pearl; aztec orange pearl; cobalt blue pearl
Number built: n/a
Price: $15,220

1999 FLTRI ROAD GLIDE
Surrey Harley-Davidson, Dorking, England.

The Buells

Buell Motorcycles, founded by former Harley engineer Erik Buell, had been building Harley-powered sportbikes since the mid-1980s. The motorcycles improved steadily, and Harley-Davidson subsequently moved from engine supplier to Buell motorcycles, to half-owner and then to full ownership of the company. The move of Erik Buell to full-time designer/engineer accelerated the development program, and Milwaukee ownership bumped up production schedules.

2000 BUELL BLAST
© Buell Motor Company

ABOVE: The single-cylinder Blast was conceived as a combination entry-level/budget machine for the youth market. With its moderate power, light weight and low price, new Harley riders were enticed.

1999 BUELL X1 LIGHTNING
Surrey Harley-Davidson, Dorking, England

ABOVE: The Lightning X1 displayed improved stream-lining and a more rigid chassis. Dynamic Digital fuel injection monitored atmospheric conditions for accurate metering. Frame and tail section were new for '99.

BELOW LEFT: Buell has been nibbling at the edges of sportbike technocracy for a decade. With the Firebolt XB9R, they have taken a large step toward the mainstream. With a short-stroke, 90-horsepower V-twin in an aluminum frame that doubles as a gas tank, it's the trickest Buell yet.

RIGHT: The Firebolt is compact; 52-inch (132cm) wheelbase, 21-degree steering head and an exceptionally low center of gravity (oil is carried in the swing arm). At under $10,000, the XB9R sets a new Yank sportbike standard.

2002 BUELL FIREBOLT
© Buell Motor Company

2000 FXSTB; 2000 FXST; 2000 FXDX

As the century turned, Harley-Davidson brought forth still another version of the latest V-twin—the Twin Cam 88B. Designed in parallel with the twin cam introduced in 1999, the B engine included twin counter-rotating balancers to quell primary vibration.

The new powerplant, aimed at making the Softail a better distance rider, appeared in the FXSTB with black-on-black motif, silver for the FXST and black-and-chrome in the other Softails. A new shifter mechanism eased gearchanges, and the chromed external oil lines recalled Harleys of yore. The new Softails also featured a new free-flow exhaust system and larger oil tank.

The Twin Cam 88B was also housed in a new frame, with overall stiffness improved by 34 percent. The frame incorporated a steering head lock and new rear suspension bushings for better suspension action. The Softies also inherited the new brake system, with four-piston fixed calipers and new brake pad material.

The FXDX Dyna Super Glide Sport, which debuted in 1999, was back with new adjustable suspension at both ends. With a cartridge-type fork, wider rear tire, free-flow ceramic-coated exhaust system and new cast-alloy wheels, the sporty Glide was ready to carve some corners.

2000 FXDX

Warr's Harley-Davidson, London, England

LEFT: *The Softail Night Train was little changed for 2000, but for the oval air cleaner.*

2000 FXSTB

Warr's Harley-Davidson, London, England

ABOVE: *Both the Softails and Dynas got the new B motor in 2000. Disc rear wheel, single front disc brake and drag-style handlebar remained standard equipment.*

LEFT: *The Dyna Super Glide Sport featured new brake discs and four-piston calipers front and rear. Cast wheels were standard, laced rims optional.*

2000 FXSTB

Engine: OHV 45° V-twin
Displacement: 88ci (1450cc)
Bore & stroke: 3.75 x 4in (95 x 102mm)
Compression ratio: 8.9:1
Torque: 85lb-ft @ 3,000rpm
Carburetion: 40mm cv/ESPFI
Transmission: 5-speed
Primary drive: Duplex chain
Final drive: Belt
Brakes: F. & R. Disc
Battery: 12-volt
Ignition: Electronic
Frame: Steel, double downtube
Suspension: F. Telescopic fork; R. Shocks
Wheelbase: 66.9in (169.9cm)
Weight: 650lb (294.8kg)
Fuel capacity: 5gal (18.9lit)
Oil capacity: 3qts (2.8lit)
Tires: F. MH90-21; R. 160/70-17
Top speed: 120mph (193km/h)
Color: Vivid black
Number built: n/a
Price: $15,825

2000 FXDX DYNA SUPER GLIDE SPORT

Engine: OHV 45° V-twin
Displacement: 88ci (1450cc)
Bore & stroke: 3.75 x 4in (95 x 102mm)
Compression ratio: 8.9:1
Torque: 82 lb-ft @ 3,500rpm
Carburetion: 40mm cv/ESPFI
Transmission: 5-speed
Primary drive: Duplex chain
Final drive: Belt
Brakes: Triple disc
Battery: 12-volt
Ignition: Electronic
Frame: Steel, double downtube
Suspension: F. Telescopic fork; R. Shocks
Wheelbase: 63.2in (160.53cm)
Weight: 640lb (290.3kg)
Fuel capacity: 4.9gal (18.5lit)
Oil capacity: 3qts (2.8lit)
Tires: F. 110/90-19; R. 150/90-16
Top speed: 120mph (193km/h)
Colors: Vivid black; luxury rich red; cobalt blue; pearl: diamond ice; orange; cobalt blue
Number built: n/a
Price: $13,595

living the dream

FAR RIGHT: *A well-lighted dresser outside the Hard Rock Café in London, a fitting symbol of Harley-Davidson's rebirth on an international scale. Sales were also strong throughout Europe, Japan and the Middle East.*

IT'S THE CLOSEST YOU'D EVER WANT TO SIT TO A PAIR OF THREE-INCH PISTONS.

IT TENDS TO MOSEY.

ABOVE: *The Sportster and the Softail had little in common in terms of form, function or ad headlines. The Softail was nicknamed "Cow Glide" for its cowhide trim.*

Harley-Davidson sailed into the 1990s on the wings of worldwide acclaim. Anyone who had predicted that Milwaukee's recovery would sputter and die had to admit they were mistaken. The Softail series was hugely successful, accounting in 1991 for more than 25,000 of the 65,500 motorcycles produced for the year.

More folks got interested in the Sportster when it was awarded a five-speed transmission, belt drive and the option of a 74ci (1200cc) engine. Noted sportbike enthusiast and *Cycle World* contributing editor Peter Egan bought a 1992 model and, as a concession to the onset of middle age (and an appreciation for his wife's comfort), added an Electra Glide Sport to his stable. While he made a few modifications to the Sportster to enhance its performance, Egan left the big twin in its original configuration. As he admitted to Harley-Davidson's historian, "I just can't find anything on it I want to change."

That ranks as high praise coming from a chronic tinkerer. But it illustrates one of the reasons for Harley's relatively swift return to credibility among touring riders. Because, compared to the sport riders, customizers and cruiser crowd, these are riders who don't relish spending a lot of time working on their motorcycles. They prefer to ride them, often quite some distances, without having to do much more than put fuel in the tank and air in the tires.

The Japanese motorcycle manufacturers, after a failed attempt to replicate the Harley-Davidson cruiser style in the 1980s, had another go at it in the 1990s. The Honda, Yamaha and Kawasaki low riders did achieve more integrated looks, and even the sound was a closer approximation of the familiar Harley rumble. But a comparison ride quickly demonstrated that the imports still didn't produce that familiar feel of mechanical unity.

The *Cycle World* editors compared the Harley Low Rider with the Honda Shadow and Kawasaki Vulcan, and admitted the imports were nicely finished. "But it's the Harley-Davidson that finally is the most appealing of the three," they concluded. "When the balloting is done, the Harley is America's number one Cruise Missle, the one that has drawn the surest bead on what it takes to cruise with class and style." While the Low Rider was the top seller in the Dyna lineup, most of the moto-scribes voted for the FXR Sport for handling qualities.

LEFT: *An early 1992 issue of* Hog Tales. *HOG was the first international, factory-directed riders' club. It helped Harley-Davidson be more effective in maintaining personal relationships with its customers.*

ABOVE: *Rock stars and Harleys have always been a good match, which didn't change in the 1990s. Jon Bon Jovi and friend are shown on the set of his music video titled "Blaze of Glory."*

The Harley Owners Group (HOG), created in 1983, had grown to more than 650 chapters worldwide and about 100,000 members. The organization was a natural corollary to the factory-dealer-rider support system, and membership included a newsletter, special premiums and organized rallies. Affiliated dealers participated in the organization of monthly meetings, local rides and associated community activities. The HOG had quickly become the largest factory-sponsored club in the world.

Harley-Davidson took another significant step in 1995 by offering fuel injection for the first time. While the big, air-cooled V-twin had been considerably refined in its evolutionary development, the electronic squirters brought it squarely into the present in terms of trouble-free motoring. Milwaukee's assertion that "things are different on a Harley" challenged the latest batch of Japanese cruisers. And it was true.

Above and Right: *Main Street in Sturgis, South Dakota becomes Harley-Davidson Boulevard every year in August. Not all the machines on hand are made in Milwaukee, but imported brands are a distinct minority.*

"Look at all that rice! I can't believe there's this much rice. Ten years ago you wouldn't see any Hondas here. It's become a tourist attraction. No wonder the Hell's Angels don't come here anymore."

Overheard at Sturgis '92

The modernization of Milwaukee achieved positive results on more than just one front. Not only did the Evo engine attract riders who had been thinking about a Harley for a long time, it also provided another platform for the aftermarket parts businesses and customizing specialists. Since most Harley riders can be counted on to accessorize their machines to personal taste, a fair number will want something other than what the factory offers in terms of add-ons. Speciality builders like California's Arlen Ness and others had no problem incorporating the new, improved line of homegrown iron into their own evolutionary creations.

The August rally in Sturgis, South Dakota had become the obligatory destination for not only Harley riders of every description, but also vendors of every conceivable accessory for bike or body, biker memorabilia and associated artifacts. The city fathers and mothers of Sturgis had imposed more stringent rules on public displays of nudity, drug possession and other assorted misdemeanors, but the party just rolled on

ABOVE: *Daytona Beach, or what some call "Sturgis South," hosts the annual rites of spring in March every year. Access to the beach is less free than it was in the old days, but the sun and sea is welcomed by northern riders.*

ABOVE: *Among the competition sidelights at Sturgis is a traditional hillclimb, which always attracts some interesting machinery and riding techniques.*

ABOVE: *Harley-Davidson advertising in Great Britain puts the emphasis on accessories, probably since the motorcycles sell well enough with little help. Most of the gear is the same as Stateside issue, but the copywriting conforms more closely to the Queen's English.*

regardless. And the Harley-Davidson showcase, including demo rides, was ever present.

The annual riders' rites of spring in Daytona also carried on as the biggest biker bash on the eastern seaboard. While parking and riding on the beach had been restricted over the years, most of the snowbirds would not be dissuaded by minor considerations. The combinations of sun, surf, racing events and the Main Street parade were attractions enough. While Harley-Davidsons didn't hold the same high ratio over other brands as Sturgis did, Milwaukee iron still held the majority.

Speaking of majorities, many riders had now reached their seniority. Those born in the '40s and '50s were now in their 40s and 50s, and many of them had traded their enthusiasm for light and middleweight roadburners for motorcycles offering more in terms of comfort and features. So Harley-Davidson had the benefit of not only a backlog of riders who had long wanted a Hog and could now afford one, but also those who had recently "matured" into the Milwaukee mode.

RIGHT AND FAR RIGHT: *Posters heralding an exhibition entitled "The Art of the Harley" staged at the Barbican Art Gallery, London in 1998, a feature of the "Inventing America: A Year of American Culture" focus.*

ABOVE: *A commemorative buckle for Harley's 90th anniversary in 1993 incorporates the eagle, bar-and-shield and a drive chain.*

ABOVE: *The Enthusiast for Summer/Fall 1994 featured the specialized art of hillclimbers, how they do it and why.*

In 1998 Harley-Davidson celebrated its 95th anniversary with a gathering of the clan in Milwaukee. The total turnout was in the neighborhood of 160,000 riders, nearly one-third of them members of the Harley Owners Group. According to the AMA magazine, the attendees deposited some $120 million in the local economy.

Harley's continuing techno-prowess was winning over even more fans as the 1990s wound down. The Twin Cam 88 engine, at a whompin' 88ci (1450cc), made more power than the original Evo powerplant, and the Dyna Glide was getting good marks for handling as well. Not that the engine made its debut in seamless fashion. Like some early inaugural editions of past Milwaukee motors, the Twin Cam exhibited some problems with the bolts that held the cams in place. Harley issued a recall on about 14,000 bikes and the problem was rectified at the dealerships.

In its long, continuing campaign to induce owners to use factory parts, Harley offered hop-up kits for several models. By offering moderate horsepower gains, with parts installed by authorized dealers, it could offer riders more invigorating performance while keeping the engine within its design limits and the original warranty. This arrangement seems to be working to the advantage of both Milwaukee and the customer so far, and has had little discernible effect on the aftermarket segment of parts and accessories.

Rolling into the 21st century, Harley-Davidson was steady on its line and in the middle of its powerband. The competition had never been stronger; the Japanese cruisers had come much closer to The Look, were eminently user-friendly and easier on the bank balance than Milwaukee iron and similar models from Ducati and BMW were attracting their fair share of riders. Plus, a new home-grown contestant appeared called the Victory—a 1500cc oil-cooled V-twin built by Polaris Industries of Iowa.

Still, Harley maintained its position as the cruiser king. When *Cycle World* passed out their awards for the Ten Best Bikes of 2000, Best Cruiser went to the Harley-Davidson Deuce. The magazine also gave Milwaukee a nod for the Buell Blast among the Honorable Mentions, citing the marketing savvy behind a moderately priced entry-level machine.

In the words of the Road Scholar, Clement Salvadori, reigning mileage master of American motojournalists, "Harleys cost a lot of money, but a lot of people want them. And they have come a long way. I rode the first Softail, 1984, to New Mexico and I hated it because of the vibration. I rode the new Twin Cam Softail and I loved it. That engine is quite an exceptional achievement. The V-Rod has a very impressive engine and it's a handsome bike. But it's an urban motorcycle, for going to the tavern and then going home; not for trips.

"As long as Americans have money to spend, Harley-Davidson will succeed. The Japanese are catching up, so it may be a different story in ten years. But if Harley can keep their production down to sensible levels, they'll sell all the Softails they can make. Their biggest success has been the Harley Owners Group. The membership is now over 500,000. A good club is going to sell a lot of motorcycles."

ABOVE: *The open road, a summer day and the rolling rhythm from a group of V-twins. In a non-helmet-law state.*

RIGHT: *Mrs. Davidson never did quite come to terms with the fact that those boys could spend so much time out in the shed.*

"FINE, WE'LL JUST EAT WITHOUT YOU THEN!"

2001-03: Evolving New Species

decade design evolution

"Boy, I hope that new V-Rod is fast and handles well, 'cause it sure is F-U-G-L-Y. Harley took their design integrity (no covers, everything looked like what it was, etc.) and turned it on its ear. An air cleaner that looks like a gas tank, a liquid-cooled engine with cooling fins? They took everything that makes a Harley a Harley and threw it out the window."

MATT GIANGRECO, BROOKLYN, NEW YORK CYCLE WORLD

"I can't believe my eyes! A water-cooled Harley? Is it finally true that Harley plans on giving us reliability and performance? Now maybe some of the Harley faithful will venture into water-cooled territory, and hooray for them."

DAVID OLSON, BROOMFIELD, COLORADO CYCLE WORLD

Most observers expected Harley-Davidson to continue the cautious development process of the century past. Production and sales figures continued to set new records, and there seemed little reason to part with tradition. No widespread rumors circulated about any revolutionary new designs from Milwaukee.

Harley's 2001 models included the Dyna Super Glide T-Sport, with quick-detach soft bags and adjustable windshield, a police model called the Dyna Defender and a lowered Dyna Low Rider. No bold or groundbreaking news there.

But the big news came at mid-year with the introduction of the 2002 V-Rod. While the name sounded like just another curious Milwaukee moniker, the motorcycle itself was a hog from a whole 'nother farm. Developed over seven years in CIA-type security, the V-Rod shared no major components with any previous Harley, although the engine design was based on the VR-1000 roadracer.

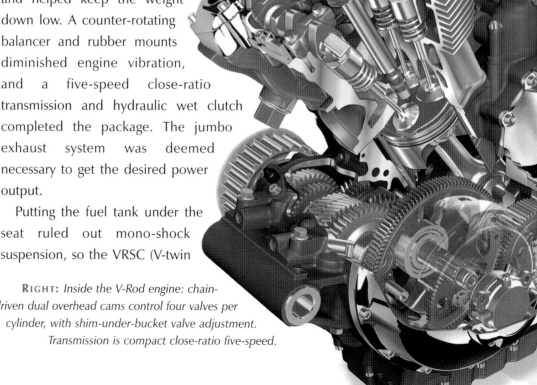

An 1130cc liquid-cooled V-twin with cylinders displaced at 60 degrees, unlike traditional Harley V-twins the V-Rod engine makes just 74lb-ft of torque at 7,000rpm. The wet-sump design eliminated the oil tank and associated plumbing, and helped keep the weight down low. A counter-rotating balancer and rubber mounts diminished engine vibration, and a five-speed close-ratio transmission and hydraulic wet clutch completed the package. The jumbo exhaust system was deemed necessary to get the desired power output.

Putting the fuel tank under the seat ruled out mono-shock suspension, so the VRSC (V-twin

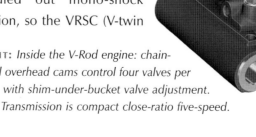

RIGHT: *Inside the V-Rod engine: chain-driven dual overhead cams control four valves per cylinder, with shim-under-bucket valve adjustment. Transmission is compact close-ratio five-speed.*

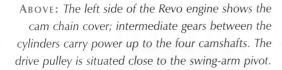

Racing Street Custom) wears standard dual shock absorbers. Up front the 49mm fork, raked at 38 degrees, carries a spun aluminum wheel and dual floating brake rotors with dual piston calipers and braided steel lines. The 34-degree steering head brought trail to 4 inches (10cm), providing some measure of low-speed turning agility. Willie G. had insisted on the extended fork to achieve the desired dragster look, though space was obviously required for the cumbersome radiator hung on the downtubes.

The perimeter frame, built up from 1.5-inch (3.8cm) hydroformed steel tubing and joined by investment castings, offered both substantial rigidity and a prominent design element. Combined with anodized aluminum panels, louvered covers and canted auto-style headlight, the V-Rod incorporates contemporary and retro styling cues in a coherent package.

Public comments on the looks of the new Harley were about equally divided between awed admiration and complete disgust. But with a scheduled production run of only 11,000 for 2002, it seemed certain that the premier V-Rod would sell out before the end of the year. Equally clear, given the time and money Milwaukee had invested in the new machine, and the pressing need to attract numbers of younger customers, was that the V-Rod was only the first of many models to be built on this platform. Its success or failure will largely determine Harley-Davidson's fortunes in its second century.

ABOVE: *The left side of the Revo engine shows the cam chain cover; intermediate gears between the cylinders carry power up to the four camshafts. The drive pulley is situated close to the swing-arm pivot.*

LEFT: *The chassis was designed around the engine. The hydroformed frame doubles as structural and design elements; the tubes are bolted together in front of and below the engine for easy access.*

ABOVE: *Below-seat fuel tank left no space for mono-shock suspension, thus the traditional swing arm with dual shocks. The extra large exhaust system was dictated by noise standards and the engine's power.*

2001 FXDXT; 2001 FXSTD

Milwaukee expanded the multiple-use machine in 2001 with the Dyna Super Glide T-Sport powered by a rubber-mount Twin Cam 88. The FXDXT carried a fork-mount fairing with a tinted windshield adjustable for both height and angle.

The T-Sport was fitted with quick-detach ballistic nylon saddlebags with watertight inner pouches, including slip-on rain covers for maximum weather-proofing. The bags could also be adjusted from narrow to wide profile according to the amount of gear the rider carried. The FXDXT also rode on adjustable front and rear suspension, and featured a larger touring seat than the standard FXDX. Both models shared the new bullet-style turn signals and 3-inch (7.6cm) diameter mufflers. The new pearl colors for 2001 were luxury blue, concord purple and suede green.

The FXSTD Softail Deuce, introduced in 2000, returned with the option of electronic fuel injection, now available on all the Softails. The Deuce also got new stacked shotgun exhaust pipes. A new 38-amp charging system was also common to the FX models, and an optional security system to disable the ignition.

2001 FXDXT

Surrey Harley-Davidson
Dorking, England

2001 FXSTD

Surrey Harley-Davidson, Dorking, England

LEFT: The T-sport maintained the all-rounder tradition of the original Super Glide Sport and the Convertible. Configured as a versatile sport-tourer, the T was a bike for most seasons.

ABOVE: The Deuce extended the tradition of the first Low Rider and the ensuing quarter-century of kicked-back cruisers with an attitude. The laced 21-inch (53.3cm) front wheel, disc rim on the rear, deeply scooped saddle and shotgun pipes combine to demand attention from pedestrians, motorists and fellow riders alike. The stretched fuel tank was new for 2001, and new fenders enhanced the leaner-is-meaner profile.

2001 FXSTD SOFTAIL DEUCE

Engine: OHV 45° V-twin
Displacement: 88ci (1450cc)
Bore & stroke: 3.75 x 4in (95 x 102mm)
Compression ratio: 8.9:1
Torque: 85lb-ft @ 3,000rpm
Carburetion: 40mm cv/ESPFI
Transmission: 5-speed
Primary drive: Duplex chain
Final drive: Belt
Brakes: F. & R. Disc
Battery: 12-volt
Ignition: Electronic
Frame: Steel, double downtube
Suspension: F. Telescopic fork; R. Shocks
Wheelbase: 66.6in (1690.3mm)
Weight: 660lb (299.4kg)
Fuel capacity: 4.9gal (18.5lit)
Oil capacity: 3qts (2.8lit)
Tires: F. MH90-21; R. 160/70-17
Top speed: 120mph (193km/h)
Colors: Vivid black; pearl: luxury blue; diamond ice; real teal; luxury rich red; concord purple
Number built: n/a
Price: $16,325

2001 FXDXT DYNA SUPER GLIDE T-SPORT

Engine: OHV 45° V-twin
Displacement: 88ci (1450cc)
Bore & stroke: 3.75 x 4in (95 x 102mm)
Compression ratio: 8.9:1
Torque: 82 lb-ft @ 3,500rpm
Carburetion: 40mm cv/ESPFI
Transmission: 5-speed
Primary drive: Duplex chain
Final drive: Belt
Brakes: Triple disc
Battery: 12-volt
Ignition: Electronic
Frame: Steel, double downtube
Weight: 660lb (299.4kg)
Suspension: F. Telescopic fork; R. Shocks
Wheelbase: 63.2in (1603.5mm)
Fuel capacity: 4.9gal (18.5lit)
Oil capacity: 3qts (2.8lit)
Tires: F. 110/90-19; R. 130/90-16
Top speed: 120mph (193km/h)
Colors: Vivid black; pearl: luxury blue; diamond ice; jade sunglo; luxury rich red; concord purple; suede green
Number built: n/a
Price: $14,925

2002 V-Rod

Harley surprised everyone with the 2002 V-Rod. Not only did Milwaukee unveil its first entirely new street model in 50 years, they had managed to keep it secret throughout the development process.

Nearly everything about the V-Rod is different from all other Harley-Davidsons. The engine, based on the design of the VR 1000 racer, is a liquid-cooled, dual overhead cam, 69ci (1130cc) 60-degree V-twin that makes 115 horsepower. The perimeter frame, built with a hydroform process, houses the fuel tank under the seat. And the 67.5-inch (171.5cm) wheelbase is accentuated by the 38-degree fork angle and spun aluminum disc wheels.

The V-Rod engine, developed in cooperation with Porsche Engineering Services, features four valves per cylinder, wet-sump lubrication and sequential-port fuel injection. Power is transmitted through a hydraulically-actuated wet clutch and five-speed close-ratio transmission.

While the power train marked a departure from Harley-Davidson tradition, the styling of the V-Rod also signified a new direction for Milwaukee-based designs. The drag cruiser motif, starkly framed by the anodized aluminum panels and powder-coat platinum surfaces, express Willie G. Davidson's continuing reverence for American industrial design as folk art. The V-Rod represents Harley's first bold design and engineering statement for the 21st century, and will serve as the platform for many models to come.

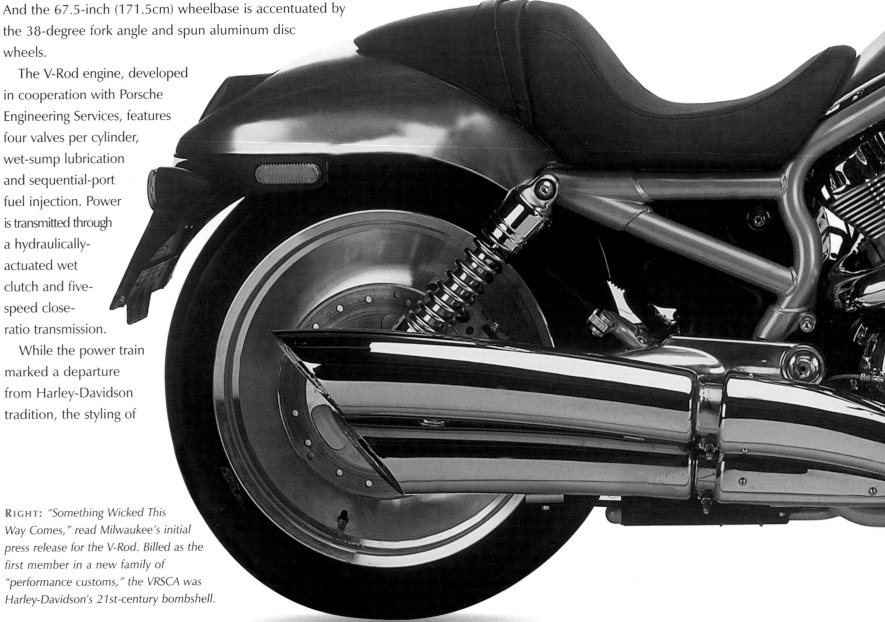

RIGHT: *"Something Wicked This Way Comes," read Milwaukee's initial press release for the V-Rod. Billed as the first member in a new family of "performance customs," the VRSCA was Harley-Davidson's 21st-century bombshell.*

BELOW: *The silver powder coated frame, aluminum bodywork and subdued engine treatment recall the Fat Boy motif. But the V-Rod, despite its weight, carries some real muscle.*

2002 V-ROD

Engine: 60° DOHC V-twin	**Frame:** Steel perimeter
Displacement: 69ci (1130cc)	**Suspension:** F. Telescopic fork;
Bore & stroke: 3.94 x 2.83in	R. Dual shocks
(100 x 72mm)	**Wheelbase:** 67.5in (171.45cm)
Compression ratio: 11.3:1	**Weight:** 615lb (279kg)
Horsepower: 115 @ 8,500 rpm	**Fuel capacity:** 4gal (15.14lit)
Torque: 74lb-ft @ 7,000rpm	**Oil capacity:** 4qts (3.8lit)
Carburetion: ESPFI	**Tires:** F. 120/70-19;
Transmission: 5-speed	R. 180/55-18
Primary drive: Spur gear	**Top speed:** 135mph
Final drive: Belt	(217km/h)
Brakes: Triple disc	**Color:** Anodized aluminum/silver
Battery: 12-volt	**Number built:** 11,000
Ignition: Electronic	**Price:** $16,995

LEFT: *Liquid cooling requires a radiator—always a problem for designers and engineers. Outboard scoops feed the air and oil coolers. Functional, yes. But attractive? C'mon.*

2002 V-ROD
Warr's Harley-Davidson, London, England

200? Pork Futures

Forecasting the look of Harley-Davidson models of the future is a dodgy enterprise. While no one outside Willie G.'s studio can make any realistic predictions, we hold a few self-evident truths. One is that model changes have never come abruptly from Milwaukee, and no doubt never will. Another is that the air-cooled V-twin will not disappear in the near future, notwithstanding any imminent federal restrictions based on dubious notions of science and the public welfare. Finally, the V-Rod is likely to be around for quite some time, joined by such future cousins as the V-Tour, V-Sport, Super Sport, etc. It should be an interesting century.

LEFT: *Designer Glynn Kerr's WC 1000 Supertracker anticipates the basic roadster version of the VR 1000 roadracer. The traditional XR 750 profile holds the liquid-cooled DOHC V-twin, inverted fork and massive front brakes.*

BELOW: *Hector Cademartori envisions the V-Rod in sport-touring trim. The windshield and driving lights add real-world functionality, while spoked wheels add sportiness. The seat, backrest, luggage rack and soft bags support the bike's touring capability, and rider/ passenger footboards enhance comfort. Straight stacked mufflers are tidy and muscular.*

OPPOSITE PAGE, BOTTOM: *Sculptor Steve Posson's design for a V-Rod sportbike subtracts about 10 inches (25.4cm) from the wheelbase. The exhaust system incorporates a finned aluminum muffler below the engine, disguised as an oil sump. Radiator and side-mount fuel tanks are aluminum. The sectional drawing shows intakes for the airbox. Instruments are behind the headlight.*

© POSSON 01

POSSON 01

LEFT: *The 1903 single was the first production Harley-Davidson. The new company turned out three motorcycles the first year, at a price of $200 each.*

LEFT: *"Have you a second-hand machine to sell? A MotorCycling classified ad will do the business for you. Advertisements of this nature cost 50¢ for 50 words or less." Classified advertising was a key revenue source for publications in the 1910s.*

| 1903 | 1904 | 1905 | 1906 | 1907 | 1908 | 1909 | 1910 | 1911 | 1912 | 1913 | 1914 | 1915 | 1916 | 1917 | 1918 | 19 |

1903 Wilbur and Orville Wright of Dayton, Ohio, achieve the first heavier-than-air plane flight at Kittyhawk, North Carolina. Henry Ford starts automobile production.

1907 Second floor added to new factory. Harley-Davidson incorporates and sells stock to its 17 employees; first V-twin prototype built.

1914 Production for the year reaches 16,247. New features include the step-starter, two-speed rear hub and footboards.

1918 World War I ends.

1905 The Harley-Davidson Motor Company hires its first outside employee. Production is up to eight machines for the year.

1908 Walter Davidson wins the national endurance run in New York with a perfect score. Milwaukee production is up to 450 machines.

1917 United States enters World War I. Racing is discontinued and Milwaukee devotes half its workforce to military production.

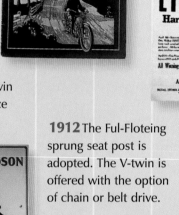

1909 Harley's first V-twin reaches the market; price is $325.

1904 The first Harley factory/shed doubles in size to 300 square feet (28m²).

1907 The first helicopter flight made in France by Paul Cornu.

1912 The Ful-Floteing sprung seat post is adopted. The V-twin is offered with the option of chain or belt drive.

1915 Harley replaces gas lights with electrical units. A new three-speed transmission is fitted, and an internal oil pump improves lubrication.

1906 Arthur Davidson produces the company's first catalog. Larger factory erected on Chestnut Street; total output rises to 50 motorcycles.

1913 The 5-35 single (5 horsepower/35 cubic inches) debuts at $290. The 8-horsepower twin sells for $350.

1916 Racing kits are offered for the V-twin. Irving Janke wins the Dodge City 300 on a Harley eight-valve.

1904 Russia and Japan go to war over Manchuria.

1919 The Sport Model opposed twin debuts to less than enthusiastic acclaim. Harley builds its own electrical system

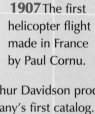

1911 Harley-Davidson manufactures a total of 5,625 motorcycles.

ABOVE: *Early advertising portrayed the gentleman rider, fashionably dressed, as an independent fellow with a sense of both adventure and style.*

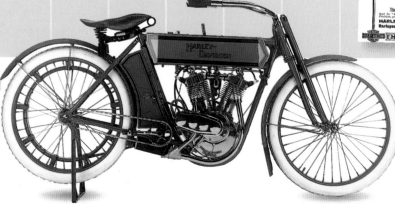

LEFT: *In 1911 the revised Harley V-twin appeared with mechanical intake valves. The belt-drive twin, magneto ignition only, was priced at $300.*

Left: *Red Parkhurst and Fred Ludlow (in sidecar) went to Daytona Beach in 1920 for a series of record runs. The eight-valve set a new mark of 84mph (135km/h) with the sidecar, although the beach had been roughened by winter storms.*

LEFT: *The 1936 booklet "Let's Visit the Harley-Davidson Factory" encouraged clubs and riders to tour the Milwaukee facility and see the manufacturing process.*

20 | 1921 | 1922 | 1923 | 1924 | 1925 | 1926 | 1927 | 1928 | 1929 | 1930 | 1931 | 1932 | 1933 | 1934 | 1935 | 1936

1921 Harley-Davidson racing team wins all championship events.

1923 The eight-valve racer, produced in limited numbers from 1916–28, sets numerous speed records on board and dirt tracks.

1931 The Servi-Car, Milwaukee's response to the Indian Dispatch Tow three-wheeler, is introduced for commercial duty and police work. Empire State Building, the world's tallest, completed in New York. Al Capone goes to slammer for tax evasion.

920 Jim Davis wins the Dodge City 300 in record time on a Harley. Teammate Ray Weishaar akes the Marion, Indiana 200-miler.

1924 Former factory rider Ray Weishaar, 34, dies in racing accident at Legion Ascot raceway in Los Angeles.

1926 With the reintroduction of singles, H-D production climbs to 22,275.

1932 Aldous Huxley publishes a startling book titled "Brave New World."

1934 Harley advertises the Servi-Car as the NEW DEAL Delivery Unit.

1921 H-D rider Otto Walker runs first race at over 100mph (161km/h) in Fresno, California.

1927 Ricardo cylinder heads are adopted on the OHV singles. Plans are announced for a new 45ci (750cc) twin.

1930 Bill Davidson wins the 420-mile Jack Pine Tour on a Forty-five. Impact of stock market crash spreads across the country.

1932 Franklin Delano Roosevelt elected U.S. President. Amelia Earhart completes transatlantic flight.

1925 "Stream-Line" styling comes to Harley-Davidson. Rounded fuel tanks, smaller wheels and a new frame bring a lower profile.

1928 The Two-cam JH (Sixty-one/1000cc) and JDH (Seventy-four/1200cc) twins reach production. Improvements drawn from racing upgrade performance.

1933 Great Depression sinks deeper. Prohibition ends. Harley-Davidson institutes two-day work week.

1922 Harley switches from olive to brewster green with gold striping.

1935 Harley-mounted Joe Petrali wins all the national dirt track races.

ABOVE AND TOP RIGHT: *The new side-valve Forty-five (750cc) appeared in standard and high-compression versions in 1929. The two-cam JDH was introduced in 1928.*

RIGHT: *In 1935 Milwaukee unveiled the OHV Sixty-one Knucklehead as a '36 model.*

LEFT: *Harley marked the first year of U.S. war involvement with an Enthusiast feature on the Army Signal Corps dispatch riders.* **RIGHT:** *1948 Panhead was the last example of the leading-link girder/spring fork.*

| 1937 | 1938 | 1939 | 1940 | 1941 | 1942 | 1943 | 1944 | 1945 | 1946 | 1947 | 1948 | 1949 | 1950 | 1951 | 1952 | 19 |

1941 U.S. enters World War II when Japanese attack navy base at Pearl Harbor. Harley builds nearly 90,000 military models during the course of the war.

1937 The eldest Davidson brother, William A., dies at 66. Joe Petrali rides Knucklehead to new record of 136mph (219km/h) at Daytona Beach.

1939 Hitler's troops invade Poland; World War II begins.

1938 Nazi Army occupies Austria. Orson Welles' radio drama "War of the Worlds" spooks America.

1940 Harley and Indian compete for military contracts. Roosevelt wins third term as president.

1945 Allied victory in Europe; U.S. drops atomic bombs on Japanese islands of Hiroshima and Nagasaki. World War II ends.

1946 The Iron Curtain partitions Europe; Cold War begins. Milwaukee resumes civilian motorcycle production.

1947 Final year for the Knucklehead engine. Marlon Brando stars in Tennessee Williams' play, "A Streetcar Named Desire."

1942 Walter Davidson, founder and company president, dies in Milwaukee. First controlled nuclear reaction.

1943 Founder and design chief William Harley dies succeeded by his son, William J. Company is awarded Army-Navy Excellence Award for contribution to war effort.

1944 Allied forces invade Europe at Normandy on June 6.

1948 First Panhead engine. Middle-aged baseball pitcher Satchel Paige signs with Cleveland Indians, who win the World Series.

1950 Arthur Davidson, last of the four founders, and his wife die in auto accident. Korean War begins.

1952 New Harley K model appears, with unit gearbox, foot shift and hand clutch. Racing KR readied for following year. Dwight D. Eisenhower elected U.S. President.

1949 Hydra-Glide telescopic fork debuts on the big twins. North Atlantic Treaty Organization (NATO) formed. Black leather jackets become fashionable.

1951 Dick Klamfoth wins his second Daytona 200 on a Norton single.

ABOVE: *Schaber's Cycle Shop of Ithica, New York also repaired lawn mowers and baby carriages in 1938.*

ABOVE: *The 1942 military XA was a clone of the BMW.*

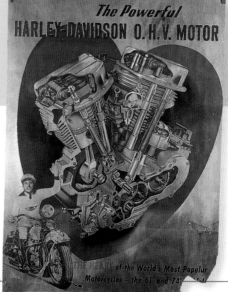

LEFT: *Cutaway drawings of the Harley-Davidson engines were popular since the first twin appeared. This illustration shows the working parts of the 1948 Panhead engine.*

LEFT: *The team of Joe Leonard and tuner Tom Sifton raised the level of competition in the early '50s with the K model.*
BELOW: *In 1958 the Hydra-Glide got rear suspension and became the Duo-Glide.*

LEFT: *Carroll Resweber won his fourth consecutive national title in 1961. Local favorite Ronnie Rall won the amateur race in the annual Charity Newsies in Columbus, Ohio.*

1963 William G. Davidson named H-D styling director. President John Kennedy assassinated. Accused murderer Lee Harvey Oswald killed by Jack Ruby.

1967 Astronauts Chaffee, Grissom and White die in launchpad fire. Richard Brautigan publishes "Trout Fishing in America."

1964 Fairings allowed at Daytona; Roger Reiman wins second 200-miler. Craig Breedlove sets new land speed record of 526mph (846.5km/h). The Beatles arrive in U.S.

1955 Brad Andres wins first of what would become seven straight Harley victories at Daytona.

1954 The K model grows to 54ci (883cc). Bobby Hills wins Daytona on a BSA 500cc twin.

1959 Carroll Resweber wins second consecutive national championship for Harley. Honda markets 50cc minibike in U.S.

1966 Shovelhead engine debuts with new aluminum heads. U.S. casualties rise in Vietnam; opposition to war grows in the States. Silent film star Buster Keaton dies at 70.

1958 Explorer I, first U.S. satellite, launched. Joe Leonard wins second Daytona in a row on KR 750.

1962 Don Burnett's Triumph breaks Harley's seven-win streak at Daytona. John Glenn is first American to orbit the earth. Barbara Tuchman publishes "The Guns of August."

1965 Last year for the Panhead engine. President Johnson authorizes combat role for U.S. troops in Vietnam. Albert Schweitzer dies at 90.

1968 Martin Luther King and Robert Kennedy assassinated. Richard Nixon elected President. Novelist John Steinbeck dies at 66.

1957 Russia launches Sputnik satellite; fearmongers proliferate in U.S.

1969 Harley-Davidson bought by American Machine and Foundry (AMF). Cal Rayborn wins second straight Daytona 200 on KR 750.

1960 Topper motor scooter introduced. Harley buys half interest in Italian Aermacchi company.

RIGHT: *The Panhead reached its development peak in 1965 with the addition of an electric starter. As the last model in an 18-year run, the final "electric leg" Pans grew in collectible status over the years and prices rose accordingly.*

ABOVE: *The K model was supplanted by the Sportster in 1957. The new roadster soon became the definite two-wheeled hot rod.*

Index

Page numbers in *italic* refer to picture captions.

bibliography

Bach, Sharon & Osterman, Ken (Editors), "The Legend Begins,"
Harley-Davidson, 1993

Bolfert, Thomas C., "The Big Book of Harley-Davidson," Harley-
Davidson, 1991

Briel, Dorothea, "Harley-Davidson," CLB Publishing, 1992

Buzzelli, Buzz, "Harley-Davidson Sportster Performance Handbook,"
Motorbooks International, 1992

Carrick, Peter, "Encyclopedia of Motor-Cycle Sport, St. Martin's Press,
1977

Emde, Don, "The Daytona 200," Infosport, 1991

Field, Greg, "Harley-Davidson Panheads," Motorbooks International, 1995

Girdler, Allan & Hussey, Ron, "Harley-Davidson: The American
Motorcycle," Motorbooks International, 1992

Ibid, "Harley-Davidson Sportster," ibid, 1995

Girdler, Allan, "Harley-Davidson Buyer's Guide," ibid, 1992

Hatfield, Jerry, "American Racing Motorcycles," Haynes Publishing
Group, 1982

Ibid, "Inside Harley-Davidson," Motorbooks International, 1990

Hendry, Maurice, "Harley-Davidson," Ballantine Books, 1972

Marselli, Mark, "Classic Harley-Davidson Big Twins," ibid, 1994

Palmer III, Bruce, "How to Restore Your Harley-Davidson," ibid, 1994

Prior, Rupert, "Motorcycling: The Golden Years," CLB Publishing, 1994

Rafferty, Tod, "Harley-Davidson: The Ultimate Machine, ibid, 1994

Ibid, "Harley Memorabilia," Chartwell Books, 1997

Ibid, "The Complete Harley-Davidson, Motorbooks International, 1997

Ibid, "The Indian," Quadrillion Publishing, 1998

Rivola, Luigi, "Racing Motorcycles," Rand McNally, 1978

Sucher, Harry, "Harley-Davidson – The Milwaukee Marvel," Haynes
Publishing, 1994

Thompson, Hunter S., "Hell's Angels," Ballantine Books, 1966

Wiesner, Wolfgang, "Harley-Davidson Photographic History," Motorbooks
International, 1989

Wright, David K., "The Harley-Davidson Motor Company," Motorbooks
International, 1993

Wright, Stephen, "American Racer," 1900–1939, Motorbooks
International, 1989

Periodicals: *American Motorcyclist*, *Bicycle Illustrated*, *Cycle and
Automobile Trade Journal*, *Cycle Guide*, *Cycle News*, *Cycle World*,
Motor Cycle Illustrated, *Motor Cycle and Motorcycling*, *The Enthusiast*

ACKNOWLEDGMENTS
Thanks are due to all the owners and restorers who volunteered their motorcycles for photography: Steve Alamango, Duane Anderson, Joy and Marv Baker, Gary Bang, Jr., Bill Bartels, Val Bassetti, Glen Bator, Dave Bettencourt, Richard Brazas, Gene Calidonna, Otis Chandler, Trev Deeley, Ray Earls, Bud Ekins, Jim and Mike Furlong, Ginger Gammon, Jeff Gilbert, Brian Holden, Doug Holden, Chuck Holenda, Dennis Huggins, Randy Janson, John Kingston, Jim Kirchner, Mike Lady, Chris Lamb, Ken Lang, Fred Lange, Armando Magri, Howard Mahler, Harold Mathews, Clay Osincup, Mike Parti, Fred Pazaski, Tom Perkins, Brad Richardson, Bob Rocchio, Dave Royal, Oliver Shokouh, Daniel Statnekov, Doug Stein, John Stratman, John Tosta, Jerry Warren, Paul Wheeler, Sam Williams, Dave Ybarra and Dwight Yoakam. Our appreciation also to the staffs of the Bartel's Harley-Davidson, Dudley Perkins Company, Farrow's Harley-Davidson, Harley-Davidson of Atascadero, Harley Davidson of EL Cajon, Harley-Davidson of Glendale, Harley-Davidson of Sacramento, Kegel Motorcycle Company, Rockford, Illinois, Los Angeles Harley-Davidson, Mathews Harley-Davidson, National Motorcycle Museum, Anamosa, Iowa, Otis Chandler

Vintage Museum, Petersen Automotive Museum, Pierce Harley-Davidson, DeKalb, Illinois, Sotheby's Auctions, Chicago, Illinois, Surrey Harley-Davidson, Trev Deeley Motorcycle Museum, Warr's Harley-Davidson and Warren's Motorcycle Service. Thanks also to Bill at Bill's Custom Cycles, Tom Brannan, Buell Motorcycle Company, Chief Blackhawk Chapter, Antique Motorcycle Club of America, Rick Cole, Peter Egan, Mark George, Allan Girdler, Ron Hussey, Don James, Larry Kahn, Reg Kittrelle of *Thunder Press*, Brian "Bob" Kovacs, Bruce Linsday, Lu and Armando Magri; Jim McClure of Vintage Cycle Promotions, Richard Messer, Milwaukee County Historical Society, Philip Mitchell, Nace Panzica and Steve Davey at Custom Chrome, Marty Rosenblum and Susan Fariss of Harley-Davidson Archives, Clement Salvadori, Mike Shattuck, Garry Stuart, Dale Walksler and his Wheels Through Time Museum, John Warr of Warr's Harley-Davidson, London, England, Jay Westerbrook and Stephen Wright.

PICTURE CREDITS
British Film Institute (BFI Stills, Posters and Designs): p. 147
Corbis: p. 19 M /Bettmann; 22 BL/Bettmann, Ezio Petersen;

81 T/© Minnesota Historical Society; 82 BR /
© Minnesota Historical Society; 102 B /Bettmann; 120
BL Bettmann; 142 BL /Bettmann; 146 T/Bettmann; 165
BR /Bettmann; 166 TR /© Ted Streshinsky; 183 TR
/Bettmann; 203 T /© Neil Preston;
Dain Gingerelli p. 162 ML, BR
Grubman p. 141 TR
© Harley-Davidson Motor Company: p. 10 BL; 15 ML, MR;
36 TR; 46 BL; 52 TR; 71 TL; 83 ML; 85 BL; 208; 209 TL
Hulton Archive: p. 14 TL/Fox Photos; 64 BR/© Getty
Images; 67 TR /Fox Photos; 101 BL; 105 T /Archive
Photos, John Margolies Collection
Hungness Publishing Co.: p. 184 BL
Kobal Collection: p. 21 T
Milwaukee County Historical Society: P. 10 TR; 47 MR
Tod Rafferty: p. 22 BR; 204 T; 205 TR; 206 BL
Reuters NewMedia Inc: 221 BL/Allen Fredrickson
James Schnepf: p. 19 TL
Sotheby's: p. 12 TL; 13 TR; 17 BR; 19 BL; 163 TL; 165 ML
Garry Stuart: back cover; p. 2–3; 7; 13 BL; 49 TR; 85 MR,
BR; 101 MR; 103 BL, BR; 125 TR, ML; 143 TL; 163 BL;
202 TR; 204 TR; 205 TL; 207 TL; 221 ML
U.S. Patent Office: p. 26 BL; 36 BL